Viktor Shklovsky

Viktor Shklovsky

A Reader

Edited and Translated by Alexandra Berlina

Mikhail Prokhorov Fund | Supporting the translation of Russian literature | transcript

Bloomsbury Academic
An imprint of Bloomsbury Publishing Inc
B L O O M S B U R Y
NEW YORK • LONDON • OXFORD • NEW DELHI • SYDNEY

Bloomsbury Academic
An imprint of Bloomsbury Publishing Inc

1385 Broadway
New York
NY 10018
USA

50 Bedford Square
London
WC1B 3DP
UK

www.bloomsbury.com

BLOOMSBURY and the Diana logo are trademarks of Bloomsbury Publishing Plc

First published 2017

The publication was effected under the auspices of the Mikhail Prokhorov Foundation TRANSCRIPT Programme to Support Translations of Russian Literature

Library of Congress Cataloging-in-Publication Data
Names: Shklovskiæi, Viktor, 1893-1984, author. | Berlina, Alexandra, translator, editor.
Title: Viktor Shklovsky : a reader / edited and translated by Alexandra Berlina.
Description: New York : Bloomsbury Academic, 2016. | Includes bibliographical references and index.
Identifiers: LCCN 2016019093 (print) | LCCN 2016020311 (ebook) | ISBN 9781501310362 (hardcover : alk. paper) | ISBN 9781501310386 (ePub) | ISBN 9781501310409 (ePDF)
Subjects: LCSH: Russian literature--History and criticism. | Criticism. | Authorship. | Opoëìiaz (Literary group) | Motion pictures–History.
Classification: LCC PG3476.S488 A2 2016 (print) | LCC PG3476.S488 (ebook) | DDC 891.73/42–dc23
LC record available at https://lccn.loc.gov/2016019093

ISBN: HB: 978-1-5013-1036-2
PB: 978-1-5013-1037-9
ePub: 978-1-5013-1038-6
ePDF: 978-1-5013-1040-9

Cover design: Andy Allen
Cover image © Nikita Shklovskiy

Typeset by Fakenham Prepress Solutions, Fakenham, Norfolk NR21 8NN
Printed and bound in the United States of America

Contents

Acknowledgments

I am deeply grateful to the Prokhorov Fund for supporting this translation, and to Viktor Shklovsky's grandson, Nikita Shklovsky, for providing priceless information as well as the cover image. Many thanks to Kevin M. F. Platt, Serguei Oushakine, Haun Saussy and Holt Meyer for their interest and input.

Translator's Introduction

The well bred contradict other people. The wise contradict themselves.

OSCAR WILDE
"PHRASES AND PHILOSOPHIES FOR THE USE OF THE YOUNG" (C. 1894)

"Give us new forms!" –
a scream resounds through all things.

VLADIMIR MAYAKOVSKY
"ORDER NO. 2 TO THE ARMY OF THE ARTS" (1921)

Let me begin by explaining the epigraphs. Shklovsky loved Wilde's writing as a teenager and was himself a master of the aphorism; in his twenties, he became a friend of Mayakovsky and a champion of his work. However, this is not the main reason for placing these lines so prominently; rather, they sum up much of what is crucial about Shklovsky. If Wilde is right, Shklovsky was both well-bred and wise: he constantly contradicted other people, and also himself. His insistence on the importance of form stood in contrast both to classical Russian criticism and to the ideological Soviet approach.[1]

[1] In *A Sentimental Journey*, Shklovsky observes, on reading prerevolutionary literary and scholarly journals: "What a strange thing; they replace the history of Russian literature with the history of Russian liberalism. / For Pypin, literary history is a subfield of ethnography."

His grandson Nikita Shklovsky, who answered my queries with great patience, believes that his grandfather "actively provoked people in order to make them listen." He goes on to say that Shklovsky only ever claimed that content didn't matter in order "to turn the listener's nose in his direction and to shake the dust off his ears." Studying form and artistic devices was Shklovsky's life work but contradicting established opinions was to him a pleasure in itself.

Disagreeing with authorities is only natural in a gifted young scholar, but Shklovsky went further. He, and other members of the Society for the Study of Poetic Language known as the OPOYAZ, also enjoyed passionately contradicting each other. More importantly still, Shklovsky was never shy of contradicting himself. One might well argue that not doing so in seventy years of scholarship would be stagnation. One of Shklovsky's closest friends and most perceptive commentators, Alexander Chudakov, observes: "The primary trait of Shklovsky's thinking [...] is its indispensable polemic quality, be it external or internal. Shklovsky's famous aphorisms, which have been quoted many thousand times, always contain 'not' and 'but'" ("Dva pervykh ...": 31).[2]

For Shklovsky, contradiction is both a device of Aesopian language in his (semi-)retractions of formalist heritage and a method of thinking. In *Hamburg Score*, he explains that he arranges his shelves so that neighboring books contradict each other (*Gamburgskiy schet* [1928] 13). In *The Third Factory*, Shklovsky writes "My work was wrong my whole life long, but I worked. It is now that I am at fault. I work little. [...] It is better to be wrong" (*Tretya Fabrika* 62). Some

---

[2]Others before him, for instance Sheldon (passim) and Lachmann (237), observed the crucial role of self-contradiction in Shklovsky's work. Striedter (*Texte der russischen Formalisten I*: xvi) stresses the importance of dialogical theory-building within the formalist group, albeit without commenting on Shklovsky's dialogue with himself.

of Shklovsky's retractions, such as "A Monument to a Scholarly Mistake" (1930), were simply a matter of self-protection, though even these might bear traces of hidden irony (cf. Boym, "Poetics and Politics …" 597). However, often, when Shklovsky contradicts or appears to contradict himself, we are actually watching him think.

Let us now turn to the second epigraph. By 1921, Mayakovsky knew and appreciated Shklovsky. It is quite probable that "Order No. 2 to the Army of the Arts" is referencing "Resurrecting the Word" and "Art as Device." The two lines cited here not only describe what became Shklovsky's most influential idea; they do so using two of his crucial keywords. *Things* (*veshchi*) must be given new *forms* (*formy*) in order to become seen, and not merely automatically recognized. When talking of things in need of formal renewal, Shklovsky can refer to literary language, genres, and conventions (in fact, *veshchi* can also mean "texts"), but also to the objects (including people, feelings, and customs) described and depicted in art. Shklovsky's first essay, "Resurrecting the Word," emphasizes the former, intraliterary aspect. His best-known text, "Art as Device"—"the manifesto of the formal method" (Eikhenbaum, *O literature* 385), "the battle cry of formalism" (Erlich, *Russian Formalism* 76)—provides examples of the latter; the two are closely connected. Openly or obliquely, Shklovsky kept returning to the idea of *ostranenie*,[3] of renewing our experience of things by changing their forms, throughout his life.

He spent seventy years writing theory, criticism, and fiction, be it under enemy fire or merely the salvos of his critics. Navigating

---

[3]This book transliterates *ostranenie*, the making strange of things in order to renew their experience, and uses Benjamin Sher's coinage "enstranging/enstrange" when *ostranyat'* is used as an adjective or verb. The translator's introduction to part I, "OPOYAZ Publications," discusses this decision in detail.

through his immense and fascinating body of work is a challenge. Things are not made easier by the existence of nonidentical twins among his books. *On the Theory of Prose*, published in 1983, includes some material from *On the Theory of Prose* published in 1925, but nine out of eleven main chapters are completely different. The same is true for *Hamburg Score* (1990) and its 1928 namesake. The present reader provides an overview, and this is one reason for its existence. Another reason is that more than half of the material excerpted here—*Technique of Writing Craft* (1927), *Hamburg Score* (1928), *Once Upon a Time* (1964), *Tales about Prose* (1966), *On the Theory of Prose* (1983), as well as most articles on cinema and letters—has never been translated into English before.

When Shklovsky says, in *Once Upon a Time*, that his books "weren't written with the quiet consistency of academic works," this is rather an understatement. Shklovsky wrote while fighting in the First World War, participating in the February Revolution, and trying to stage an anti-Bolshevik coup. He wrote while hiding in a mental ward and while starving in Petrograd. He wrote while in hospital, almost shredded by a bomb, and while torn between an unrelenting love object in Berlin and an imprisoned wife in Russia. Originally, the structure of this reader was meant to pair scholarship with autobiographical writing dedicated to that time. However, soon it became clear how wrong any attempt to separate Shklovsky's scholarly, autobiographical, and fictional writing would be: this would mean cutting texts into pieces.

In revolutionary times, many things became intermixed, including genres. Shklovsky was not the only Russian writer working outside of the usual categories. He himself cited Dante's *Vita Nova* as an example of a text which combines meditations on the theory of art with memories and poems (*Tetiva* 160). When looking for a comparable contemporary work, Ali Smith's *Artful* comes to mind. Still, among scholarly writing of his time, his texts were the most daring crossbreeds. Trying to neatly structure them is counterproductive.

But precisely this hybridity makes it helpful to know what was happening to Shklovsky while a particular text was written. Difficult as it is to condense his extraordinary life into a timeline, here is an attempt to do so. A bibliography of Shklovsky's work published eight years before his death takes up 85 pages (Sheldon, *Viktor Shklovsky*). The following short biography includes only a very small selection of Shklovsky's writings.

Viktor Shklovsky: Life and Work

1893 (January 25): Viktor is born in St. Petersburg to the math teacher Boris Shklovsky and his wife Varvara (née Bundel).

1908: Shklovsky's short story "The Right to Grieve" is published in the magazine *Vesna*; he is fifteen. In the same year, he is expelled from school (and accepted at another).

1912: Shklovsky enters the Philological Faculty of Petersburg University, where he studies for a year and a half (he never receives a higher education diploma).

1913–14: Shklovsky gives talks in literary cafes and schools, most famously on "The Place of Futurism in Language History" and "Resurrecting the Word." The group of philologists which is to become the OPOYAZ begins to condense around Shklovsky. In 1914, he publishes "Resurrecting the Word" and a poetry collection, *The Lot of Lead*.

1914 (28 July): the First World War begins. In fall 1914, Shklovsky joins the army as a volunteer.

1916: usually regarded as the birth year of the OPOYAZ. While proceeding with his military service in Petrograd, Shklovsky writes "Art as Device."

1916–17: Shklovsky edits and publishes the first and second volume of the *Collection on the Theory of Poetic Language* (*Sbornik po teorii poeticheskogo yazyka*), which features several of his articles.

1917: Shklovsky participates in the February Revolution as a member of the Socialist-Revolutionary (SR) Party.

In spring, at the Southwestern Front, he receives the Cross of St. George for courage from General Kornilov, Supreme Commander-in-Chief of the Provisional Government.

In fall, he leaves for Persia (North Iran) to participate in the Caucasus Campaign.

1917 (7 November) (new style): October Revolution.

1918: Shklovsky returns and works in the SR underground, attempting an anti-Bolshevik coup. When it fails, he seeks refuge in a mental hospital in Saratov. In fall, he proceeds to Kiev, fighting for Ukraine's independence. His brother Nikolai (aged twenty-eight) is executed. His half-brother Evgeny (aged c. thirty) is killed while helping the wounded.

1919: After an amnesty for SR members, Shklovsky returns to Petrograd, where he leads an active life despite the cold and hunger—teaching, writing, discussing literary matters with OPOYAZ members, and marrying Vasilisa Kordi, a sick nurse and stage designer. His sister Evgeniya (aged 27) dies from malnutrition, leaving behind two daughters.

1920: After participating in a duel, Shklovsky follows his wife to Ukraine, where he fights in the Red Army against the White Guard. He is wounded dismantling a grenade; eighteen splinters remain in his body. He returns to Petrograd and is elected Professor for Literary Theory at the State Art History Institute.

1922: The official amnesty is unofficially revoked, and Shklovsky's SR connections nearly get him arrested. In spring, he flees, crossing the frozen Gulf of Finland. In Berlin, he falls in love with Elsa Triolet. In fall, he solicits the right to return to Soviet Russia, partly because his wife is imprisoned there.

1923: *Zoo. Letters not about Love, or The Third Heloise* (*Zoo*), *A Sentimental Journey* (*Sentimental'noye puteshestviye*) and *A Knight's Move* (*Khod konya*) are published. In September, Shklovsky returns to Russia and is reunited with his wife in Moscow. A year later, their son Nikita is born.

1925: *On the Theory of Prose* (*O teorii prozy* [1925]). For financial reasons, Shklovsky begins working at the Third State Cinema Factory as a screen writer and film editor.

1926: *The Third Factory* (*Tretya Fabrika*).

1927: His daughter Varvara is born. *Technique of Writing Craft* (*Tekhnika pisatel'skogo remesla*).

1928: *Hamburg Score* (*Gamburgskiy schet*).

1930: Stalinist repressions intensify. Shklovsky publishes "A Monument to a Scholarly Mistake" ("*Pamyatnik nauchnoy oshibke*").

1932: Shklovsky travels to the White Sea–Baltic Canal, constructed by Gulag prisoners, one of whom is his brother Vladimir. Shklovsky succeeds in helping him, but in 1937 Vladimir is rearrested and shot (aged forty-eight).

1939: Shklovsky is decorated with the Order of the Red Banner of Labor (two more will follow).

1945: Shklovsky's only son, Nikita, is killed on the German front aged twenty-one.

1949: Following an article on Shklovsky's "antipatriotic and anti-Soviet" writing, his work is boycotted for years.

1952: Shklovsky's grandson, also named Nikita, is born.

1956: Shklovsky divorces Vasilisa and marries his typist Serafima Suok.

Beginning of de-Stalinization under Khrushchev.

1963: *Lev Tolstoy* (a biography).

1964: *Once Upon A Time* (*Zhili-byli*).

1965: *Théorie de la littérature: textes des formalistes russes*, translated and edited by Tsvetan Todorov and prefaced by Roman Jakobson, includes "Art as Device." In *Russian Formalist Criticism: Four Essays* (ed. Lemon and Reis), two of the four essays are by Shklovsky: "Art as Device" and "Sterne's *Tristram Shandy*."

1966: *Tales about Prose* (*Povesti o proze*).

1970: *Bowstring. On the Dissimilarity of the Similar* (*Tetiva*).

1981: *Energy of Delusion. A Book on Plot* (*Energiya zabluzhdeniya*).

1982: Shklovsky's wife Serafima dies.

1983: *On the Theory of Prose* (*O teorii prozy*).

1984 (5 December): Viktor Shklovsky dies in a Moscow hospital, aged 91.

Selected posthumous publications: *In 60 Years. Works on Cinema* (*Za 60 let*); *Hamburg Score* (*Gamburgskiy schet*; 1990).

Shklovsky lived to be ninety-one. The life spans of his half-brother, his sister, and one of his brothers make up less—taken together. All of them died between 1918 and 1919, the time when he was working on the most detailed version of "Art as Device." His son, too, died young. Shklovsky's life was tragic, but also rich. He was, to quote Erlich's epithets in *Russian Formalism* (1955), "fellow-traveller of the futurist

Bohemia" (67), "formalist chieftain" (68), "chief trouble-shooter of Opoyaz" (76), and "the *enfant terrible* of Russian Formalism" (68, 265). Being a movement's patriarch and its *enfant terrible* is quite a feat, and yet Erlich's description isn't wrong.

There being "nothing more wonderful than a catalogue, an instrument of wondrous hypotyposis" (Eco 79), let us proceed with two more. Shklovsky was "the founder of the OPOYAZ and an officer of the Provisional Government; instructor of an armored division and guerilla fighter of the Socialist-Revolutionary Party; professor at the Art History Institute and political émigré; writer and scholar; literary critic and reeditor of foreign films; screenwriter, film critic, even actor" (Kalinin), and also the protagonist of his own work, be it obviously or obliquely. Due to his wide-ranging interests and his experience as a reporter, his literary scholarship contains passages on "the construction of rotary motors, on rat migration, on necktie salesmanship, on 'furniture made from old frigates' [...], on methods of horse coupling ('—this is terribly indecent, but otherwise there'd be no horses'), on the differences between linseed flax and fiber flax"—Chudakov ("Dva pervykh ..." 31) goes on with this list.

Shklovsky's life experience, combined with his self-fashioning as both a literary scholar and literary figure, make his life endlessly fascinating. Nevertheless, Shklovsky's only biography so far was published in 2014 (by Berezin), and there is no English translation yet. This biography is guided by the premise that Shklovsky has been dramatically misunderstood: he was, argues Berezin, a writer, a poet in prose, not a scholar. This is perhaps a deliberate overstatement intended to direct attention to Shklovsky's fiction, which certainly deserves it. Attempting to imitate Shklovsky's style, Berezin might have also adopted his penchant for provocative exaggeration. Still, Shklovsky clearly was both writer and scholar; more than that, he was both simultaneously, not in turns.[4] Berezin's emphasis on the literary milieu is perhaps the reason why Mayakovsky's alleged syphilis receives more attention than Shklovsky's theoretical work. Still, the biography is a great source of information, to which I am deeply indebted.

To flesh out the CV on the preceding pages, here are a few details, beginning with Shklovsky's childhood. You might be familiar with Nabokov's magical infancy and dreamy adolescence. The nannies, the doting if distant parents, the holidays at sea … Well, Shklovsky's childhood was nothing like it. He was born in the same city and in the same decade as Nabokov, but he never had reason to miss his early years. In *On the Theory of Prose* (1983), in a passage which hasn't made it into this reader, he writes:

> My mother whipped me and exhibited the weals to the rest of her progeny as a deterrent.
>
> I remember a wolf cub sitting under the table looking at boots confidently walking away.
>
> Even now, I'm jealous of the way she talked to my elder brother.

Later, the violence was rechanneled. Shklovsky told his friend, the writer Viktor Konetsky, about family fights in his teenage years:

> It was usually my mother who hurled the samovar. My father started with the dishes. Then, my elder brother would tear down the curtains. I darted through the door into the next room or onto the staircase. I literally went *through* the door, not opening it, but ramming it out with my breast or shoulder, panels and all.

---

[4] Apart from his trademark mixture of autobiography, scholarship, and fiction, Shklovsky wrote short stories, poems, screenplays, and even co-authored a detective/sci-fi novel (*Iprit*, i.e. *Mustard Gas*, with Vsevolod Ivanov, 1925).

> Sometimes, the panels stayed in place. Then, we drank tea from the samovar that mother was trying to repair.
>
> Then, everything became well, leaving no marks.
>
> Two or three times, I refrained from ramming doors. These times remained as weals, as eternal scars in my soul. (Konetsky 495)

Shklovsky's was not a literary household (though not without cultural interests: his mother cared for music, his father adored the cinema). In *Once Upon a Time*, Shklovsky explains how he learned to love books, first Jules Verne, then Gogol and Tolstoy. While escaping into fiction from the mundanity of his home, Shklovsky was dreaming of becoming a sculptor or a boxer. He dabbled in writing, even getting a short story published at the age of fifteen, but only turned to literary scholarship when he saw something he could contradict, namely the traditional emphasis on content, and something he could fight for, namely futurist art. In 1971, Shklovsky wrote to a friend:

> The formal method was born from futurism. It results from understanding futurism, from finding parallels to it in folk art and in old novels. This was the birth of the formal method and with it, of *ostranenie*. The formal method enabled analysis outside of content, it even negated content. It created a crystallography of art.
>
> This was the OPOYAZ.
>
> In its turn, it gave birth to structuralism. (Shklovsky and Maryamov)

"Resurrecting the Word" was an attempt to understand futurism and other experimental writing. It attracted the attention of young scholars who had a more solid philological background than the young Shklovsky, but who shared his hunger for a new approach. In an unpublished chapter of *The Third Factory* (Galushkin, "Footnotes" 487), Shklovsky remembers: "The day when I met Lev [Yakubinsky] was a good day. We talked about theory for an hour or two every day. Lev explained to me the difference between the poetic and prosaic functions of language. There were now two of us. Later, we were joined by Evgeny Polivanov, and there were three of us." These three friends were the kernel of what came to be known as the OPOYAZ. They were soon joined by Roman Jakobson, Boris Eikhenbaum, Yury Tynyanov, Osip Brik, and others.

The OPOYAZ had no card-carrying members. Jakobson spent most of his time not in Petrograd but in Moscow, where he presided over another formalist-minded linguistic circle, later resurrected in Prague; Vladimir Propp never referred to himself as part of the OPOYAZ, but was interested in its ideas. It was a formalist organization, but never a formal one (though there is a list of members submitted to Petrograd authorities in 1921, which lists Shklovsky as chairman).[5] Neither the date of its foundation nor even the exact meaning of the abbreviation is clear. Most publications agree on 1916 as the beginning of the OPOYAZ, but one could also cite 1914, when "Resurrecting the Word" was published and the friendship between Shklovsky, Yakubinsky, and Polivanov began. Shklovsky says that OPOYAZ was short for "Society for the Study of Poetic Language Theory," several others skip the word "theory."

Whatever the OPOYAZ was, it worked. It even had a hymn, a long jocular affair which can help imagine the excited crowd of wild

---

[5] Needless to say, the label "formalism," originally coined by adversaries of the OPOYAZ, is merely convenient shorthand for the kind of work that consisted in analyzing not ideology but artistic form (a concept which includes, as a subfield, that which is usually called "content"). Names are a matter of convention, including even Shklovsky's own: he officially adopted his wife's last name, Kordi, when he married, but went on signing his works "Shklovsky."

philologists around Shklovsky. In the following, you'll find an excerpt from it, based on several sources (primarily Khmel'nitskaya). I have attempted to recreate the rhymes and meter; the absence of musical notation should not prevent you from joining in the song. The versions of the text differ (as you will shortly see from its rendition in Kaverin's novel), but all allude to the laying bare of devices as well as to the Latin meaning of Shklovsky's first name.

The rowdy Shklovsky is our father,
the strict Tynyanov is our minder.
Not like them Eikhenbaum; rather,
he's our good mommy, so much kinder.

Oh, the device was such a fay kid,
a cheerful, beautiful creation!
But now, behold, we've stripped it naked,
bedecked in naught but motivation.

Love, just as any other object,
is known to us with all its vices.
But passion, from a formal viewpoint,
is the convergence of devices.

No matter if the boa constrictor
of our detractors is a mutant—
still "ave Shklovsky, ave Viktor,
formalituri te salutant!"

It might be difficult to imagine that, during a World War, a civil war and two revolutions, literary theories could be emotionally explosive, but they were. Kalinin writes "in Greek, the word *skandalon* referred to a trap or an obstacle intended to make the victim trip into a trap. [Shklovsky] used the scandal as an inalienable principle of producing the new [...] Consciously and passionately, he made different planes of his existence collide." Though Shklovsky flunked Greek at school, he was a master of the *skandalon* as a device, particularly in association with the futurists. In *The Third Factory*, he recalls the aftermath of a reading: "Mayakovsky went through the crowd like a steam iron through snow. Kruchenykh fought back with his galoshes." Shklovsky is the prototype of the eponymous hero of Kaverin's novel *The Troublemaker* (*Skandalist* in Russian). Once, he challenged a stranger to a duel merely for being vulgar. It ended with very little bloodshed, and, to be fair, this was not as exotic an event as it might seem. Affaires d'honneur weren't infrequent in the feverish era around the revolution, as witnessed by an attempted duel between Mandelstam and Khlebnikov (Vitale 102–3), with Shklovsky a second.

Shklovsky remembers the OPOYAZ as a paragon of dedicated teamwork amid heated discussions. In *On the Theory of Prose* (1983), he writes: "We worked tremendously quickly, tremendously easily, and we had agreed that everything said within our team was unsigned—our common work. As Mayakovsky put it, let's add the laurel leaves of our wreaths to our shared soup." In *The Third Factory*, Shklovsky uses the image of soup in reference to formalism less joyfully: "Vegetables are sometimes cooked in soup, but not eaten. [...] Probably, it is us who were the vegetables." Even if the soup would have been impossible without "the vegetables", it still hurts to be thrown out. Besides, while "formalism" became a term of abuse in Soviet Russia.

Another informal Petrograd circle of literary friends close to Shklovsky was the Serapion Brotherhood. Consisting mostly of Zamyatin's and Shklovsky's students, this group of writers met to master literary techniques and not to discuss ideology. Each "brother" (and the only "sister," Elizaveta Polonskaya) had a nickname; Shklovsky's was *skandalist*. Like the OPOYAZ, the

Serapion Brotherhood was unofficially and gradually shut down in the late 1920s due to censorship pressure.

But before that, in 1922, Shklovsky had to flee from Russia as a member of the Socialist-Revolutionary Party who had conspired in an anti-Bolshevist coup. He left behind his wife and his friends, the OPOYAZ and the Serapion circle. His friendships with fellow-minded scholars and writers, their passionate arguments about literature, were immensely important to Shklovsky, and he suffered without them. Almost as soon as he left Russia, biding his time in Finland, he began writing *A Sentimental Journey*, some passages of which are so nostalgically lyrical that they suggest years, not weeks of separation:

> I shall not be happy.
>
> I won't be sitting in my room, at the stone table, drinking sugared tea from saucerless glasses with my friends, not anytime soon; I won't see the circles left by glasses on the table.
>
> Boris Eikhenbaum and Yury Tynyanov won't come to me, won't discuss the essence of "rhythmic-syntactic figures."

In 1922, while in Berlin and in love, Shklovsky writes to Gorky: "I'm lonely. I don't tell anybody anything. I've immersed myself into studying 'the plot' like a maniac so as not to cry my eyes out. Don't wake me up" (Frezenskiy 167).

But, despite his scholarship, he was painfully awake in Berlin. In the open letter to Soviet authorities at the end of *Zoo*, he begs to be permitted to return home, stating, "My whole everyday life, all my habit patterns connect me to today's Russia." The original words *byt* and *navyki*, translated here as "habit patterns," could also be rendered as "my way of life and skills," or "the quotidian and my experiences." *Byt* is what Mayakovsky's love boat crashed against in the poem part of which became his suicide note; Jakobson spends a page discussing the untranslatability of this word with its suggestions of "narrow petrified molds", "stagnant slime," and, significantly, automatization (Jakobson 13; cf. Steiner 48). Psychological dictionaries translate *navyki* as "learned behaviors" or "habit patterns." Shklovsky is disconnected from the everyday, saved from automatism—this sounds very much like *ostranenie*. But he is not at all happy.[6]

At another point in *Zoo*, describing a fellow émigré crying, he uses one of these words again: "*Byt* [everyday life] here defrosts us." This defrosting is very much like what the process of writing about his most painful experiences does to him: "I shouldn't have written this. My heart has warmed. It hurts" (*A Sentimental Journey*). But is being defrosted and liberated from everyday routine not Shklovsky's greatest goal? Well, no. It is, to his mind, the greatest goal of art. A book might be the ax for the frozen sea within us—but if life itself unfreezes it, there might be a flood. What is happening to Shklovsky in Berlin is exactly what art should do, but he prefers a return to automatism when *ostranenie* is created through alienation, when strangeness encroaches upon reality.

This doesn't mean that Shklovsky is always unhappy when his real life is made strange. The February Revolution, and the first mad postrevolutionary years, were a painful but exhilarating time for Shklovsky. He was in the midst of it. Emigration, however, was a tortuous experience. The failed courtship of Elsa Triolet and the imprisonment of his wife certainly contributed to his desire to return home, but he—a scholar of world literature who spoke no foreign language—also felt out of place in Berlin, despite its brilliant émigré

---

[6] The narrator of *Zoo* and *A Sentimental Journey* is so closely modeled on the author that I permit myself to factor out the difference between them here: it is not larger than the difference between Shklovsky at twenty and Shklovsky at ninety, or Shklovsky's experience and the autobiographical anecdotes he told his friends.

community. In her insightful "Estrangement As A Lifestyle," Boym (515–16) writes that "*Ostranenie* means more than distancing and making strange; it is also dislocation, *depaysement.*" This might be debatable etymologically, but the connection between alienation and *ostranenie* is an intriguing topic. In 1922, Shklovsky experienced the former, while for the first time putting into practice the latter: *Zoo* is an exercise in the *ostranenie* of love.

The decade between 1914 and 1924 was the most eventful by far in Shklovsky's life, and he wrote several books about it. The introduction to the chapter "Autobiographic Hybrids" provides some more background. But what happened after Shklovsky returned to Russia? "Nothing good" is a popular answer. When writing Shklovsky's biography, it is impossible to circumvent the accusation of mimicry. Vitale (19–20) observes that many Russian intellectuals looked down on Shklovsky from the 1930s on, considering him a turncoat. But even the most ardent of his detractors and the most disappointed of his friends could hardly call his behavior opportunistic. It was a matter of avoiding danger, not of gaining favors; for several decades, an open embracement of formalism could have cost Shklovsky his head.

It seems almost fantastic that, in the early 1920s, Shklovsky could have an open discussion with one of the leading Bolsheviks on the virtues of formalist and Marxist literary studies. Leon Trotsky published an article called "The Formal School of Poetry and Marxism" in the leading Soviet newspaper, *Pravda*, in 1923.[7] Trotsky was on the verge of becoming the leader of the USSR (later, he lost the fight), and yet he found the time to analyze *Knight's Move* in considerable detail, albeit misreading many key ideas, and spewing sarcasm:

[7]Many leading Bolshevik figures were interested in literary scholarship. Trotsky went on discussing the matter in his book *Literature and Revolution*. Bukharin was present at an OPOYAZ lecture (Vitale: 92).

> Viktor Shklovsky is a theorist of futurism, and at the same time the head of the formal school. According to his theory, art has always been the creation of self-sufficient pure forms, and futurism was the first movement to recognize it. This makes futurism the first instance of conscious art in history, and the formal school the first scientific art theory. Thanks to Shklovsky's extraordinary services, art theory and partly art itself have finally been transformed from alchemy into chemistry.
>
> […]
>
> What, then, is the formal school?
>
> In the form in which it is now represented by Shklovsky, Zhirmunsky, Jakobson etc., it is first and foremost extremely insolent and premature. (Trotsky)

The original is harsher than this rendition: the final word in the excerpt is *nedonosok*, a term of offense usually translated as "bastard" or "jerk," but literally meaning a prematurely born child. Shklovsky's "A Response to Lev Davidovich Trotsky" has not been preserved, but most of it is incorporated in another article written in the mid-1920s. Shklovsky addresses one of the most powerful men in Soviet Russia as a fellow literary critic, though not a very intelligent one:

> We never claimed that only sound mattered in poetry.
>
> This is a most vulgar misunderstanding of a scholarly theory whose only fault is that it is being misread.
>
> […]
>
> Your mistake is based on our differing definitions of the word "form."

> For you, forming a text means working on its message.
>
> We consider the semantic material of a text extremely important, but we know that meaning, too, is given an artistic form.
>
> [...]
>
> "Content" is a phenomenon of semantic form. The ideas contained in a text are material, their relationship is form. (*Gamburgskiy schet* [1990] 279)

One can hardly call the author of these lines a coward or a traitor. A few years later, when finishing *The Third Factory*, he would be more circumspect, but still unbroken.

> There are two ways now. One is to leave, to dig yourself in, to make money with something other than literature and to write privately, at home.
>
> The other way is to dedicate yourself to describing life, conscientiously looking for the new way of life and the right world view.
>
> There is no third way. This is the way to go.

But in 1930, Shklovsky published a self-accusatory article, whose title can be rendered as "A Monument to a Scholarly Mistake," "A Memorial to a Scientific Error," or a combination of these (Shklovsky, "Pamyatnik").[8] He was the only OPOYAZ member to officially denounce formalism—unless one reads "A Monument" as veiled defense (cf. Sheldon, "Ostensible Surrender") or even as parody, as suggested by Serguei Oushakine, who also points out parallels to Eisenstein's repentant writing (personal communicaton).

---

[8] A translation by Maria Belodubrovskaya is available at www.davidbordwell.net/essays/shklovsky.php.

In 1932, Shklovsky traveled to the White Sea–Baltic Canal, which was being constructed by Gulag prisoners. Armed with an official journalistic mission, he went there to see his brother, the linguist Vladimir Shklovsky. The price he had to pay for doing so and eventually (though temporarily) helping to liberate him was the publication of several articles in a collective volume glorifying the building of the Canal. Though he wrote almost exclusively about technical details of the project, his name appears under some unsavory articles on Stalin and the Gulag system. The visit to the Canal gave rise to further alienation from active dissidents, and also to this anecdote: "The guard who had escorted me asked: 'And now, how do you feel after your reunion?' 'Like a live fox in a fur shop'" (Vitale 28).

This quip is very well-known in Russia. In his writing, too, Shklovsky often makes light of terrible things. He is a performer, and he performed his story for Serena Vitale—but then broke down crying (ibid.). His brother was afraid to show recognition when they met. You can hardly call Shklovsky a turncoat considering his chance of turning into a coat.

Indeed, it is close to a miracle that an active member of the Socialist-Revolutionary party, a man who, in *A Sentimental Journey*, called the Bolsheviks bacilli infecting Russia, was never actually arrested. His brother, though—his only sibling not killed during the civil war, the one whom he visited at the Canal—was shot in 1937. Shklovsky became more cautious. Later, he deeply regretted not having tried to protect Zoshchenko, having joined the attack on Pasternak in print (Vitale 29–30). Sometimes fear triumphed, but kindness and friendship won more often. As Nadezhda Mandelstam (409) wrote, "only one home in Moscow was open to outcasts," and it was Vasilisa's and Viktor's home. From 1949 on, Shklovsky's work remained unpublished for years. The question is, though: was all the work he did publish after the mid-1920s only an exercise in mimicry?

The short answer is "no." It is conventionally assumed that Shklovsky began to return to formalist studies in 1953, after Stalin's death (cf. e.g. Sheldon, "The Formalist Poetics of Victor Shklovsky" 368). A few years later, Sheldon convincingly analyzed how Shklovsky smuggled formalist ideas into his post-1953 work, introducing irony and contradiction into seemingly conformist texts. He argues that Shklovsky

> reached the nadir of his existence as critic and writer in 1953 with the book *Remarks on the Prose of the Russian Classics*, a dismal product of this difficult period. But in his writing since the death of Stalin he has returned at least partially to his earlier positions and has produced work of high quality. ("Ostensible Surrender" 108)

Indeed, *Notes on the Prose of the Russian Classics* is one of Shklovsky's greatest regrets. As he said in a dangerously sincere interview, "in that book I rejected everything: father, mother, dog and cat" (Vitale 97). Sheldon's observation has attracted expressions of moral outrage on Shklovsky's "double-edged loquacity" (Erlich, "On Being Fair" 108): yet again, the discussion of devices proved inseparable from the discussion of ideology.[9] Right as Sheldon is in general terms, the account given by him is somewhat cursory. Chudakov ("Dva pervykh …" 29) writes:

> In any of his texts written before 1953, there are many statements and instances of analysis which are quite in the vein of

[9] Far be it from us to discuss how closely Erlich's reaction is connected to Sheldon's critical treatment of his own work. In fact, Erlich was close to the main idea of Sheldon's article back in 1955: if Shklovsky's "confessions need not be taken too literally"(Erlich, *Russian Formalism*: 79) because of their ironic and playful nature, why should his surrenders be treated differently?

> the OPOYAZ. His thinking fell apart into two spheres that were, to him, incompatible—the formalist approach, and the rest. [...] Did he ever "really" doubt the work of the OPOYAZ and its main scholarly results? In many conversations, in which the present author participated for over twenty years, Shklovsky never expressed even a shadow of such a doubt.

What Shklovsky wrote between 1930 and the late 1950s is indeed much blander and tamer than the rest of his work, which is why the present collection includes no specimen from this time. As Shklovsky put it, "I wrote so much just to survive. I've written mediocre, even terrible things. There's only one thing future generations won't find my name on: reports and denunciations" (Vitale 29). But if one looks closely, one does find thinly veiled examples of Shklovskyan thinking in almost all of them. Shklovsky spent much of his time with what he called *podenshchina*, potboiler work, for instance, producing screenplays for such Soviet movies as *Chuk and Gek* (1953)—but then again, much of what he did on and in cinema was worthwhile, as witnessed by this reader's final chapter.

In his seventies, Shklovsky became famous, first in the West, and then at home. The year 1965 saw the publication of "Art as Device" and other articles in English and French. Shklovsky could publish almost anything he wrote now, and he wrote a lot. He took to moving his table when he finished a book. "Initially, Shklovsky stumbles into the table in its new, unusual place," describes Ognev (284), and comments "it seems that he always starts from scratch." There is also another explanation: Tolstoy, Shklovsky, and many others described furniture as an object of automatization. Perhaps Shklovsky celebrated each new book by enstranging his furniture, albeit at the risk of hurting his foot.

As an old man, Shklovsky was a docile husband and a doting grandfather. His granddaughter Vasilisa adored him, but there was one thing she didn't like: the way he read fairy tales (see Lazarev). Aged four, she complained that he kept changing the story. Despite all criticism, he preferred variation to repetition.

Interviewing Shklovsky in 1979, Serena Vitale (13) observed: "His curiosity was voracious. Shklovsky was like an eighty-six-year-old boy." He lived in the Writers' House at the time, a building whose raison d'être he explained to Vitale (25) thus: "You see, a hundred and forty writers live in this building. They put us all together to keep an eye on us more easily. Like in *1984*." And then he went on to say: "You know, I believe I'll make it to the year 1984 … I would like that. I want to live." He did make it.

Ostranenie and Other Key Concepts

In a way, this reader's index is the best foreword. It shows how certain topics—*ostranenie*, literary genealogy, plot and story, literary language vs. everyday language—surface in Shklovsky's work again and again. The introductions to different chapters provide more context. Still, for readers as yet unfamiliar with formalism (and I'd be overjoyed if this book attracted such readers), some points of clarification might be useful.

First, Shklovsky (unlike Jakobson) believes that literary, "poetic" language is principally different from the everyday variety, which he first called "prosaic" and then "practical." It doesn't have the goal of economy and easy understanding; rather, it makes the reader struggle in order to reward her with experience. I say "reader" and "language" because this is the way Shklovsky puts it. However, he also refers to film and sometimes to visual arts, and seems to be assuming a similar distinction between images as sources of information and images as art.

Second, Shklovsky differentiates between "story" (*fabula*) and "plot" (*syuzhet*). The story is what happens in a text; "the plot is a construction which uses events, people and landscapes, which shrinks time, extends time or shifts time, and thus creates a phenomenon which is felt, experienced the way the author wants it" (Shklovsky, *Tetiva* 85).

Third, there is Shklovsky's arguably most important contribution: the concept of *ostranenie*, of making the habitual strange in order to reexperience it. The register of key terms in the 1929 edition of *On the Theory of Prose* features "seeing" (*videnie*), defined as "the goal of *ostranenie*, a feature of artistic perception opposed to the 'recognition' of a thing." *Ostranenie* can be extraliterary, applying to the world, and also intraliterary, applying to "poetic" language, genres, and devices. Most examples in "Resurrecting the Word" concern ways of foregrounding language. Most examples in "Art as Device" concern new ways of seeing things. In neither text does Shklovsky seem to be fully aware of his concept's ambiguity, but the examples he cites illustrate all its forms. Futurism is to a large degree an exercise in the *ostranenie* of language and poetry; Sterne and Cervantes enstrange the novel by parodying its conventions; Tolstoy makes strange the world he describes. Needless to say, this is a matter of tendency, not an absolute distinction—there is some intraliterary *ostranenie* in Tolstoy, and much of the extraliterary variety in Sterne and Cervantes.

When a book on Russian formalism states that *ostranenie* is far from being a wide-spread device, that it is merely typical of Russian avant-garde art (Hansen-Löve 21), it seems to have intraliterary forms in mind. These, too, are typical of all experimental and unusual writing, not only of Russian provenance. More to the point, the extraliterary form is even more widespread. This is not to say that every literary work *must* contain it, but it is at the heart of a great many images.[10]

---

[10] The claim in "Art as Device" that every image contains *ostranenie* is arguably overstated.

Boym ("Estrangement As a Lifestyle …" 515) observes that "the theory of estrangement is often seen as an artistic declaration of independence, the declaration of art's autonomy from the everyday. Yet in Shklovsky's 'Art as a Device' (1917), estrangement appears more as a device of mediation between art and life." Indeed, almost every example from Tolstoy provided in "Art as Device" serves as a critique of society. "The main function of *ostranenie* in Tolstoy is consciousness," he'd say later (*Tetiva* 75). Even the passages which do not seem obviously critical become so in context. The scene in which opera is made strange by Natasha Rostova, for instance, can be productively read as follows: "the confused, humiliated heroine, fresh from her disastrous encounter with her future father- and sister-in-law and eager to blunt her sense of the real, rejects artistic sincerity and welcomes operatic 'falsehood' as a portal into her seduction by Anatol Kuragin" (Emerson 644).

"Art as Device" never explicitly comments on the social function of the examples, but it is Shklovsky who chose them. The idea of art enstranging the habitual is much older than the concept of *ostranenie*: the belief that poetic language should be somewhat strange is at least as old as Aristotle, and the Romantics sought to "lift the veil from the hidden beauty of the world, and makes familiar objects be as if they were not familiar" (Shelley 642).[11] Coleridge (308) describes poetry as "awakening the mind's attention from the lethargy of custom, and directing it to the loveliness and the wonders of the world before us; an inexhaustible treasure, but for which in consequence of the film of familiarity and selfish solicitude we have eyes, yet see not, ears that hear not, and hearts that neither feel nor understand."

---

[11] Much has been written on the parallels between Romantic ideas of art and *ostranenie* (e.g. Todorov, "Poetic Language"; Robinson: 80–1, 153–8).

Shklovsky himself mentions Novalis' idea of "making things pleasantly strange" in *Tales about Prose*. Indeed, both Novalis' *Befremdung* and Brecht's *Verfremdung* are semantically and etymologically close to *ostranenie*. However, there are differences: unlike the Romantics, Shklovsky saw art as a way to reawaken the mind not only to the beauty of the world, but also to its horrors. Unlike Brecht, he did not believe that restricting feelings was necessary in order to promote critical thought. Indeed, he saw emotion and cognition as closely connected, and contemporary empirical research shares this view (cf. Storbeck and Clore and on Shklovsky and cognitive studies, Berlina, "To give back…"). *Ostranenie* is a multifaceted concept, and at different times Shklovsky was more interested in some aspects than others. But he never lost interest entirely (see the Index for the discussions of *ostranenie*, both veiled and direct, in the seventy years of his work). As he put it (Vitale 175), "Tolstoy […] wants to shake people and say 'Stop, return to your selves, wake up!'" And so does Shklovsky.

Shklovsky in the West: Reception and Heritage

In 1965, Shklovsky's work was first published in English and French (Lemon and Reis; Todorov, *Théorie de la littérature*). Having already influenced Jakobson, Bakhtin, and Lotman, it went on to attract the attention of Todorov ("Poetic Language") and other structuralists (see Striedter, *Literary Structure*; Scholes). Shklovsky was flattered, but he disagreed with some key structuralist concepts and was disdainful of jargon as well as wary of theory unaccompanied by practice: "If literature is an exclusively linguistic phenomenon, how is translation possible?"; "the structuralists, who filled the world with terminology […] don't know this thing [the experience of literary writing]" (Vitale 80, 85).

Shklovsky's young self was resurrected in foreign languages (which he never learned), while he himself remained shut off from the world. "I doubt that most of us who were enthusiasts of the handful of essays available in the West were aware that he was not only still alive, but still publishing," writes Gorman (133). In 1972, *Twentieth Century Studies* dedicated a special issue to Russian formalism, which included three articles by Shklovsky and one on him. Gradually, Shklovsky's success in the West led to the acknowledgement of his work in the Soviet Union. Today, he is perhaps better known in the Anglophone world than he ever was.

But what happens if a contemporary student, one who doesn't speak Russian, hears Shklovsky's name mentioned in a lecture, and develops an interest? First, she'll probably Google him and find quite a competent (as of June 2016) Wikipedia article. And what if she is so diligent as to use literary dictionaries and compendia? There is usually no entry on Shklovsky there, but almost always one on Russian formalism.

Now, Shklovsky doesn't equal the whole of formalism, which is usually defined to include Jakobson's school; moreover, both changed with time (cf. Steiner). Still, dictionary definitions of "formalism" often rely on "Art as Device" as their key text, and it would be nice if they got it right. *The Oxford Dictionary of Literary Terms* (2015) states that formalism "deliberately disregard[s] the content of literary work"; the entry in *The Penguin Dictionary of Literary Terms and Literary Theory* (2013) adds that, for formalists, "the writer is of negligible importance." Often, it is assumed that the reader doesn't matter, either—only the devices do.

Partly, this image stems from Jakobson's concept of "literariness," *literaturnost'*—the quality of a text which makes it literary and is the object of literary studies. Partly, the image is based in Shklovsky's own writing, but it disregards two things: when young, Shklovsky was prone to aphoristic overstatements; when old, he was made to publicly chastise himself for mistakes he never made. Looking closely at, say, "Art as Device," we see that it deals with *devices* created by a *writer* to combat automatism, to make the *reader* sensitive to the "*content.*" Shklovsky takes into consideration all four aspects (though he wouldn't separate "devices" from "content"). In fact, formalism can be regarded as a forerunner of reader-response criticism (cf. Tompkins) along with New Criticism.

According to *Literary Theory and Criticism: An Oxford Guide* (Morson 217–18), formalism sees literary history thus:

> Literary change always goes through four stages. First, literary devices defamiliarize the world. Next, a readership becomes familiar with the devices of defamiliarization, and so these devices cease to perform their function. Next, writers start defamiliarizing these very devices. [...] Finally, new devices replace old ones, the new ones typically coming from a past now out of the readers' sensibility (from "the grandfathers") or from popular literature (from "the uncles").

The references to literary "uncles" and "defamiliarization" point to Shklovsky, but he never described such a four-stage-model. (I couldn't find it in other formalist texts, either, though I'd be happy to be corrected.) First, "uncles" is not shorthand for "popular literature." In "Literature beyond 'Plot,'" Shklovsky says that "it is not sons who inherit from their fathers, but nephews who inherit from their uncles." He envisions a spiral development of literature, with writers borrowing not from the greatest among the immediate predecessors in their genre (as was universally assumed), but from adjacent strands—poetry from prose, for instance, or prose from journalism. "Highbrow" literature using devices from "popular" literature is but one of the examples he cites (though he does concentrate on it in several texts, for instance, *A Sentimental Journey*). More importantly, the extraliterary and the intraliterary functions of *ostranenie* do not appear in any particular succession. A single text and, more to the point, a single reading can contain both.

To conclude: our student might end up somewhat confused by reference books. Still, let's assume her interest is growing. If so, she has many opportunities to pursue an acquaintance with Shklovsky. First of all, there is his writing. Between 1990 and 2012, eleven books by Shklovsky were published in English. In 2005–6, a special double issue of *Poetics Today—Estrangement Revisited*—was dedicated to Shklovsky's heritage. In 2013, Serena Vitale's book-length interview with Shklovsky was published in English. The conversation was a risky affair for both; Vitale was traced by eight KGB escorts. Nevertheless, Shklovsky is very sincere in it; charming and crabby by turns, he shows through the printed page as a living being.

The year 2014 saw the death of two brilliant Shklovsky scholars, Alexander Galushkin and Richard Sheldon, the latter also a translator of his work. In the same year, Shklovsky's biography appeared in Russian (Berezin). In 2015, Columbia University hosted an international conference "On Strangeness and the Factory of Life: Viktor Shklovsky Then and Now" (organized by Rad Borislavov). Next year, another international conference took place in Erfurt, Germany (organized by Holt Meyer and myself). Entitled "One Hundred Years of Ostranenie", it attracted not only Slavicists, but scholars of different literatures and other disciplines. In 2016, OPOYAZ (arguably) and the talk (1916) that became "Art as Device" (1917) (certainly) turned one hundred. This reader is a way to celebrate these birthdays.

The Poker of Russian Formalism: Shklovsky as Protagonist

Shklovsky was a source of aphorisms and a force of nature, the father of formalism and its enfant terrible, its "trouble-shooter" (Erlich, *Russian Formalism* 76) and "trouble-maker" (Kaverin, *Skandalist*). He is mentioned in almost every memoir about Russian émigré Berlin or the intelligentsia in Petrograd, a city which existed from 1914 to 1924. His portraits appear not only in his own novels, but also in up to a dozen others.[12] In at least four novels, Shklovsky's role as a prototype is clearly established.

The best-known among these, and the only one translated into English, is Bulgakov's *White Guard*, in which Shklovsky's name is only thinly veiled. Shpolyansky is a provocative figure whom another (admittedly, mentally unstable) protagonist believes to be the devil incarnate. Demonic features are not necessary negative in Bulgakov's work, as witnessed by Woland in *The Master and Margarita*. However, Shpolyansky (unlike Shklovsky) is also a Bolshevik, which is more problematic from Bulgakov's perspective. The present chapter cites the passage in which Shpolyansky appears for the first time, wearing sideburns, as did Shklovsky during the Russian Civil War in 1918, in Kiev. With its repetitions of "moreover" and the list intermingling habitual and one-off actions, the introduction of Shpolyansky parodies Shklovsky's style.[13]

---

[12] The number partly depends on interpretation. Very probable instances not included here are Zhukanets in *The Mad Ship* by Olga Forsh, Andreishin in Vsevolad Ivanov's *U* (Shklovsky and Ivanov also co-authored the science-fiction novel *Mustard Gas*, in which both make cameo appearances), and Serbinov in Andrei Platonov's *Chevengur*. A very well-researched Russian article on Shklovsky as a protagonist in Kaverin and Ginsburg also briefly mentions other texts (Razumova and Sverdlov).

[13] In Michael Glenny's translation, all these are smoothed into utter neutrality. Those

While *White Guard* features Shklovsky during the Civil War, *The Troublemaker, or Evenings on the Vasilievsky Island* deals with his fate as a scholar. In fact, Kaverin only wrote this book because Shklovsky doubted his talent as a writer. On the passage cited in this chapter, Kaverin comments as follows:

> One of the chapters of *The Troublemaker* conveys the real state of things. To celebrate the arrival of Nekrylov ["The Troublemaker" identified with Shklovsky], his former students organize a party. Pretending that everything is all right, they sing the young formalists' hymn. We were still the "formalituri," but Viktor had stopped being a Caesar for whom it was worth it to die. The whole scene is not invented, but written down immediately after the event. (Kaverin, *Epilog* 34)

The main theme of Kaverin's novel is automatization and *ostranenie*. One of its protagonists is a literary scholar plagued by the feeling that his life—his books, his lectures, his wife—are becoming too familiar. Shklovsky liked the novel on the whole but complained (perhaps not quite sincerely, for he was often weary of his cinematic work) about one aspect: "Kaverin thinks that I return from the cinema factory tired—like a lion who crawls into his lair, takes off his hide and sighs with relief. Or like an old Jew. They believe that all people speak Yiddish at home but some pretend otherwise in company"(Shulman).

Belinkov's novel whose title is clumsily translated here as *Surrender and Death of [One from] the Soviet Intelligentsia,*[14] is subtitled "Yury Olesha." While the title openly refers to the author of Envy and

---

wishing to read Bulgakov's brilliant novel on the Russian Civil War are much better served with Marian Schwartz's rendition.

[14] The original *sovetskogo intelligenta* can refer both to a single person and to the intelligentsia as a class.

Three Fat Men, Shklovsky's surrender is also a prominent motif. "Razdvatris," who is closely modeled on Shklovsky (cf. Sarnov), is condemned as a Soviet opportunist. In 1944, the contact to Shklovsky played a role both in Belinkov's arrest under the charge of anti-Soviet agitation, and in his release. Even in the chaos of Soviet imprisonment, it was rare for one person to play two opposing roles. Interrogating Belinkov, the investigator said: "It is commonly known that Shklovsky has a hostile stance toward the world around him and it is also commonly known that he has engaged in anti-Soviet activities for some time" (Vitale 33). And yet, soon after Shklovsky wrote a letter of support, Belinkov was let free (see Belinkov and Belinkova).

Not only those who met Shklovsky felt drawn to write about him; Dmitry Bykov, a present-day Russian author, includes a very Shklovsky-like figure in his 2003 novel *Orthography*. Needless to say, the borderline between novels and "nonfiction"—diaries, memoirs, autobiographies—is artificial, all the more so in regard to writings from the 1920s. Still, it seems to make sense to separate books featuring a man named "Shklovsky" from others; the excerpts in each category appear in order of publication.

As befits texts dealing with Shklovsky, these contain many contradictions. Osip Mandelstam and his wife Nadezhda, for instance, have rather different things to say about him; Nina Berberova[15] believes *Zoo* to be "a game" written merely to entertain, while Lidiya Ginzburg[16] calls it "the tenderest book of our times," brimming with

---

[15] The writer and biographer Nina Berberova left Russia in 1922 with the poet Vladislav Khodasevich; she met Shklovsky both in their native St. Petersburg and in Berlin. She left for the United States in 1950 where she taught Russian literature at Yale and Princeton. An English translation of her autobiography *The Italics Are Mine* by Philippe Radley was published in New York in 1969—before the book appeared in the original Russian.

[16] The literary critic and historian Lidiya Ginzburg studied with Tynyanov and Eikhenbaum in Leningrad and was considered one of the leading young formalists before formalism was officially eradicated.

passion. Even a single diary can veer from "one cannot imagine him unhappy" to "Shklovsky is actually a sad person." Happy or sad, hero or traitor, guerilla fighter or scholar, Shklovsky remains memorable. All excerpts below are translated by Alexandra Berlina.

In Fiction

Mikhail Bulgakov, *White Guard* [1925]

Mikhail Semenovich [Shpolyansky] was swarthy and clean-shaven, with velvety sideburns, an exact copy of Eugene Onegin. Mikhail Semenovich made himself known to the whole City as soon as he had arrived from St. Petersburg. Mikhail Semenovich became famous as an excellent reader of his own verse "Drops of Saturn" at the Ashes club and as a fantastic organizer of poets, the chairman of the poetry sect "The Magnetic Triolet." Moreover, Mikhail Semenovich was an unrivalled orator; moreover, he operated military as well as civilian vehicles; moreover, he kept Musya Ford, a ballerina from the opera theater, and another lady, whose name Mikhail Semenovich, being a gentleman, revealed to nobody; he had much money and generously lent it to members of "The Magnetic Triolet"; moreover, he

drank white wine,

played baccarat,

acquired the painting "The Bathing Venetian,"

lived on the Khreshchatyk street at night,

in the cafe Bilbocquet in the morning,

in his cozy room at the city's best hotel, Continental, in the afternoon,

in the Ashes club in the evening,

and composed the scholarly work "The Intuitive in Gogol" at dawn.

The Hetman's City perished about three hours earlier than it should have, and this was because on December 2, 1918, during an evening at the Ashes club, Mikhail Semenovich said to Stepanov, Sheyer, Slonykh and Cheremshin (the heads of "The Magnetic Triolet"): "They are all scum. Both the hetman and Petliura. But Petliura is also a pogromist. This is not the main thing, though. I'm bored. I haven't thrown a bomb for ages."

(Bulgakov 94)

Veniamin Kaverin, *The Troublemaker* [1929]

Nekrylov was saying that you couldn't just keep rejecting everything; that once, they had written in order to turn around art, and also, "the game we play must be chess, not backgammon, a matter of luck and confusion." He said that his heart ached from the complacency of those at that very table, that Dragomanov had no right to be eating fish with such a placid air if he believed our literature to be a catastrophe …

Dragomanov left the fish alone and began to stir his concoction with a coffee spoon.

—You shouldn't have smashed that drinking glass, he replied quietly.

—A single glass! Go ahead and count all the glasses I had to smash so that you could talk …

[…]

It was very late when a graduate student, blond and long-legged, somewhat giraffe-like, proclaimed that he wished to sing.

He was drunk; perhaps this is why he sang mezzo-soprano.

Love, just as any other object,
is known to me with all its vices,

but passion, from a formal viewpoint,
is the convergence of devices.

He didn't finish. The roar of laughter had such force that the silk lampshade lost its balance and flew above the table like a butterfly, noiselessly.

The long-legged student stood in the middle of the room on broken bottles, swinging his endless arms, the cuffs of his sleeves as hard as iron. After a bass warble, he changed back to mezzo.

No matter if the boa constrictor
of our detractors is a mutant—
still ave Caesar, ave Victor,
aspiranturi te salutant!

But had Viktor really won?

(Kaverin, *Skandalist* 99–100)

Arkady Belinkov, *Surrender and Death of [One from] the Soviet Intelligentsia. Yury Olesha* [1968]

A writer, once brilliant (let's call him "the dance instructor Razdvatris in new circumstances"),[17] a great and bitter sinner of Russian literature, a man whose every new book crossed out his every old book, a smiling man dangling between lie and half-truth, was nodding his head in understanding.

People were drinking tea.

This man believes that time is always right: when it makes mistakes, and when it admits them. Many people visit him. Some hold him in contempt; some drink his tea and laugh at him [...]

---

[17] A protagonist of Olesha's *Three Fat Men*, the dance instructor Razdvatris was largely on the side of the title heroes. Though these stood for capitalism, here Belinkov seems to be referring to Shklovsky's connections with the Soviet apparatus.

"In times of the personality cult," the smiling man was saying, "sometimes the publisher made one write that Russia was the motherland of elephants. Well, you understand—it wasn't debatable. Such things are not discussed. Odysseus didn't choose whether he wanted to land on Circe's island. Many wrote that Russia was indeed the motherland of elephants. As for me, I expressed my indignation, almost spontaneously. I broke a chair. I came to these people. I made a statement. I said: 'You don't understand anything. Russia is the motherland of mammoths!' A writer can't always do as he is told. He can't be always saying yes."

(Belinkov 163–4)

Dmitry Bykov, *Orthography* [2003]

The idol of this young public was, for some reason, Lgovsky, whose "Problems of Structure" Yat couldn't finish, as he didn't believe that poetry could be approached statistically. Lgovsky recognized many on sight (it seemed to be his regular audience); he was saying that only a hundred years later the reality of Petrograd life as they knew it would seem like fantasy.

"Few facts will survive," he said, his eyes gleaming, conspiratorial smiles flying hither and thither, "Nobody writes prose today, and it would be well if at least diaries remained from our epoch. Keep diaries, this is the literature of the future! Prose has no power today, is it yet to be rewritten. You can't write 'Ivan Ivanovich walked' or 'Anton Antonovich said' anymore. Conventional conditionality has been exceeded. You could write 'Petr Petrovich flew,' that would be more believable."

(Bykov)

In Diaries and Memoirs

Korney Chukovsky [1917]

When telling something terrible, Shklovsky smiles and even laughs. This is very attractive. "Luckily, I was wounded, or else I'd have shot myself!" He's been shot, the bullet went right through his stomach, but he seems just fine.

(Chukovsky 216)

Lidiya Ginzburg [1920s–1930s]

Shklovsky's interest in Sterne isn't a matter of chance. But shifts, displacements and digressions are perhaps much less of a literary device for him than they were for Sterne; they derive from the construction of his thinking apparatus.

When Rina Zelenaya and I were walking back from Shklovsky's, she said: "Here is a man who cannot be unhappy." This is a very true observation. Really, one cannot imagine him unhappy, embarrassed or frightened—this might well be the essence of his charm.

Apropos of Rina: about her, he said crossly, "So she read *Zoo* and decided that I must be thin and sentimental!" "No, Viktor Borisovich, I warned her that you're quite corpulent."

[…]

"Failing to understand is my profession," says Shklovsky.

He says that all his talent for unrequited love has been spent on the heroine of *Zoo*; that he can only love happily now.

He says that this book, *Zoo*, was so full of love in its first (Berlin) version that you couldn't hold it in your hands without burning yourself.

It's quite wrong to believe (as many do) that Shklovsky is a cheerful person; Shklovsky is actually a sad person. To make quite sure, I asked him, and he gave me his word of honor that he was sad.

[…]

I said to [Osip] Brik:

—V. B. [Shklovsky] talks just the way he writes.

—Yes, exactly the same way. But the difference is huge. He talks in earnest and writes in jest. When Vitya says "I'm suffering," it means there is a human being who suffers. But when he writes it, it means "Look, I'm *suffering*."

[…]

Shklovsky once said that formalism, idealism and such are like tins bound to a cat's tail. The cat flings itself about, and the tin keeps clattering after him. "The whole life long …"

[…]

During a dispute in the twenties, Shklovsky told his opponents:

There's only four of us, and you, you've got an army and a fleet. Why are you worried?

[…]

Shklovsky told me how he managed to receive permission to return to Russia. He sent twelve copies of *Letters not about Love*, including the famous final letter, to the VTsIK [All-Russian Central Executive Committee]. "Once in their lives, the people at VTsIK had some fun, so they let me in."

Shklovsky is, without a doubt, a man with a defective thinking apparatus.

From his intellectual stammer, he has created a new kind of literary article.

[…]

I've heard Shklovsky being called (perhaps not without reason) a traitor, a ruffian, a philanderer, a negligent worker—but I won't stand, I just cannot stand people considering him a clown. Do they really believe that he wrote *Zoo*, the tenderest book of our times, according to the formal method?!

(Ginzburg 133 et seq.)

Roman Gul [1927]

Viktor Shklovsky was walking through the night with the walk of a neurotic, hopping on his toes. He walked and sang. He stopped at the window of a book shop. There he remained standing, smiling at something.

When he was gone I saw what he had been looking at in the window: *A Sentimental Journey*. Writers are most sincere when alone with their own books.

(Gul)

Osip Mandelstam [1927]

His head resembles the wise cranium of a baby or a philosopher. It's a laughing, thinking pumpkin.

I imagine Shklovsky giving a talk on the Theater Square. The crowd surrounds him and listens, as if he was a fountain. Thought is shooting from his mouth, his nostrils, his ears; the fountain keeps playing, indifferently and constantly, continuously self-renewing and equal to itself. Shklovsky's smile is saying: all things will pass, but I'll never run dry, for thought is running water. Everything will change, new buildings will rise on the square, but still the stream will shoot from my mouth, my nostrils, my ears.

There's something about it—something indecent, if you will. Typists and stenographers in particular love to take care of Shklovsky, they feel tender toward him. I believe that, taking down his speech, they experience sensual pleasure.[18]

(O. Mandelstam 459)

Evgeny Schwartz [1954]

I'm afraid of him, of his snub-nosed mask, always ready to smile. He suspects that I'm not a writer. [...] He really loves literature, more than anyone I know in his profession. He tries to understand it, he seeks its laws—because he loves it. He loves passionately, organically. He remembers every story, whenever he read it. He doesn't like books about books, like his brethren. No. His connection to literature is organic. This is why he is better as a writer than a scholar.

(Schwartz, diary entry from August 5, 1954)

Nadezhda Mandelstam [1960]

Only one home in Moscow was open to outcasts. [...] When the doorbell rang, they hid us in the kitchen or the nursery before opening. If it turned out that the visitors were friends, we were liberated from captivity amid happy screams [...] The Shklovsky home was the only place where we felt human. This family knew how to deal with the doomed. In the kitchen, we discussed where to stay overnight, how to go to a concert, whence to get money and what to do. We tried not to sleep at the Shklovskys' because their house was full of lift operators, yard cleaners and concierges. These kind-hearted and wretched women have always worked for the secret police. [...] The circle of those who shared with us grew ever smaller. We waited for Shklovsky's pay packet. He came home with money stuck into all his pockets, and shared his booty with us.

(N. Mandelstam 409–13)

---

[18] Shklovsky would indeed marry one of his typists.

Valentina Khodasevich [1960]

Sometimes I seem to get out of breath when listening to him, as if from running or great excitement. I don't know how to describe it, but I strongly feel the very process of his brain working.

(Khodasevich 180)

Nina Berberova [1969]

Shklovsky was a round-headed, short, cheerful man. There was always a smile on his face, and this smile showed the black roots of his front teeth and the intelligence of his sparkling eyes. He could be brilliant, and he was full of mockery and wit; he could be impudent, particularly in the presence of an "important person," a phony celebrity or anyone whose pedantry, self-assurance or stupidity got on his nerves. He was an inventive soul, brimming with energy, discoveries and phrases. Life was humming within him, and he loved life. His *Letters not about Love* and other books he wrote at that time were a game; he amused others and himself.

(Berberova 230)

Mikhail Kozakov [1979]

When Boris Mikhailovich [Eikhenbaum] was driven out of the university for his "comparativism" and "formalism," Viktor Borisovich [Shklovsky] came to Leningrad at once. "Viten'ka" reacted to "Borechka's" banishment as follows: on entering the apartment, he threw off his coat with much vigor, kissed Eikhenbaum hello and quickly strode into his study; he walked around it excited, agitated, wide-shouldered, squarely built; on his strong neck set a clean-shaven head whose unique form always reminded me of a fetus in the womb. There he was, walking, panting; then, finding no words, he strode to the stove, grabbed the poker, placed it behind his neck and, using all his force, bent it double. This wasn't enough to him! He took it by the ends, crosswise, and pulled them apart! It was a strange object he ended up with. He presented it to Eikhenbaum and said, breathing heavily:

—Borechka, this is the poker of Russian formalism.

(Kozakov 47)

Shklovsky's Shorts

If you ask Russians about Shklovsky, you often hear: "Isn't he the one who, at some Gulag camp, said he felt like a live fox in a fur shop?" or "Wasn't it him who said that Soviet authorities had taught literary scholars subtle differentiation between different shades of shit?"

The latter quip is variously ascribed to Andrei Sinyavsky and Shklovsky, but much more often to the latter. This doesn't prove he really said it, though: Shklovsky is the (anti)Soviet Oscar Wilde, to whom witticisms are often ascribed by default. His contemporary Chukovsky even had the habit of adding "not by Shklovsky!" to aphorisms and puns in his almanac, the *Chukkokala*. Most of the following phrases are taken from Shklovsky's published texts and letters that didn't make it into this reader; some are gleaned from notes taken down by his students and friends (Chudakov, "Sprashivaya Shklovskogo"; Shulman; Adamovich; Galushkin, "Razgovory"). Here they are, in no particular order:

I'm both a fish and an ichthyologist.

I'm afraid to accidentally say something which resembles a rule.

I'm a very unpractical man. There are only three things I can do: write, talk and make a scene.

Gronsky said from the podium:

—We'll be clubbing Shklovsky's cranium until he recognizes his mistakes!

Shklovsky shouted from his seat:

—You've got it easy: you have nothing but a club, and I have nothing but a cranium!

In English homes, on the staircases, there are special niches in the walls, for people to stand in while a coffin is being carried out. Our literature reminds me of such a niche.

Derzhavin said that formalists were impotent. I answered: Ask your wife.

It's brains that burn, not rooftops.
It's heads that lie in ruins, not the loos.[19]

The "two brothers" scheme, with "red and white" instead of "good and bad," now continues the rather worn-out anecdote about Cain.

The world that has lost the sensation of life along with art is about to commit monstrous suicide. In our times of dead art, war circumvents consciousness; this explains its brutality, which is greater than the brutality of religious wars.

I don't believe in wonders, which is why I'm not an artist.

Sometimes, books can be created by budding, like the lower lifeforms, without fertilization. Most scholarly work on Shakespeare belongs to his category.

Creating a plot means cutting a diamond. You can only talk of a

---

[19] The first line is from Dostoyevsky's *Demons*, the second from Bulgakov's *The Dog Heart*. A thriftier literary critic would have based an article on the observation of this parallel; Shklovsky created a two-line poem.

plot if it refracts the material over and over. The facets refract the light, and another reality is created. The ray of perception changed its way.

We must study old forms the way we study frogs. A physiologist examines a frog not because he's learning how to croak.

In art, we use things of the past by rejecting them.

The plot is a method of character analysis.

You need to have an idea of anatomy to understand your own heart.

New thoughts grow not from books, but from the spaces between books.

I'm sad like an unfinished book with missing leaves.

Love is a play with short acts and long intermissions. The most difficult thing is to learn how to behave in the intermissions.

To become the member of a party, when it's the only one around? Never had such a thought.

One of the ways to kill a writer is to candy him in honey.

Literary creation is compulsory youth. An old man cannot write.

They say: your youth is over. I have the feeling that my old age is over, as well.

I'm flying between the gaps in my education like a grey-haired bat.

Shklovsky's Style

Gorman (138) describes Shklovsky's style with great insight: "He rejects smooth, transparent, and tidy expression. His goal is to force his reader to *work* to understand him; the reason for this, presumably, is that his thoughts will have greater impact. This is the doctrine of defamiliarization, which thus finds its true application on the stylistic level."

Shklovsky's style isn't easy. Often, it's purposely unidiomatic; almost always, it's nonacademic. If Shklovsky does sound dry and scholarly, this is usually either when he's writing something he doesn't want to be writing (such as "Monument to a Scientific Error") or when he's being facetious: "I had a grandmother who wore a little velvet hat [...] I was convinced (I was seven) that such little hats characterize the structure of grandmothers" (Tetiva 118). When Vitale (25) mentions parataxis while interviewing him, his reaction is: "What the devil is that? A pair of taxes? Or basset hounds (*taks*)?"

The style of his scholarly writing is very close to that of his poems. "Russians die like wolves, and wolves—as either Aksakov or Brehm says somewhere—die silently" is taken from a poem ("Verstovyye stolby"), but it could be from any article. Such (pseudo)citation of unclear provenance is vintage Shklovsky, as is the use of *ostranenie*, parody, allusion, word play, even rhyme. One might wonder,

> Is Shklovsky perhaps simply a very theoretical, very conscious writer, who creates his own traditions based on his literary taste and opinions?
>
> It seems at the end that Shklovsky observes only such devices and principles which he uses himself.
>
> [...]

> If Shklovsky writes in an ambiguous context and with an air of significance "here, I made a blot on my manuscript," we'll suspect that blot of actually existing (Khmel'nitskaya)

Shklovsky's writing is also very rich in images. Some are from what Shklovsky describes, in "A Letter to Roman Jakobson," as "the thick book which my father read from right to left, my mother read from left to right, and I do not read at all" (his father was Jewish). Most are Shklovsky's own idiosyncratic creatures. Many images become leitmotifs. Shklovsky shares the penchant for animalistic comparisons with Wittgenstein, and one could write a book on his menagerie: there are cats in *Bowstring*, beavers in *Tales about Prose*, and horses everywhere. Sometimes, images travel from text to text. *Technique of Writing Craft* (1927) features the following example:

> A book describes a soldier returning from the front and riding on the roof of a train; the soldier is so cold that he even wraps himself in a newspaper.
>
> Gorky read through this passage and changed it as follows [...]: "I was very cold even though I had wrapped myself in newspapers."
>
> The thing he creates here is this: a man wrapped in newspapers seems to consider himself lucky; it's only the reader who sees his grievous state.

This seems to be an impersonal suggestion in a manual of literary devices. But almost forty years later, in *Once Upon a Time*, Shklovsky remembers the war:

> Every man has his measure of grief, his measure of weariness, and if he is filled with grief, you can pour another bucket of it over him—he won't absorb more. I had lost all my papers and all my

friends. I came back cowering on the roof of a train, wrapping myself in a newspaper.

Did Shklovsky integrate the book into his biography, or did he smuggle his biography into the manual? Was the book shown to Gorky Shklovsky's own draft? Or were rooftop travelers wrapped in newspapers simply an everyday occurrence in postrevolutionary Russia? Be it as it may, it's worthwhile to read different works by Shklovsky in immediate succession. Only connect.

Selection, Translation, and Formal Remarks

If the structures are interconnected, and the style is intricate, how do you select and translate? I tried to include at least glimpses from all key texts and also as much previously untranslated material as possible. Texts published in English for the first time make up about half of the selection.

Only two crucial articles—"Resurrecting the Word" and "Art as Device"—and some very short ones are published in full. In all other texts, elisions are indicated with "[...]" (elision marks without square brackets are Shklovsky's own). Cutting Shklovsky's texts feels both painful and presumptuous, but it was impossible to condense his seventy years of writing otherwise.

Despite all my attempts to preserve connections and leitmotifs, some were lost; others became more obvious in abbreviation—in Shklovsky, interconnected images can be a hundred pages or even a dozen books apart. Attention was paid to Shklovsky's key themes and ideas: if a certain thought occurs in many texts, I use at least one. Initially, I wanted to avoid repetitions and was worried about Shklovsky's inconsistencies—but changing variations on the same theme are part of his style. However, I did homogenize the spelling of certain keywords: Shklovsky sometimes capitalizes "OPOYAZ" and sometimes doesn't; the editors of his later books add an "n" or, occasionally, a "t" to *ostranenie*. Orthographically, this reader aims at uniformity. In all other respects, authenticity matters more.

I realize how audacious it is to translate into what is not my native language. Shklovsky's Russian is often unidiomatic: should my English sound foreign, I could always claim that this was intentional. To put it more seriously, I feel that, not being a native speaker, I have fewer qualms about enstranging the target text. With Shklovsky, this is not even a case of foreignizing the translation—merely of recreating the original effect.

To me, the main challenges in translating Shklovsky were not his unidiomatic turns of phrase, or his allusions and puns, or his elliptic, aphoristic style, but the seemingly least important English words, namely articles and prepositions. Russian uses none of the former and fewer of the latter; this makes original ambiguities difficult to recreate. Every Russian noun has the potential of turning into a bifurcating puzzle: should it be preceded with "a" or "the"? I was lucky with most titles: "Art as Device," for instance, can do without articles. But is *ostranenie* "*a* goal of art" or "*the* goal of art"? Word order and context suggest the stronger claim—this is the translation I chose, losing a grain of ambiguity inherent in the original. The same is true of the essay's crucial statement: "Art is the means to live through the making of a thing." Here, too, the bolder claim seems more probable, but it might be just "*a* means."

A similar problem arises with prepositions. Does "art exist in order to return the sensation *of* life" or "*to* life"? The original can mean either. In context, "of" seems more probable. Still, Shklovsky might have well intended a double meaning. If art exists to "return sensation *to* life," the *after*-effects of reading become most important:

the reader, her senses refreshed, is ready to encounter reality; the ultimate effect of *ostranenie* is extraliterary.

I attempted to always use the same translation for what seem to be Shklovsky's crucial key words, not shying away from repetition when he doesn't. The excel file entitled "Shklovsky dictionary" on my desktop contains 112 words. Still, uniform translation wasn't always possible. *Veshch'*, for instance, is a crucial word for Shklovsky; it normally translates as "thing," and this is what it usually means in his texts. It is the *things* of the world that art enstranges. However—and here we return to the question of intra- and extraliterary *ostranenie*—*veshch'* is also an idiomatic, if somewhat elevated, way of referring to texts (comparable to "work" or "oeuvre").

Another keyword connected to *ostranenie* is *perezhivat'*, lit. "live through." The closest equivalent is, I believe, the psychological term *erlebnis*: "the mind's identification with its own emotions and feelings when it consciously 'lives through'" (Runes). However, replacing a Russian word with a German one in an English text would be just silly, and I settled for "experience"—but the verb can also mean "sense," "feel," as well as "be in emotional turmoil" and "survive." *Syuzhet* usually means "plot," but sometimes it also refers to a theme. Shklovsky's favorite term of disparagement is *poshlost'*. I render it as "vulgarity," but am aware that Nabokov, who punningly transliterates it as *poshlust*, spends five pages on discussing its untranslatability (in *Nikolai Gogol* 63–7).

Russian writers and scholars tend to disregard gender bias even now, and Shklovsky began publishing a hundred years ago. Hence, abstract entities such as "the reader" and "the author" are always male. However, Shklovsky was no sexist, as witnessed by his admiration for many female writers, first and foremost Anna Akhmatova. He never calls her simply "Anna," always "Anna Andreevna." The use of the patronymic suggests respect and a degree of formality, which is why patronymics are preserved throughout the text, confusing as they might be to an Anglophone reader.

Each text title is accompanied by the date of its first release and, if applicable, of the alternative version used for this reader. I didn't always choose the primary publication, as Shklovsky often expanded his texts. One of the most interesting parts of *Zoo*, for instance, is a preface added forty years later. When Shklovsky quotes heavily abbreviated translations of Anglophone texts, the present version provides back-translations in order to show in which form foreign writers came to influence Shklovsky. The BGN/PCGN Romanization system is used, with the exception of names whose transliteration is established ("Shklovsky," not "Shklovskiy").

All footnotes and all translations (also of texts which are not by Shklovsky) are by me, unless noted otherwise.

Alexandra Berlina

Part One

OPOYAZ Publications

Part One: Introduction

Based on Shklovsky's 1913 talk in the "Stray Dog" café, "**Resurrecting the Word**" (*Voskreshenie slova*) is arguably the first document of formalist theory, self-published in 1914 in St. Petersburg; some of the copies were decorated by the avant-garde artist Olga Rozanova and the futurist Alexey Kruchenykh. A translation of the essay by Richard Sherwood is included in the *Russian Formalism* collection (Shklovsky, "The Resurrection of the Word").

This essay is a strange mixture of futurist provocation (Shklovsky ridicules the reverence for "old art") and conservative dogmatism (he also claims that "the heydays of art knew no vulgarity")—despite which it manages to be brilliantly original. As a twenty-one-year-old student, Shklovsky was still not daring enough to throw all academic conventions overboard: this article is more quotationist and respectful than anything else he published in his formalist youth. Instead of his later "I seem to have read somewhere," there are direct references, some even containing page numbers. Among them, there are respectful mentions of many scholars he'd be harsh about only a few years later: for instance, Ovsyaniko-Kulikovsky, whose attitude toward literature he'd soon compare to a person "who came to look at a flower and, to make [himself] comfortable, sat down on it" (Shklovsky, *Gamburgskiy schet* [1990] 163).

Others Shklovsky cites in these early essays—most prominently Polivanov and Yakubinsky—were his close friends; together, they were what was to become the OPOYAZ. They were young and hungry—for bread, but, even more, for ideas. We will encounter these figures in Shklovsky's autobiographic writing, but here are some notes to flesh out the references: Polivanov lost a hand as a boy—to imitate a character from the *Brothers Karamazov*, he laid it on the tracks as a train passed over.[1] He also ate opium and went to present his doctoral thesis in his underwear. As a linguist, he was, in Shklovsky's opinion, a genius (Vitale 79). About Yakubinsky, Shklovsky says this: "The best year of my life was the one when I spent an hour, two hours every day talking to Lev Yakubinsky on the phone. We set up little tables by the phones" (*Gamburgskiy schet* [1990] 423). Many of Shklovsky's ideas were born of notes jotted down on these tables.

Without yet coining the term *ostranenie*, "Resurrecting the Word" lays the groundwork for the concept. It has been pointed out in regard to "Art as Device" that *ostranenie* has two functions: "to force a new way of seeing things upon the reader," but also "in a kind of counter-movement, to steer perception toward the enstranging and complicating form itself" (Striedter, *Texte der russischen Formalisten I* xxiii). I'd venture to disagree with Striedter's subsequent claim that, in "Art as Device," Shklovsky only regards the second effect as relevant. He might be disregarding the ambiguity of his concept—but most of the examples he discusses in "Art as Device" deal with a new way of seeing things. The *ostranenie* of language itself, on the other hand, is the key topic of his first essay, "Resurrecting the Word." The choice of literary material in these two articles, too, is symptomatic: though "Resurrecting the Word" cites very few examples, toward the end it rather suddenly turns into a futurist manifesto. "Art as Device," on the other hand, partly reads as a commented Tolstoy anthology. While futurist poetry concentrates on enstranging language, Tolstoy

[1] At least, according to Shklovsky; other sources offer less romantic explanations.

enstranges the world. It might be added that two others writers crucial to Shklovsky—Sterne and Cervantes—enstranged genres. Needless to say, these distinctions are anything but absolute, but they point to the multifaceted nature of Shklovsky's key concept. *Ostranenie* appears (often in disguise) in most of Shklovsky's writing, but, for better or worse, almost all attention is captured by "Art as Device."[2]

Nevertheless, there has been no textological work on it. Naiman (346) made this observation in 1998, and it still largely holds true, with the exception of some passages in Naiman's article itself. The present translation follows the longest version of the essay—the one published in the third volume of the OPOYAZ *Collection on the Theory of Poetic Language* (*Sbornik po teorii poeticheskogo yazyka*; 1919). The first version appeared in the second volume in 1917, without the material on erotic *ostranenie*. Apparently, the addition was deemed important enough to justify the repeated publication of the whole article. As Shklovsky puts it in regard to another text, "I wanted to make a splash, shock people. As I've said, this was the era" (Vitale 81). Later reprints of "*Iskusstvo[,] kak priem*" differ in minor aspects such as punctuation and fail to include a Belorussian fairy tale.[3] These reprints formed the sources of the existing English translations (Shklovsky, "Art as Technique"; Sher). Which brings us to the question: if there already are two translations,[4] why attempt a third? One answer is: perhaps this is one of those texts which every

---

[2] Or else, "Art, as Device": in the 1919 edition, the original title reads "Iskusstvo, kak priem," but the comma does not appear in *Poetika*'s table of contents. Shklovsky being Shklovsky, the possibility of a pun cannot be excluded: *kak priem?* means as much as "can you hear me?," "how is the reception?"

[3] This fairy tale is included in the German translation (Striedter, *Texte der russischen Formalisten I*: 29), where a Kafkaesque transformation takes place: in Russian, the wife gets on her hands and knees (*stala rakom*: "doggy-style" is literally "crayfish-style" in Belorussian); in German, she "turns into a crayfish" (*wurde ein Krebs*).

[4] There are actually two and half translations available already: an excerpt was published in English under the title "Poetic Diction" in 1933 (Reavey and Slonim: 420–2).

generation needs to translate again. I'm looking forward to reading a version produced in 2040.

There are also more concrete reasons, but before explaining these, I'd like to say how much I appreciate Benjamin Sher's work. I felt tempted to come up with another title (art "as method," or perhaps "as tool"?)—but soon realized that my alternatives were not as good as Sher's "device." His "e**n**strangement," too, captures the strangeness of *ostranenie.* It is an unintentional neologism, an orthographical mistake on Shklovsky's part: derived from *strannyi* (strange), it should feature a double "n." Sixty-seven years later, Shklovsky commented: "it went off with one 'n,' and is roaming the world like a dog with an ear cut off" (*O teorii prozy* [1983] 73). The missing ear draws attention: the word's incorrectness refreshes language and stimulates associations connected to strangeness. The alternatives—"defamiliarization" and "estrangement"—don't.

Moreover, these terms are associated with Brecht's *Verfremdung* and interpersonal estrangement (as in "she is estranged from her family"). These two concepts suggest decreased emotional connection to people, fictional or real, which is the opposite of *ostranenie.* The ambiguity of "defamiliarization" and "estrangement" is not entirely out of tune with the original term, as Shklovsky well realized: "I have many creations, some legitimate, some not; strangely enough, both survive. '*O***t***stranennyi*' and '*ostrane***n***nyi*'—both spellings make sense" (*Izbrannoe v dvuhk tomakh* v.2, 327). Still, it is confusing. *O***t***stranenie* suggests a withdrawal, a stepping back—an effect closer to Brecht's than to Shklovsky's own ideas. Sher (xviii) believes the original missing letter to be a conscious pun on Shklovsky's part and accordingly does not attempt a solution which treats it as a typo (it is easier to leave out a letter by mistake than to add one). Still, in terms of effect his "e**n**strangement" is close to Shklovsky's neologism.

Despite my admiration for many other of Sher's solutions, a new translation seems useful. For one thing, Sher's version exhibits some difficulties in handling Shklovsky's examples of erotic *ostranenie*. In one tale, the husband fails to recognize his wife who is dressed up as a warrior and refers to herself using the masculine form; in English, she calls her husband "dear" in the very first line, immediately signaling her real identity. In another story, a sexual denouement is replaced with a beating because of a linguistic misunderstanding. Moreover, Shklovsky's diction is rendered more academic and less categorical in translation: for instance, the device of *ostranenie* in an erotic folktale is described as "similar" to Tolstoy's in English where the original says "identical." The essay's key sentence is rendered as "*Art is a means of experiencing the process of creativity*" (Shklovsky, "Art as Device" 6). A closer translation is, I argue, "*Art is the means to live through the making of a thing.*"

By using the most basic words, such as *perezhit'* (live through), *delan'e* (making) and *veshchi* (thing), Shklovsky enstranges this very sentence, removing it from academic diction, and making the reader sit up and see. Moreover, art exists not "in order to return sensation to our limbs" (Shklovsky, "Art as Device" 6) but to return the sensation to life—or, more probably, *of* life. Still, Sher's version of Shklovsky's maxim is a vast improvement over the previous translation: "*art is a way of experiencing the artfulness of an object*" (Lemon and Reis 12).[5] Instead of this apparent tautology, the original speaks of the cognitive act—of things being made by the mind in the process of reading. Even more problematically, a scholar quoting Shklovsky in her own translation renders the same maxim as: "*Art is a means to experience*

[5] The translation by Lemon and Reis also has difficulties with the verb *uznavat'*, which can mean both "recognize" and "get to know," meanings that are functionally opposed in the context of *ostranenie*. They do offer some beautiful solutions for word play, though, such as "butterfingers" (child with fingers covered in butter; clumsy person) for *shlyapa* ("old hat" in the present translation).

the creation of things which have been made insignificant in art" (Haber 51). Shklovsky says the very opposite: things have been made insignificant in automatized life; it is art which creates significance.

I have tried to refrain from smoothing out Shklovsky's stubbly texts. When he repeats a word thrice in a line, this is not for lack of synonyms. When something sounds strange, the translator can edit tacitly, but should she really? Still, the temptation to clarify has not been resisted fully; a few long sentences are divided in two in translation. But what about the key word, *ostranenie*? Why transliterate rather than translate it? Let us begin with the current usage as measured by a Google Scholar search on July 15, 2016 (the widest use in each category in bold; the results include books and articles; I haven't included "foregrounding," the meaning being somewhat different):

Chart I: Current Usage[6]

In conjunction with Shklovsky	In conjunction with Brecht	In psychological and psychiatric publications
Shklovsky's/Shklovskyan ostranenie: 62	Brecht's/Brechtian *ostranenie*: 0	familial/interpersonal *ostranenie*: 0
Shklovsky's/Shklovskyan defamiliari[z/s]ation: 38	Brecht's/Brechtian defamiliari[z/s]ation: 63	familial/interpersonal defamiliari[z/s]ation: 0
Shklovsky's/Shklovskyan estrangement: 31	**Brecht's/Brechtian estrangement: 300**	**familial/interpersonal estrangement: 426**
Shklovsky's/Shklovskyan making strange: 8	Brecht's/Brechtian making strange: 5	familial/interpersonal making strange: 0
Shklovsky's/Shklovskyan **en**strangement: 4	Brecht's/Brechtian **en**strangement: 0	familial/interpersonal **en**strangement: 0

[6]For both Brecht's device and interpersonal difficulties, "alienation" is used far more often than any of the terms listed above (but never in regard to *ostranenie*). For *Verfremdung*, the original term, "V-effect" and "distancing" are also popular; still, "defamiliarization" and "estrangement" appear in conjunction with Brecht's name more often than with Shklovsky's. A look at recent publications reveals no significant trend changes—understandably, as the most recent translation of "Iskusstvo kak priem" was published in 1990.

The method of this survey is far from faultless. A few articles which mention several terms have been counted twice; moreover, the relative influence of publications is not measured here. An important example is the special double issue of *Poetics* (2005–6) dedicated to Shklovsky's heritage and entitled *Estrangement Revisited*. It's hardly surprising that every article in it uses the term "estrangement" (sometimes interchangeably with "ostranenie," "defamiliarization," and "making strange"). "E**n**strangement" is only mentioned when terminology is being discussed, for instance in this statement: "There is estrangement and enstrangement, making it strange, defamiliarization, and de-automatization. [...] the many overlapping, contentious, and complicit terms for *ostranenie* suggest that there are many 'different kinds' of estrangement" (Vatulescu). This is correct—but not all forms of estrangement constitute *ostranenie*.

Unfortunately, "e**n**strangement," a choice convincingly explained both in the translator's foreword and elsewhere (Sher), did not catch on; even publications directly quoting Sher often leave out the "n," seemingly unintentionally. It is indeed easy not to notice the "n" (witness the need for emphasis in this introduction). What do we take from this, combined with the chart above? Another chart, I'm afraid (see page 60).

Chart II: *Ostranenie* Translated—Congeniality and Functionality

	ostranenie	enstrange-ment	defamilia-rization	estrange-ment	making strange
Risk of confusion with partially antonymous concepts	none	none[7]	high	very high	low
Currency in English in regard to Shklovsky's work[8]	43%	3%	26%	22%	6%
Etymological correspondence to the original	[x]	x	-	x	x
Original effects of strangeness and difficulty recreated	x	x	-	-	-
Self-reflexive effect recreated: a "normal" word made strange	-	x	-	-	-
International usage	x	-	-	-	-

All things considered, "ostranenie" and "e**n**strangement" seem like the best solutions. Unfortunately, the latter is too often confused with "estrangement." Still, as using *ostranenie* as anything but a noun would be, well, the *ostraneniest* thing to do, I decided to employ verbal and adjectival forms of "e**n**strange" alongside it in the hope that this book could contribute to finding a shared terminology and giving *ostranenie* the momentum it merits. If the scholarly pendulum really is "swinging once more from the historical to the formal" (Otter 123), it makes sense to keep in mind that *ostranenie* is a highly productive concept combining the two: while the device appears to be universal, its application—as

[7] This is, unless "n" goes unnoticed, as it often does.

[8] Percentage of the total number of terms used in immediate conjunction with "Shklovsky's/Shklovskyan" from chart I (109), rounded off to full percentage points.

witnessed by the *ostranenie* of social norms in "Strider"—is historical. The study of *ostranenie* is a field where researchers of poetics and aesthetics can look into cultural matters and vice versa—it is, after all, a change of perspective which makes things new.

Ostranenie makes an appearance toward the end of "Literature beyond 'Plot'": the writer's work consists in "violating categories," in "wrenching the chair out of furniture." Yet again, furniture is used as an example, perhaps because it is so usual and unnoticeable—at least until it is enstranged by being burnt for warmth, as happened in Shklovsky's lifetime. In "Art as Device," *ostranenie* was introduced by means of Tolstoy's sofa; in "Literature beyond 'Plot,'" it sits in Rozanov's chair.

The writer and philosopher Vasily Rozanov is a constant presence in this article; in fact, it first appeared under the title "Theme, Image and Plot in Rozanov," but then developed into a more general study. The present selection follows the 1925 version published in *O teorii prozy*. Very little of Shklovsky's close readings of Rozanov, fascinating as they are, has been preserved in the present selection. They formed the transitions between different theoretic themes; in their stead, subtitles in square brackets have been added in translation.

One of the crucial ideas of "Literature beyond 'Plot'" is that "it is not sons who inherit from their fathers, but nephews who inherit from their uncles." The assumption that every great writer descends directly from a previous great writer was an axiom in Russian criticism before Shklovsky suggested that it was wrong. He envisions a spiral development of literature; in his critical work, he often analyzes such literary "family trees."

He does not inquire into the psychology of the process here, but his suggestion bears a resemblance to a concept developed fifty years later—Harold Bloom's "anxiety of influence." The form of "inheritance" Shklovsky describes might be explained thus: gifted writers try to avoid the influence of immediate predecessors, borrowing instead from those farther removed in time, space, or style. Those who try to "inherit" directly from the greatest writer in their line usually fail. As Shklovsky puts it in a 1925 feuilleton (*Gamburgskiy schet* [1990] 295),

> The monument [to Pushkin] is now a gag in the throat of the boulevard. It's ruining people who want to write like the classics.
>
> It's ruining Esenin, who's clambering onto its pedestal like a kitten.

Like most of Shklovsky's work, "Literature beyond 'Plot'" uses the literary devices it discusses. It enstranges literary criticism by inserting expressions from domains as different as the army and agriculture, such as *uiti v zapas* (leave military service) and *pod parom* (fallow, resting fields). Some of these have been weakened in translation, but most are recreated. Shklovsky was a master of meta-devices; the digression on digressions is a particular gem—even if, as you will see, Shklovsky puts words into Fielding's mouth to make his point.

Shklovsky was made to retract many of his formalist ideas, and genuinely reconsidered some. But he never stopped fervently believing what he said in almost every early article—that art is our *memento vivere*. As he puts it in one of his latest and most candid interviews, "What do we do in art? We resuscitate life. Man is so busy with life that he forgets to live it. He always says: tomorrow, tomorrow. And that's the real death. So what is art's great achievement? Life. A life that can be seen, felt, lived tangibly"; "we struggle with the world, but we don't see it [...] To touch, see, perceive, this is the strength of art, which looks at the things outside with wonder. Art is continuous astonishment" (Vitale 53; 91).

Resurrecting the Word (1914)[1]

The image-word and its fossilization. The epithet as a means of renewing the word. The history of the epithet as the history of poetic style. Old works of verbal art experience the same fate as the word itself: they journey from poetry to prose. The death of things. The aim of futurism: resurrecting things—returning the sensation of the world to the human being. The connections between futurist poetic devices and cognitive linguistic devices in general. Semi-comprehensible language of ancient poetry. Futurist language.[2]

The most ancient human poetic creation was the creation of words. Today, words are dead, and language resembles a graveyard, but newly-born words were alive and vivid. Every word is originally a trope. For instance, *moon*: the original meaning of this word is "measurer"; *weeping* is cognate with the Latin for "to be flogged"; *infant* (just like the old Russian synonym, *otrok*) literally means "not speaking." One could cite as many examples as there are words in language.[3] And often, when you get through to the lost, effaced image

[1] Source: *Voskreshenie slova*. Tipografiya Sokolinskogo, 1914.

[2] This verbless abstract precedes the article in the original publication.

[3] Contemporary etymology can hardly cite "as many examples as words in language," but reasonable substitutes could be found for all examples, which speaks for the abundance of dead tropes in language. The original *mesyats* (sickle moon/month) might be cognate with the English "moon"; the theory invoked by Shklovsky argues that both derive from

which was the original source of the word, you find yourself struck by its beauty—the beauty which existed once, and is no more.

When words are used as general concepts, when they serve, so to speak, as algebraic symbols devoid of imagery, when they are used in everyday speech, when they are neither fully spoken nor fully heard—then they become familiar, and neither their internal forms (images), nor the external one (sounds) are experienced anymore. We do not experience the familiar; we do not see but only recognize it. We do not see the walls of our rooms, we find it hard to spot a misprint in a proof, particularly in a familiar language—because we cannot make ourselves see, read a familiar word instead of "recognizing" it.[4]

Searching for a definition of "poetic" and, more generally, "artistic" perception, we're bound to arrive at this one: "artistic" perception is such perception in which form is experienced (not just form, perhaps, but form for certain). It's easy to demonstrate the correctness of this "working" definition in instances when a poetic expression becomes prosaic. It is clear, for example, that such expressions as "the foot" of a mountain or "the head" of a table did not change their meaning when they left poetry for prose, but merely lost their form (their internal form, in this case). An experiment proposed by A. Gornfeld confirms the correctness of the proposed definition. He suggested changing the word order in a poem by Nekrasov in order to realize that, with the loss of form (in this case, external form), it becomes a trivial didactic aphorism:

---

the Proto-Indo-European **mē-* (to measure): a month is measured according to the moon cycle. *Weeping* has been substituted for a Russian word meaning "sad" and connected to burning. However, etymology is not always so logical: *sadness*, for instance, derives from the Proto-Germanic **sadaz* (satisfied), with *sated* progressing to *weary*. *Infant* (French *enfant* in the original) does indeed derive from the Latin *in* (not) and *fari* (speak).

[4] Shklovsky is speaking from experience here; he was notoriously inattentive to typos.

Mint the poem, your coin:
let words on the page be dense,
let them closely conjoin –
leave all the room to sense.

Ergo: the word, losing form, makes its unavoidable journey from poetry to prose (cf. Potebnya, *Notes on Literary Theory*).

This loss of the word's form considerably simplifies thinking and may be a necessary condition for the existence of science, but art could never be satisfied with the worn-out word. It could hardly be said that poetry has made up for the damage suffered through the loss of verbal vividness by replacing it with a higher kind of creation—for example, the creation of types—because in such a case poetry would not have held on so greedily to the image-word even at such high stages of its development as the epoch of epic chronicles. In art, material must be alive, precious. And thus, the epithet appeared, the epithet that does not introduce anything new into the word, but simply refreshes the deceased image: for instance, mucky muck, sorrow sore, broad daylight, or pouring rain.[5] Muck is always mucky, but the image has died, and the desire for the concrete, which is the soul of art (Carlyle), requested its renewal. The word, enlivened by the epithet, became poetic again. Time passed—and the epithet, now familiar, ceased to be experienced. It began to be handled habitually, by virtue of scholastic tradition and not living poetic sense. Used this way, the epithet is experienced so weakly that its application often contradicts the general situation and hue of the image, for example:

---

[5] Almost all Shklovsky's examples are directly borrowed from Veselovsky's *From the History of the Epithet*, which, in its turn, owes some examples to Potebnya (cf. Cassedy: 62; Paulmann: 418) and Gerber's *Die Sprache als Kunst* (1885). Potebnya's "foot of a mountain" (the image is identical in Russian) is also taken up in Bely's "The Magic of Words." Shklovsky's whole discussion of the pleonastic epithet is very similar to Veselovsky's.

Don't you burn the tallow candle,
the tallow candle of ardent wax ...

(folk song)

... or a moor's "lilywhite hands" (Serbian epic), or "my true love" of Old English ballads, applied indiscriminately, be the love in question true or untrue, or Nestor, raising his arms to the starry sky in broad daylight, and so on ...[6]

Stable epithets have worn smooth; they fail to create an experience of image and to satisfy the demand for such experience. Within their limits, new epithets are created and accumulate; definitions become diversified by descriptions borrowed from the material of sagas or legends (cf. Veselovsky's article on the history of the epithet). Complex epithets, too, belong to this later era.

"The history of the epithet is an abridged history of poetic style" (Veselovsky, *Sobraniye sochineniy* v. I, 51). It shows us how all forms of art leave life; like the epithet, they all live, fossilize and finally die.

Too little attention is paid to the death of art forms, the old is all too flippantly contrasted with the new without considering if the old is alive or has vanished, as the sound of the sea vanishes for those who live by the shore, as the thousand-voiced roar of the city has vanished for us, as everything habitual, too familiar, disappears from our consciousness.[7]

Not only words and epithets fossilize, whole situations can fossilize too. For instance, in a Bagdad edition of Arab fairy tales, a traveler who was robbed naked climbs upon a mountain and "tears apart his

---

[6] Shklovsky uses the expression *sredi belogo dnya* (in broad daylight), which he had just cited as an example of a pleonastic epithet.

[7] In the 1919 article "On the Great Metalworker," Shklovsky puts it even more categorically: "The thing is that so-called old art does not exist; it objectively does not exist, which is why it is impossible to create a work of art according to its canons" (*Gamburgskiy schet* [1990]: 93).

clothes" in despair. In this passage, a whole image has fossilized into unconsciousness.

Old works of verbal art experience the same fate as the word itself. They journey from poetry to prose. They stop being seen and begin being recognized. Classic works have become covered with the glass armor of familiarity—we remember them too well, we've heard them as children, we've read them in books, we've quoted them in passing, and now we have calluses on our souls—we no longer experience them. I'm speaking of the masses here. Many believe that they do experience old art. But mistakes are so frequent here! It is not by chance that Goncharov skeptically compared the experience of a classicist reading a Greek drama with the experience of Gogol's Petrushka.[8] It is often impossible to directly inhabit ancient art. Have a look at the books of famous experts in classicism—what vulgar vignettes, what decadent sculptures do they place on their covers! Rodin spent years copying Greek sculptures and finally had to resort to measurement to render their forms; it turned out that he has been making them too thin all the time. Thus, a genius could not simply repeat the forms of another age. The museum delights of ignoramuses can only be explained by their thoughtlessness and the low demands they make on their own ability to inhabit ancient times.

The illusion of experiencing ancient art is supported by the fact that it often contains elements alien to art. Such elements are most frequent in literature; therefore, literature now has hegemony in art and the largest number of followers. Artistic perception presupposes our material disinterestedness. Exhilaration at the

---

[8]Petrushka, a lackey in *Dead Souls*, is rather smug about what he considers to be his education. Goncharov is talking about *modern* readers enjoying ancient drama mostly as self-congratulation on the very ability to do so. Shklovsky uses the word *klassik*, which means "classic writer" in contemporary Russian but could also refer to a classic scholar in 1916; this latter meaning fits in better with Goncharov's text.

speech of one's defense counsel in the court of law is not an artistic experience, and our experience of the noble, compassionate thoughts of our poets, the most human in the world, has nothing in common with art.[9] They have never been poetry and therefore could not have journeyed from poetry to prose. The fact that some people place Nadson higher than Tyutchev also shows that writers are often judged according to the number of noble thoughts contained in their work—a form of measurement which happens to be very wide-spread among young Russians. The apotheosis of experiencing "art" in terms of "nobility" is to be found in Chekhov's "Old Professor,"[10] in which two students have the following conversation in the theater: "What is he saying? Is it noble?"—"It's noble alright."—"Bravo!"

This is the scheme of the critics' attitude toward new artistic movements.

Go out into the street and look at the houses: how do they use old artistic forms? You'll see things which are straight out terrible. For instance (a house on the Nevsky by Lyalevich): semicircular arcs are placed on pillars, and between their imposts, lintels are rusticated as flat arcs. This whole system has a sideways thrust, but it is not supported on the sides; thus, there is a perfect impression of the house falling apart.

This architectural absurdity (which fails to be noticed by both critics and the wider public) cannot, in this case (such cases are many) be explained by the ignorance or talentlessness of the architect.

---

[9] The epithet "the most human in the world," used ironically by Shklovsky, was popular in Soviet times—but apparently also before.

[10] Shklovsky is actually referring to "Skuchnaya istoriya," variously translated as "A Boring/Dull/Dreary Story."

Apparently, the form and the meaning of the arc (just like the form of the column; this could also be proven) is not experienced; therefore, its use is as nonsensical as the epithet "tallow" in regard to a wax candle.

Look at the way old authors are quoted.

Unfortunately, nobody has yet made a collection of incorrectly and inopportunely used quotations; this is interesting material. During the performances of a futurist drama, the public was shouting "madmen!," "lunatics!," and also "Ward No. 6!," and newspapers happily printed these exclamations—but there are neither madmen nor lunatics in Chekhov's "Ward No. 6," but only a doctor who had been ignorantly placed there by idiots and a suffering philosopher of sorts. Thus, this work has been dragged in by the shouters quite malapropos. What we see here is, so to speak, a fossilized quotation, which means the same as a fossilized epithet: missing experience (in this case, a whole work of art is fossilized).

The broad masses are content with marketplace art, but marketplace art shows the death of art. Once upon a time, we greeted each other with *zdravstvui* [a wish of health], now the word is dead, and what we say is *asti* [an abbreviated "hello"]. The legs of our chairs, the patterns of fabric, the ornaments of houses, paintings by the "Petersburg painters' society," Ginzburg's sculptures—all these say *asti*. The ornament is not made, it's "told," it is intended not to be seen but to be recognized as the right thing. The heydays of art knew no vulgarity. The pole of a soldier's tent in Assyria, the statue of Hecuba meant to guard over a cesspit in Greece, medieval ornaments placed so high that they were hard to spot—all this was made, was intended for affectionate contemplation. In the epochs when forms of art were alive, no one would have brought home vulgar rubbish. When icon painting became a trade in XVIIth-century Russia, and "on icons, such rampant absurdities appeared which were not even fit to be looked at by a Christian,"[11] this meant that old forms were becoming outdated. Nowadays, old art has already died, new art has not yet been born, and things have died—we have lost our awareness of the world; we resemble a violinist who has ceased to feel the bow and strings; we have ceased being artists in everyday life, we do not love our houses and our clothes, and we easily part with life, for we do not feel life. Only the creation of new art forms can restore to man the experience of the world, can resurrect things and kill pessimism.

When, in a fit of affection or rage, we want to say something tender or insulting, then we are not content with worn-out, gnawed words, and so we crumple and break words to make them touch the ear, to make them seen and not recognized.[12] This includes all the countless mutilated words which we use in moments of affect and which are so hard to recall subsequently.

And now, today, when the artist wants to deal with living form, with the living—not the dead—word, he breaks it up and distorts it in his desire to give it a face. The "arbitrary" and "derived" words of the futurists are born. They either form new words from old roots (Khlebnikov, Guro, Kamensky, Gnedov), or split the word up by rhyme, like Mayakovsky, or give it a wrong stress with the rhythm of the verse (Kruchenykh). New, living words are created. The ancient diamonds of words recover their former brilliance. This new language is incomprehensible, difficult, it cannot be read like the *Stock Exchange Newspaper*. It does not even resemble Russian, but

[11] The source could not be established.

[12] In this key phrase, Shklovsky uses the word "seen" (*uvidali*), not "heard," though he is talking about oral speech—his own formula of *ostranenie*, stated in writing for the first time, already has a ritualized, fixed aspect and could benefit from enstranging. Further in this sentence, the translation leaves out Shklovsky's example of intentionally using the wrong grammatical gender for emotional effect in Russian folk speech.

we've become too used to regarding comprehensibility as a necessary requirement of poetic language. The history of art shows us that (at least, very often) the language of poetry is not comprehensible but semi-comprehensible. Thus, savages often sing in an archaic or foreign language, sometimes so incomprehensible that the singer (or, rather, the lead singer) must translate and explain to the choir and listeners the meaning of the song he just composed (Veselovsky, *Tri glavy iz istoricheskoi poetiki*; Grosse).

The religious poetry of almost all peoples is written in such semi-comprehensible language. Church Slavonic, Latin, Sumerian (a language dead since the 20th century before Christ and used in religious contexts until the third century), German language for Russian stundists (according to Dostoyevsky's *A Writer's Diary*, for a long time, the Russian stundist sect chose not to translate German hymns into Russian, but to learn German instead).

Jacob Grimm, Hoffman, and Hebel all note that folk songs are often sung not in dialect but in a "heightened," quasi-literary language; "the Yakut song language differs from the everyday variety about as much as Old Slavonic from today's Russian" (Korolenko, *At-Davan*). Arnaut Daniel with his dark style, his complicated art forms ("Schwere Kunstmanier"), his hard forms which presuppose pronunciation difficulties (Diez, *Leben und Werk der Troubadours* 285), the Italian *dolce stil nuovo* (XIIth century)—all these are semi-comprehensible languages, and Aristotle in his *Poetics* (Chapter 23) recommends making language seem foreign. This is because such semi-comprehensible language, being unusual, appears more image-sated to the reader (this has been pointed out, for instance, by Ovsyaniko-Kulikovsky).

The writers of yesterday wrote too smoothly, too sweetly. Their texts were like that polished surface of which Korolenko said: "across it, the plane of thought runs touching nothing." There is a need for the creation of new, "tight" language (Kruchenykh's expression), aimed at seeing instead of recognizing. This need is unconsciously felt by many.

The paths of new art have only been lightly traced. Not theorists but artists will be the first to travel these paths. Whether the new forms will be created by the futurists, or by others—in any case, the futurists are on the right track: they judged the old forms correctly. Their poetic devices are general devices of linguistic thought which they introduced into poetry, just as rhyme, which probably always existed in language, was introduced into poetry in the first centuries of Christianity.

Consciously comprehending new creative devices which the poets of the past (the symbolists, for instance) used only by chance—this alone is a great deed. A deed done by the futurists.[13]

[13] Shklovsky uses the self-appellation of the Russian futurists, *budetlyane* (from *budet*: will be). This grammatically highly unusual neologism illustrates his point about futurist language renewal.

Art as Device (1917/1919)[1]

"Art is thinking in images." You can hear his phrase from a schoolboy, and it also the starting point for a philologist beginning to construct a literary theory. This idea has been planted into many minds; Potebnya must be considered one of its creators. "Without images, art—including poetry—is impossible" (Potebnya, *Iz zapisok ...* 83), he writes; and elsewhere: "Poetry, like prose, is first and foremost a certain way of thinking and understanding" (ibid. 97).

Poetry is a particular method of thinking, namely, thinking in images; this method creates a certain economy of intellectual energy, "the sensation of relatively easy processing," with the aesthetic sense being a reflex of this economy. This is how the Academy member Ovsyaniko-Kulikovsky sums it up, and he must be right in his summary—after all, he has certainly read his mentor's books with attention. Potebnya and his numerous followers consider poetry to be a special kind of thinking, namely, thinking in images; they believe that imagery is intended to bring together heterogonous acts and objects, explaining the unknown via the known. Or else, to quote Potebnya: "The image relates to the object of explanation as follows: a) the image is a constant predicate of variable subjects, a constant

---

[1] Source: "Iskusstvo kak priem" in *Sborniki po teorii poeticheskogo yazyka III*. Tipografiya Sokolinskogo, 1919.

means of attracting[2] variable objects of apperception …; b) the image is much simpler and clearer than the object of explanation" (ibid. 314), i.e. "the goal of imagery is to bring the meaning of the image closer to our understanding, without which imagery would have no sense; therefore, the image must be better known to us than the object of explanation" (ibid. 291).

One might wonder how this law applies when Tyutchev compares summer lightning to deaf-mute demons, or when Gogol likens the sky to God's chasuble.

"No art is possible without an image." "Art is thinking in images." Monstrous twists have been made in the name of these definitions; people have attempted to analyze music, architecture, lyrical poetry as "thinking in images." After wasting his energy for a quarter of a century, Ovsyaniko-Kulikovsky was finally forced to single out lyric poetry, architecture, and music as special, imageless art forms, to define them as lyric arts that immediately appeal to emotion. Thus, an enormous sphere of art turned out not to be a method of thinking; one of the arts constituting this sphere, lyric poetry, is nevertheless very similar to "image-bearing" art: it uses words in the same way; most importantly, image-bearing art flows into imageless art quite imperceptibly, and we experience the two in similar ways.

Still, the definition "art is thinking in images"—and therefore (I'm leaving out the intermediate links of well-known equations), "art is, above all, the creator of symbols"—persists, surviving the collapse of the theory on which it was based. Most of all, it's alive in the symbolist movement. Particularly in the work of its theoreticians.

Thus, many people still believe that thinking in images—"ways and shadows," "furrows and boundaries"—is the main characteristic of

---

[2] The rare term *attraktsia* usually denotes the absence of grammatical connections between neighboring words; in this case, the missing connections seem to be semantic.

poetry.[3] They should have expected the history of this image-bound art to be a history of changing imagery. But images turn out to be almost immobile; they flow, unchanging, from century to century, from country to country, from poet to poet. Images belong to "nobody," to "God." The better you comprehend an epoch, the better can you see that the images you believed to be created by a particular poet are actually borrowed from others and almost unchanged. The work done by schools of poetry consists in accumulating verbal material and finding new ways of arranging and handling it; it's much more about rearranging images than about creating them. Images are a given, and poetry is not so much thinking in images as remembering them.

In any case, thinking in images is not what unites all arts or even all literature; images are not the thing whose change drives poetry.

*

We know that expressions not created for artistic contemplation are often nevertheless experienced as poetic; compare Annensky's belief in the poetic qualities of Slavonic or Andrey Bely's admiration for the way Russian eighteenth-century poets place adjectives after nouns. Bely admires this as art, or rather as intentional art, though in reality it is merely a particularity of language (the influence of Church Slavonic). Therefore, a thing can be 1) created as prosaic and experienced as poetic; 2) created as poetic and experienced as prosaic. This suggests that a given work depends in its artistry—in whether or not this work is poetry—on our perception. In the narrow sense, we shall designate as "works of art" only such works which have been created by special devices intended to have them perceived as artistic.

---

[3] Allusions to symbolist writing: *Furrows and Boundaries* (1916) is a book of essays by Vyacheslav Ivanov; "ways and shadows" have been identified (Galushkin, "Footnotes" 490) as an ironic montage of Valery Bryusov's collections *Ways and Crossroads* (1908) and *The Mirror of Shadows* (1912).

Potebnya's conclusion, which can be put as "poetry = imagery," has given rise to the whole theory of "imagery = symbolism," of the image as the invariable predicate of various subjects (this conclusion forms the basis of the theory of Symbolism; leading Symbolists—Andrey Bely and Merezhkovsky with his "eternal companions"—fell in love with it because of its similarity to their own ideas). This conclusion partly stems from the fact that Potebnya made no distinction between the language of poetry and the language of prose. This is why he failed to notice that two kinds of images exist: the image as a practical means of thinking, as a means of grouping objects—and the poetic image, as a means of intensifying an impression. Let me clarify with an example. Walking down the street, I see a man wearing an old crumpled hat drop his bag. I call him back: "You, old hat, you've dropped your bag!" This is an example of a purely prosaic trope. Another example. "This joke is old hat, I heard it ages ago."[4] This image is a poetic trope. (In one case, the word "hat" was used metonymically, in the other, metaphorically. But this is not what I want to point out here.) The poetic image is a way to create the strongest possible impression. It is a device that has the same task as other poetic devices, such as ordinary or negative parallelism, comparison, repetition, symmetry, hyperbole; it is equal to that which is commonly designated as rhetorical figures, equal to all these methods of increasing the impact of a thing (words and

---

[4]To recreate the pun, the translation had to stray away from the original, which uses the double meaning of *shlyapa*—"hat" and "clumsy person." The use of metonymy, such as "[you] hat" or "[you] glasses," as a somewhat rude form of addressing strangers is more usual in Russian than in English. The fact that Shklovsky uses a dead metaphor as an example of a poetic image is problematic, as is the citing of clichéd sexual euphemisms as examples of *ostranenie* later in the essay. At other points, however, Shklovsky shows awareness of the fact that the effect of *ostranenie* can easily evaporate.

even sounds of the text itself are things, too). But the poetic image bears only superficial resemblance to images as fables, to patterns of thought,[5] such as a girl calling a sphere "a little watermelon" (Ovsyaniko-Kulikovsky 16–17). The poetic image is a device of poetic language. The prosaic image is a device of abstraction: a watermelon instead of a round lamp shade, or a watermelon instead of a head, merely abstracts a particular quality of an object. It's like saying: head = sphere, watermelon = sphere. This is thinking, but it has nothing in common with poetry.

*

The law of the economy of creative effort is also generally accepted. Spencer, in his *Philosophy of Style*, wrote:

> As the basis of all rules designating the choice and use of words we find one and the same main requirement: economy of attention … . Leading the mind to the intended concept by the easiest route is often their only and always their most important goal.[6]

And R. Avenarius (8):

> If the soul possessed inexhaustible strength, then, of course, it would be indifferent to how much might be spent from this inexhaustible source; only the expended time would play any role. But since its strength is limited, we can expect that the soul seeks

---

[5] *Obraz myslei* (lit. the *image* of thought) is the Russian for "thought patterns" or "mentality."

[6] The translation used by Shklovsky departs from the original in many aspects, for instance, downplaying the fact that Spencer refers to speech as much as to writing: "On seeking for some clue to the law underlying these current maxims, we may see shadowed forth in many of them, the importance of economizing the reader's or the hearer's attention. To so present ideas that they may be apprehended with the least possible mental effort, is the desideratum towards which most of the rules above quoted point" (Spencer 7).

> to carry out apperceptive processes as purposefully as possible—that is, with, in relative terms, the least expenditure of energy, or, to put the same thing differently, with the greatest result.

With a single reference to the general law of mental economy, Petrazhitsky dismisses James's theory of the physical basis of affect, a theory which happened to be in his way. The principle of the economy of creative effort, a seductive theory—particularly in the study of rhythm—has been affirmed by Alexander Veselovsky who followed in Spencer's footsteps: "The merit of style consists precisely in delivering the greatest amount of thoughts in the fewest words." Andrey Bely, who in his better works gave numerous examples of challenging, stumbling rhythm and (for instance, in the work of Baratynsky) showed the laboriousness of poetic epithets—even he believes it necessary to speak of the law of the economy in his book, which constitutes a heroic effort to create a theory of art based on unverified facts from outdated books, on his vast knowledge of poetic techniques and on Krayevich's high school physics textbook.

Regarding economy as a law and goal of creation might be right for a particular linguistic case, namely "practical" language, but ignorance of the differences between the laws of practical and poetic language led to the idea of economy being applied to the latter. When Japanese poetic language was found to contain sounds never used in practical Japanese, this was one of the first, if not *the* first factual indication that these two languages are not identical (Polivanov 38). Yakubinsky's article (13–21), which states that the law of liquid consonant dissimilation is missing from poetic language and that in poetic language such hard-to-pronounce sound combinations are possible, is one of the first scientifically sound indications of the opposition (in this case, at least) between poetic language and practical language.

Therefore, we need to discuss the laws of spending and economy in poetic language based on its own workings, not on prosaic language.

Considering the laws of perception, we see that routine actions become automatic. All our skills retreat into the unconscious-automatic domain; you will agree with this if you remember the feeling you had when holding a quill in your hand for the first time or speaking a foreign language for the first time, and compare it to the feeling you have when doing it for the ten thousandth time. It is the automatization process which explains the laws of our prosaic speech, its under-structured phrases and its half-pronounced words. This process is ideally expressed in algebra, which replaces things with symbols. In quick practical speech, words are not spoken fully; only their initial sounds are registered by the mind. Pogodin (42) gives the example of a boy imagining the phrase "Les montagnes de la Suisse sont belles" as a series of letters: L, m, d, 1, S, s, b.

This property of thinking has suggested not only the path of algebra, but even the particular choice of symbols (letters, and especially initial letters). This algebraic way of thinking takes in things by counting and spatializing them;[7] we do not *see* them but recognize them by their initial features. A thing passes us as if packaged; we know of its existence by the space it takes up, but we only see its surface. Perceived in this way, the thing dries up, first in experience, and then its very making suffers;[8] because of this perception, prosaic speech is not fully heard (cf. Yakubinsky's article), and therefore not fully spoken (this is the reason for slips of the tongue). Algebraizing,

---

[7] The original *berutsia schetom i prostranstvom* (lit. "taken by counting and space") is highly unidiomatic. It appears to mean "we recognize the object by its quantity and position in space" (without really seeing it)—but other readings are possible.

[8] This phrase might appear puzzling to a Russian reader, too; "the making of a thing" seems to refer to artistic creation and perhaps also to artistic perception.

automatizing a thing, we save the greatest amount of perceptual effort: things are either given as a single feature, for instance, a number, or else they follow a formula of sorts without ever reaching consciousness. "I was dusting in the room; having come full circle, I approached the sofa and could not remember if I had dusted it off or not. I couldn't because these movements are routine and not conscious, and I felt I never could remember it. So if I had cleaned the sofa but forgotten it, that is if this was really unconscious, it is as if this never happened. If somebody had watched consciously, reconstruction would have been possible. But if nobody watched, if nobody watched consciously, if the whole life of many people is lived unconsciously, it is as if this life had never been" (Tolstoy 354; diary entry, February 29, 1897).[9]

This is how life becomes nothing and disappears. Automatization eats things, clothes, furniture, your wife and the fear of war.

"If the whole complex life of many people is lived unconsciously, it is as if this life had never been."

And so, what we call art exists in order to give back the sensation of life, in order to make us feel things, in order to make the stone stony. The goal of art is to create the sensation of seeing, and not merely recognizing, things; the device of art is the "*ostranenie*" of things and the complication of the form, which increases the duration and complexity of perception, as the process of perception is its own end in art and must be prolonged. Art is the means to live through the making of a thing; what has been made does not matter in art.[10]

---

[9] Actually, March 1.

[10] This sentence (italicized in other publications) seems to be echoing the words of a poet: "Khlebnikov told me that the making matters, and not what has been made; what has been made are but wood shavings" (Shklovsky, *Gamburgskiy schet* [1990] 469). Khlebnikov was talking about the process of writing; while the completed text might not matter to the

The life of a poetic (artistic) text proceeds from seeing to recognizing, from poetry to prose, from the concrete to the general, from Don Quixote—a scholar and poor aristocrat, half-consciously suffering humiliation at a duke's court—to Turgenev's generalized and hollow Don Quixote, from Charles the Great to the mere name of "king."[11] Art and its works expand when dying: a fable is more symbolic than a poem, a saying more symbolic than a fable. This is why Potebnya's theory is least self-contradictory when discussing the fable, a genre which he was, in his own view, able to analyze in full. His theory did not fit "thingish" artistic texts, and thus Potebnya's book couldn't be finished.[12] As we know, *Notes on Literary Theory* were published in 1905, thirteen years after the death of their author. Potebnya himself could only complete the chapter on the fable (Potebnya, *Iz lektsii ...*).

Things that have been experienced several times begin to be experienced in terms of recognition: a thing is in front of us, we know this, but we do not see it (Shklovsky, *Voskresheniye slova*). This is why we cannot say anything about it. Art has different ways of de-automatizing things; in this article I would like to show one of the methods very frequently used by L. Tolstoy—the writer who, in Merezhkovsky's judgment, presents things the way he sees them, who sees things fully but does not change them.

Tolstoy's device of *ostranenie* consists in not calling a thing or event by its name but describing it as if seen for the first time, as if

---

writer, it certainly does to the reader. Alternatively, "what has been made" could refer to the images created by the reader in the process of reading.

[11] Shklovsky is referring to the essay "Hamlet and Don Quixote" (Turgenev); the Russian word for "king" (*korol*) derives from "Karl."

[12] The word *veshchnyy* ("material," "concrete," lit. "thingish") appears as a neologism to most Russian readers. However, Shklovsky probably was familiar with its use by Russian philosophers, above all the existentialist Nikolay Berdyaev. Shklovsky and Berdyaev shared in the tight-knit Russian community in Berlin; Shklovsky has listened to at least one of his lectures (Gul 223).

happening for the first time. While doing so, he also avoids calling parts of this thing by their usual appellations; instead, he names corresponding parts of other things. Here is an example. In the article "Ashamed," L. Tolstoy enstranges the concept of flogging: "people who have broken the law are denuded, thrown down on the floor, and beaten on their behinds with sticks," and a couple of lines later: "lashed across their bare buttocks." There is a postscript: "And why this particular stupid, barbaric way of inflicting pain, and not some other: pricking the shoulder or some other body part with needles, squeezing arms or legs in a vice, or something else of this sort."

I apologize for this disturbing example, but it is typical of Tolstoy's way to reach conscience. The customary act of flogging is enstranged both by the description and by the proposal to change its form without changing its essence. Tolstoy used the method of *ostranenie* constantly: in one case, "Strider",[13] the narrator is a horse, and things are enstranged not by our own perception, but by that of a horse. Here is what the horse made of the institution of property:

> What they were saying about flogging and Christianity, I understood well, but I was quite in the dark about the words "his own," "his colt," which made me realize that people saw some kind of connection between me and the equerry. What this connection was, I just couldn't understand back then. Only much later, separated from the other horses, did I begin to understand. But back then I simply could not understand what it meant when they called *me* someone's property. The words "*my* horse" described me, a living horse, and seemed as strange to me as the words "my land," "my air," "my water."
>
> However, these words had a strong effect on me. Thinking about this all the time, and only after the most diverse experiences with

[13] The short story has also been published in English under its original title, "Kholstomer."

people, did I finally understand what meaning they ascribe to these strange words. Their meaning is this: in life, people are ruled not by acts but by words. They love not so much the possibility of doing or not doing something as the possibility of talking about different things using certain words, on which they agree beforehand. Such are the words "my" and "mine," which they use to talk about different things, creatures, topics, and even about land, about people, and about horses. They agree that only one person may say "mine" about any particular thing. And the one who says "mine" about the greatest number of things, in this game whose rules they've made up among themselves, is considered the happiest. Why this should be so, I don't know, but this is how it is. For a long time, I've been trying to explain it to myself in terms of some direct benefit, but this turned out to be wrong.

For instance, many of those who called me their horse never rode me, while completely different people did. Neither did they feed me, but yet others did. The ones who were good to me were not those who called me their horse, either, but the coachman, the horse doctor, and people who didn't know me at all. Later, having widened the scope of my observations, I realized that, not only in relation to us horses, the notion of *mine* had no basis apart from a low animal instinct people have, which they call property sense or property right. A man says "my house" and never lives in it but only worries about its building and upkeep. A merchant says "my shop," "my cloth shop," for instance, and does not have any clothes made from the best cloth in his own shop.

There are people who call a piece of land their own, but they have never seen this piece of land and never walked upon it. There are people who call other people their own though they have never seen these others, and all they do to these other people is harm

> them. There are people who call women their women or their wives, but these women live with other men. And people do not strive to do what they consider good but to call as many things as possible their own. I am convinced now that this is the essential difference between people and us. This alone, not to mention other things in which we are better than people, is reason enough to say that we are higher up in the chain of being: their doings—at least to judge by those I knew—are guided by words, ours by deeds.

Toward the end of the story, the horse is killed, but the narrative method, the device, does not change:

> Much later, Serpukhovsky's body, which had been walking about in the world, eating and drinking, was put into the ground. His skin, his meat and his bones were of no use.
>
> Just as his dead body had been a great burden to everyone for 20 years while it was still walking about, so the putting away of this body into the ground created nothing but trouble. No one had cared about him for a long time, all this time he had been a burden to everyone; and yet the dead who bury their dead found it necessary to dress this bulky body, which had begun to rot so quickly, in a good uniform and good boots, to lay it in a new, good coffin with new tassels at all 4 corners, then to put this new coffin in another, leaden one, and to ship it to Moscow, and there to dig out old human bones and then use this particular place to hide this body, putrefying, swarming with maggots, in its new uniform and polished boots, and strew earth all over it.

Thus we see that at the end of the story, the device is liberated from the accidental motivation for its use.

Tolstoy also applies this device to all battles in *War and Peace*. They are all presented as, first and foremost, strange. I will not quote these long descriptions—this would mean copying out quite a considerable part of a four-volume novel. Tolstoy also uses this method in describing salons and the theater:[14]

> Most of the stage was covered with flat boards; by the sides stood painted pictures showing trees, and at the back, a cloth was stretched on boards. Girls in red bodices and white skirts were sitting in the middle of the stage. A very fat one in a white silk dress was sitting separately on a narrow bench, which had some green cardboard glued behind. They were all singing something. When they had finished their song, the girl in white approached the prompter's box, and a man in silken pants stretched tightly over his fat legs, with a plume, approached her, and began singing and spreading his arms. The man in the tight pants sang first, and then the girl sang. After that, both stopped, music boomed out, and the man began to finger the hand of the girl in the white dress, apparently waiting, as before, to begin singing his part with her. Then they sang together, and everyone in the theater began to clap and shout, and the men and women on stage, who had been pretending to be lovers, were bowing, smiling and spreading their arms.
>
> In the second act, there were paintings pretending to be monuments, and there were holes in the cloth pretending to be the moon, and the shades on the footlights were raised, and trumpets and basses were playing, and from right and left came many people wearing black gowns. The people started waving their arms, and they were

[14] None of the existing translations of *War and Peace* fully recreates the *ostranenie* of such intentionally clumsy expressions as "painted pictures." The quotation below follows Shklovsky's text, which makes several omissions and differs from Tolstoy's in using figures instead of words in reference to numbers. However, I did take the liberty to correct the most obvious typos such as "ramke" (*frame*) instead of "rampe" (*footlights*).

> holding daggers of sorts; then still more people came running out and proceeded to drag away the girl who had been wearing a white dress, but now had on a blue one. They did not do so at once, though, but first sang with her for a long while, and only then dragged her away, and then something metallic was struck three times in the back, and everybody got down on their knees chanting a prayer. Several times, these activities were interrupted by exultant shouts from the spectators.

Same in the third act:

> But suddenly there was a storm, chromatic scales and diminished seventh chords resounded from the orchestra, and everybody ran off, again dragging one of the people present backstage, and the curtain came down.[15]

In the fourth act, "there was some devil who sang, waving his arms, until boards were pulled out from under him and he descended down there."

This is also how Tolstoy described the city and the court of law in "Resurrection." This is how he describes marriage in "The Kreutzer Sonata." "Why, if people are soul mates, are they meant to sleep together." But he used the device of *ostranenie* not only in order to let his readers see things he disapproved of.

> Pierre rose and walked away from his new comrades, between the fires onto the other side of the street where, he was told, the captive soldiers were staying. He wished to talk to them. But on the way a French sentinel stopped him and ordered him to return. Pierre returned, but not to the fire and his comrades, but to an

---

[15] One might wonder how the sophisticated discussion of music and the correct use of such concepts as "orchestra," "prompter's box," and "theatre curtains" accord with *ostranenie*.

> unharnessed carriage with no people near it. He sat down on the cold earth by the wheel of the carriage, his legs tucked under and his head bowed, and sat there immobile for a long time, thinking. More than an hour passed. Nobody disturbed Pierre. Suddenly he broke out in his thick good-natured laugh, so loudly, that the evident strangeness of this laughter made people turn and look from all directions.
>
> Ha, ha, ha, Pierre laughed. And he began to say to himself: the soldier didn't let me through. I'm caught, I'm shut in. I. Me—my immortal soul. Ha, ha, ha, he laughed while tears came to his eyes …
>
> Pierre looked up at the sky, at the depth of receding sparkling stars. "All this is mine, all this is in me, all this is me," thought Pierre, "and all this, they caught and put into a barracoon, shut off with boards." He smiled and started walking toward his comrades, ready for sleep.

Anybody who knows Tolstoy well can find many hundreds of such examples in his work. This method of seeing things outside of their context led Tolstoy to the *ostranenie* of rites and dogmas in his late works, to the replacement of habitual religious terms with usual words—the result was strange, monstrous; many sincerely regarded it as sacrilegious and were deeply offended. But it was the same device that Tolstoy used elsewhere to experience and show his surroundings. Tolstoy's perception unraveled his own faith, getting to things he had been long unwilling to approach.

*

The device of *ostranenie* is not particular to Tolstoy. I described it using Tolstoy's material for purely practical reasons, because this material is familiar to everyone.

And now, having elucidated the essence of this device, let us try to delineate the limits of its use. I personally believe that *ostranenie* is present almost wherever there is an image.

Accordingly, we can formulate the difference between Potebnya's perspective and our own as follows: the image is not a constant subject with changing predicates. The goal of an image is not to bring its meaning closer to our understanding, but to create a special way of experiencing an object, to make one not "recognize" but "see" it.

The goal of imagery can be traced most clearly in erotic art.

Here, the erotic object is commonly presented as something seen for the first time. Take Gogol's "Night before Christmas":

> He then came closer, coughed, chuckled, touched her full naked arm and said both slyly and smugly:
>
> —What have you got here, then, magnificent Solokha?—Having spoken thus, he jumped back a little.
>
> —What a question! My arm, Osip Nikiforovich!—replied Solokha.
>
> —Hm! Your arm! Heh-heh-heh!—replied the sexton, heartily content with his opening move, and made a tour of the room.
>
> —What have you got here, dearest Solokha!—said he, still with the same expression, approaching her again, lightly putting his hand around her neck, and then jumping back, as before.
>
> —As if you couldn't see, Osip Nikiforovich!—replied Solokha,—my neck, and on my neck a necklace.
>
> —Hm! A necklace on your neck! Heh-heh-heh!—and the sexton proceeded to take another tour of the room, rubbing his hands.

—What have you got here, then, incomparable Solokha ... ?— Who knows what the sexton was about to touch this time with those long fingers of his ...[16]

Or in Hamsun's *Hunger*:

"Two white marvels showed through her chemise."

Or else, erotic objects are paraphrased, clearly not with the goal of "bringing [the reader] closer to our understanding."

In the same vein, we find the depiction of sex organs as a lock and key, as devices for weaving (Sadovnikov 102–7, 588–91), as a bow and an arrow, or a ring and a spike, as used in a game in the epic of Staver (Rybnikov 30).

In it, the husband fails to recognize his wife who is dressed up as a warrior. She poses him a riddle:

"D'you remember, Staver, can you not recall
How we went into the street, we little ones,
How we played the game of spikes in the open street,
And you had a silver spike, and I a gilded ring?
And I hit the ring only now and then,
But you hit the ring every single time."
Staver, Godin's son, gives a strict reply:
"I have never played rings and spikes with you!"
Vasilisa, daughter of Mikula,
speaks again to ask him and challenge him:
"D'you remember, Staver, can you not recall
How we learned to write, me and you the same,
And I had a silver inkwell, you a gilded quill?

[16] It could be argued that neither the reader nor the protagonist experience *ostranenie* here. Rather, the latter coyly pretends to experience it, putting the "sex" in "sexton."

And I dipped the quill only now and then,
But you dipped the quill every single time." [17]

Another version of the epic provided a solution:

Then the fearsome ambassador Vasily
Raised his clothes up, raised them all the way.
And the young Staver, Staver Godin's son,
Recognized the familiar gilded ring.

But *ostranenie* is not only used in euphemistic erotic riddles, it is also the basis and the only sense of all riddles. Every riddle describes an object with words which define and depict it but are not usually used in reference to it ("two stings, two rings, a nail in the middle" for scissors), or else it is a kind of *ostranenie* through sound, a parroting parody—"tloor and teiling" instead of "floor and ceiling" etc.

Erotic images which are not riddles are still examples of *ostranenie*, such as all cabaret "maces," "aeroplanes," "little dolls," "little brothers" etc.

They have much in common with the folk image of trampled grass and broken viburnum bushes.[18]

The device of *ostranenie* clearly appears in another wide-spread image—the motif of the erotic pose, in which a bear or another animal (or the devil, as another motivation for non-recognition)

---

[17] Sic; the fact that the sexual imagery seems somewhat confused here (with "Vasily" "hitting the ring") is not a matter of translation. Arguably, the less-than-obvious meaning of "now and then" versus "every time" makes the image more difficult to process and therefore more attractive to Shklovsky.

[18] It could be argued that these traditional images are the very opposite of *ostranenie*: after all, they are so familiar that the reference to sexuality is immediately "recognized," not "seen." "Trampled grass" is obvious enough; red viburnum berries ("kalinka," as in the song "Kalinka-Malinka") refer to defloration in Russian folklore. On the other hand, when used—or heard—for the first time, such an image can indeed be enstranging.

fails to recognize a human. This is how the non-recognition, the strangeness of this pose, is presented in a Belorussian fairy tale (Romanov 344):

> He then led his wife to the bathhouse, and, before having quite reached the steam room, spoke: "Now, wife of mine, take off all your clothes and remain as naked as your mother bore you!" "How can I strip naked before we reach the steam room?" "Well, you have to!" So she shames him: how can she strip naked before they reach the steam room? But he says: "If you don't, you'll be a widow, and I'll kick the bucket." So the wife undressed, let her hair loose and went down on her hands and knees; he sat down on top of her, facing her behind. The door was opened. The devils looked: who is he riding? He said: "Look here, you devils—if you can tell who I'm riding, I'm yours; and if not, get out of here, all of you!" And he slapped [his wife's] behind. They walked around and around—and couldn't guess. They could tell there was a tail—but what was that other thing? "Well, that's a piece of work, you dear; we'll give you whatever you want, and we'll stay away from here!"

Very typical is non-recognition in the following fairy tale (Zelenin N70):

> A peasant was plowing his field with a piebald mare. A bear came to him and asked: "uncle, who has made this mare piebald for you?" "I myself." "But how?" "Shall I make you piebald, too?" The bear agreed. The peasant tied up his legs, took the ploughshare, heated it in the fire and went on to apply it to the bear's flanks: the hot ploughshare scorched off his fur right to his flesh, making him piebald. He untied the bear, and the bear went away to lie under a tree. A magpie came down and wanted to peck at some meat on the peasant's field. The peasant caught it and broke its leg. The magpie

> flew away and alighted on the tree under which the bear was lying. Then, after the magpie, a spider (a big fly)[19] flew onto the peasant's field and began biting the mare. The peasant took the spider, shoved a stick up its bum, and let it go. The spider flew off to the tree where the magpie and the bear were. So there they were, all three of them. The man's wife came to the field, bringing him lunch. The husband and his wife had their lunch in the fresh air, and then he toppled her onto the ground. The bear saw this and said to the magpie and the spider: "oh my! He's about to make someone piebald again." The magpie said: "no, he's about to break someone's leg." And the spider: "no, he wants to put a stick up someone's bum."

This device is identical to the one used in "Strider": this, I believe, is obvious to everyone.[20]

Ostranenie of the act itself is very frequent in literature. Decameron is an example: "the scraping of the barrel," "the catching of the nightingale," "the merry wool-beating work" (the latter image is not developed into a plot line). Sexual organs are enstranged just as frequently.

A whole series of plots is based on their "non-recognition." Afanasiev's fairy tales such as "The Bashful Lady" provide examples:

---

[19] Sic; all original absurdities are preserved. The word *pauk* (spider) is rendered as "fly" in both published translations. The addition of "a big fly" in brackets refers to a somewhat more plausible version of the tale. Still, penetrating an insect with a stick is a feat worthy of Leskov's "Lefty," the master who horseshoed a fly.

[20] It does not actually seem that obvious how the depiction of human society from an alien perspective is "identical" to the punchline of a joke in which sexual intercourse is mistaken for violence (the acts of laying bare the skin on someone's flanks, putting their legs at an angle and sticking a lengthy object into their lower parts are united in a denouement which each animal associates with his own misadventure). Though animal perspectives are employed in both cases, it is doubtful whether the bawdy tale leads the reader (or, originally, listener) to perceive the strangeness of sex as intensely as Tolstoy's readers might perceive the strangeness of society. The device—showing something familiar as unfamiliar—is indeed arguably identical; the effect isn't.

the whole tale consists of not naming the object,[21] of pretending not to recognize it. Same in his "The Bear and the Hare." The Bear and the Hare mend "a wound." Same in Onchukov's "A Woman's Blemish."

Constructions such as "the pestle and the mortar" or "the devil and hell" (*Decameron*) are also devices of *ostranenie*.

Ostranenie in psychological parallelism is discussed in my article on plot formation.

Here, let me repeat that, in a parallelism, the sense of non-identity despite affinity is crucial.

The goal of parallelism—the goal of all imagery—is transferring an object from its usual sphere of experience to a new one, a kind of semantic change.

When studying poetic language—be it phonetically or lexically, syntactically or semantically—we always encounter the same characteristic of art: it is created with the explicit purpose of de-automatizing perception. Vision is the artist's goal; the artistic [object] is "artificially" created in such a way that perception lingers and reaches its greatest strength and length, so that the thing is experienced not spatially but, as it were, continually.[22] "Poetic language" meets these conditions. According to Aristotle, "poetic language" must have the character of the foreign, the surprising.[23] It often is quite literally a foreign language—Sumerian for Assyrians, Old Bulgarian as the basis of literary Russian—or else, it might be elevated language, like the almost literary language of folk songs. Here, we can also name

---

[21] Shklovsky applied this device to romantic love rather than sexuality in his novel *Zoo, or Letters not about Love*. By attempting to refrain from talking about love, the narrator does nothing but talk about love.

[22] The somewhat puzzling opposition of space and continuity is reminiscent of a state Shklovsky would later ascribe to his toddler son: "He doesn't walk yet: he runs. His life is still continuous. It doesn't consist of single drops. It's experienced as a whole" (Shklovsky, *Tretya Fabrika* 134).

[23] Shklovsky appears to be referring to the concept of *xenikón* (Aristotle XXII).

the widespread use of archaisms in poetic language, the difficulties of the *dolce stil nuovo* (XII), Arnaut Daniel's dark style, and hard forms *which presuppose pronunciation difficulties* (Diez 213). Yakubinsky in his article proved the law of phonetic difficulty in poetic language, using the example of sound repetition.[24] The language of poetry is difficult, laborious language, which puts the brakes on perception. In some particular cases the language of poetry approaches the language of prose, but this does not violate the law of difficulty. Pushkin wrote:

> Tatyana was her name ... I own it,
> self-willed it may be just the same;
> but it's the first time you'll have known it,
> a novel graced with such a name.
>
> (translation by Charles H. Johnston)[25]

For Pushkin's contemporaries, Derzhavin's elevated diction was the usual language of poetry, so that Pushkin's style was unexpectedly difficult for them in its triviality. Recall that Pushkin's contemporaries were horrified by his vulgar expressions. Pushkin used the vernacular as a device to arrest attention, just as his contemporaries used *Russian* words in their everyday French speech (for examples, see Tolstoy's *War and Peace*).

Today, an even more characteristic phenomenon takes place. Russian literary language, originally alien to Russia, has penetrated into the human masses so deeply as to level many dialectical varieties. Literature, meanwhile, began to care for dialects (Remizov, Klyuev,

---

[24] Expressions such as "proved the law" are worth noticing, being typical of the young formalist.

[25] This version was chosen from the many English translations of *Eugene Onegin*, as in this particular stanza it arguably mirrors best the original light tone and playful rhyming—features crucial to this example. Tatyana was a "simple" name, not considered elegant enough for poetry—just as Pushkin's style itself was too colloquial for his time.

Esenin, and others, unequal in talent but close in their intentionally provincial language) and barbarisms (which made Severyanin's school possible). Maxim Gorky, too, is making a transition from literary language to dialect, not any less literary, in the manner of Leskov.[26] In this way, folk language and literary language have changed places (cf. Vyacheslav Ivanov and many others). Moreover, there is a strong tendency to create new language specifically intended for poetry; as we know, Vladimir[27] Khlebnikov is leading this school. Thus, we arrive at a definition of poetry as decelerated, contorted speech. Poetic speech is constructed speech. Prose, on the other hand, is ordinary speech: economical, easy, correct (*dea prosae* is the goddess of correct, easy birth, of the baby's "straight" position). I will speak in more detail about deceleration and delay as a general *law* of art in my article on plot construction.

In regard to rhythm, the position of people who believe economy to be a driving and even defining force in poetry seems strong at first sight. Spencer's interpretation of the role of rhythm seems incontestable: "Irregular blows force us to keep our muscles in excessive, sometimes unnecessary tension as we cannot foresee the repetition of the blow; regular blows help us economize energy."[28] This seemingly

---

[26] In Russian, *barbarizmy* refer exclusively to the use of foreign words or calqued expressions (of which Severyanin was particularly fond). Shklovsky uses the word *govor* (idiom, dialect); however, as he talks not of authentic dialect but of its literary imitation, he appears to be anticipating the concept of *skaz* (Eikhenbaum, "Kak sdelana 'Shinel' Gogolya") which describes the literary approximation of "folksy" speech.

[27] Khlebnikov's real name was Viktor, but he began calling himself Velimir in 1909. Shklovsky's slip of the pen (or tongue, as he dictated the text) might be connected to Khlebnikov's patronymic: his father's name was indeed Vladimir.

[28] Shklovsky is quoting an abbreviated paraphrase of Herbert Spencer's *The Philosophy of Style* (Veselovsky, *Sobraniye sochineniy* 445). The original is as follows: "Just as the body, in receiving a series of varying concussions, must keep the muscles ready to meet the most violent of them, as not knowing when such may come; so, the mind in receiving unarranged articulations, must keep its perceptives active enough to recognize the least easily caught sounds. And as, if the concussions recur in definite order, the body may husband its forces

convincing observation suffers from the usual fallacy—the confusion of the laws of poetic and prosaic language. In *The Philosophy of Style*, Spencer made no distinction between them, though there might well be two kinds of rhythm. The rhythm of prose, of a work song like "Dubinushka," can replace a command;[29] it also simplifies work by automatizing it. It really is easier to walk with music than without it, but it's just as easy to walk while engaged in animated conversation, when the act of walking vanishes from our consciousness. Therefore, prosaic rhythm is important as an automatizing factor. The rhythm of poetry is different. There is "order" in art, but not a single column of a Greek temple corresponds to it exactly; poetic rhythm consists in the distortion of prosaic rhythm. Attempts to systematize such distortions have been made; they are the current task of the theory of rhythm. It seems probable that such systematization will not succeed, for we are talking not of complicating but of disrupting the rhythm, of disrupting it unpredictably; if such a disruption is canonized, it will lose its power as a device of deceleration. But I will not discuss rhythm in more detail; a separate book will be dedicated to the topic.[30]

---

by adjusting the resistance needful for each concussion; so, if the syllables be rhythmically arranged, the mind may economize its energies by anticipating the attention required for each syllable" (Spencer 51).

[29] The song's refrain can be very roughly translated as "Move it!"; it was used as a signal for strenuous collective actions. "Dubinushka" is similar to such work songs as sea shanties and African-American call-and-response songs.

[30] Shklovsky never came around to writing that book.

Literature beyond "Plot" (1921/1925)[1]

Literature beyond Theme; Non-Linear Inheritance[2]

[...]

Analyzing a literary work and regarding its so-called form as a sort of veil which needs to be penetrated, the contemporary literary theorist jumps over the horse while trying to mount it.

A literary work is pure form; it is not a thing, not a material, but the relation of materials. Like any other relation, this one is zero-dimensional. The scale of the work—the arithmetic value of the numerator and denominator—does not matter; what matters is their relation. Jocular, tragic, world-wide and room-wide works; a world juxtaposed to a world, a cat juxtaposed to a stone—they are equal.

This is why art is harmless, self-contained, nonimperative. The history of literature moves forward along a truncated, broken line. If we line up, say, all the literary saints canonized in Russia between the XVIIth and XXth century, we won't see a line allowing us to

---

[1] Source: "Literatura vne 'syuzheta' in *O teorii prozy*. Moscow/Leningrad: Krug 1925.

[2] The subtitles are added by Alexandra Berlina.

study the history of developing literary forms. What Pushkin says about Derzhavin is neither sharp nor true. Nekrasov obviously does not follow Pushkin's tradition. In prose, Tolstoy doesn't descend from Turgenev or Gogol, and Chekhov doesn't come from Tolstoy. The breaks do not come from the chronological gaps between these writers.

No, the reason is this: as literary schools change, it is not sons who inherit from their fathers, but nephews who inherit from their uncles. Let us unpack this formula. Every literary epoch contains not one, but several literary schools. They co-exist, and one forms the canonized crest. Others are not part of the canon but exist obscurely, the way Derzhavin's tradition remained alive in Küchelbecker's and Griboedov's poetry during Pushkin's times, along with the Russian vaudeville poetry school and a number of other traditions, such as that of the adventure novel, which lived on in Bulgarin.

Pushkin did not start a tradition—a phenomenon of the same kind as the absence of genius and great gift among the children of a genius.[3]

But at the same time, in the lower strata new art forms are created instead of old ones, which, like grammatical forms in speech, are not experienced, which have stopped being elements of art and became unfelt, functional phenomena.[4] The young line rushes in, taking the place of the old one, and the vaudeville writer Belopyatkin becomes Nekrasov (Osip Brik's work), while Tolstoy, a direct descendant of the XVIIIth century, creates a new kind of novel (Boris Eikhenbaum), while Blok canonizes the themes and tempos of Gypsy romances, and Chekhov introduces the feuilleton into Russian

---

[3] The idea that people of genius never have gifted children is a wide-spread adage in Russia, possibly derived from Erasmus von Rotterdam's *The Praise of Folly* (chapter XXIV).

[4] Here and in the final sentence of this excerpt, Shklovsky uses the word *sluzhebnyi* which can mean "official," "work-related"; in context, it appears to refer to the concept of *sluzhebnye slova*, function words.

literature.[5] Dostoyevsky elevates the devices of dime novels to literary norm. Each new literary school is a revolution, something like the creation of a new class.

But this is only an analogy. The defeated line is not destroyed; it doesn't cease to exist. It only plummets from the crest, rests and may rise again; it remains an eternal contender for the throne. Moreover, matters are complicated by the fact that the new hegemon usually does not simply canonize an established form but also adds features borrowed from other young schools, and even features (albeit functionally used) inherited from its predecessor on the throne.

[...]

Literature beyond Genre; Digressions

As a genius, Tolstoy had no pupils. Without a new list of forbidden themes, his work left service.[6] What happened then is what Rozanov describes happening in marriage when the feeling of difference between the spouses disappears:

> The teeth of the gearwheel (the difference) are ground down, smoothed, they don't engage anymore. And the crankshaft stops, the work stops, because the machine of juxtaposition has disappeared.
>
> Love, once it dies naturally, will never be reborn. This is why, before all is over (before midnight), infidelities flare up as the

---

[5] Actually, this line reads "Chekhov introduces *Budil'nik* into Russian literature." *Budil'nik* ("The Wake-up Clock") was the journal in which Chekhov published his early feuilletons, which were deemed rather low-brow.

[6] Earlier in the article, Shklovsky mentions that Tolstoy forbade himself to write about Romantic things like the Caucasus and moonlight, not unlike the key device in Shklovsky's *Zoo, or Letters not about Love*.

> last hope of love; nothing separates (creates a difference between lovers) as well as infidelity. The last tooth that has not yet been fully smoothed down grows again and catches the opposite tooth (Rozanov, *Opavshie Listya* 212).[7]

The change of literary schools is such an infidelity.

It's a well-known fact that the greatest literary works (I am speaking of prose here) do not fall into the definition of any particular genre. It is difficult to say what kind of book *Dead Souls* is, hard to define its genre. Lev Tolstoy's *War and Peace* and Sterne's *Tristram Shandy* with their near-absence of a frame story can be called novels only because it's the laws of the novel that they break. The very concept of genre purity—for instance, in the "pseudo-classical tragedy"—is understandable only as the juxtaposition of this genre, which may be still searching its essence, to the canon. But the canons of the novel can change again and again in parodies and re-parodies, perhaps more often than in any other genre.

Following the canon of XVIIIth-century novels, I'll digress.

Apropos of digressions. In Fielding's *Joseph Andrews,* there is a chapter following the description of a fight. This chapter contains a dialogue between a writer and an actor; it's entitled "*Included only for the sake of delaying action.*"[8]

There are three roles digressions can play. Their first role is to enable the introduction of new material into the novel. Thus, Don Quixote's speeches allowed Cervantes to introduce critical, philosophical, and

---

[7] The translation follows Shklovsky, who leaves out and changes several words but preserves the overall meaning.

[8] In the original, Chapter 10 in part III is actually subtitled "A discourse between the poet and the player; of no other use in this history but to divert the reader." Volpin's Russian translation, which appears to have been the only one available to Shklovsky, is close to the original. "Delaying action" thus seems to be Shklovsky's own invention, in tune with his key concepts and terms.

similar materials. Much more important is the second role of digressions—it consists in delaying, slowing down the action. This device was widely used by Sterne, as I've discussed in an unpublished study.[9] The essence of Sterne's device is that a single plot motif is developed in different ways, be it the exposition of characters, the introduction of new material in discussions, or the insertion of a new theme (this is how Sterne introduces a story about the protagonist's aunt and her coachman).

Playing with impatience, the author keeps reminding the reader about the abandoned character but does not return to him after the digression, so that the very reminders only serve to renew the reader's impatience.

In novels with parallel intrigues, such as Victor Hugo's *Les Misérables* or Dostoyevsky's novels, the digression material is formed by one plot line interrupting another.

The third role of digressions consists in creating contrasts. This is what Fielding has to say on this:

> And here we shall of necessity be led to open a new vein of knowledge, which if it hath been discovered, hath not, to our remembrance, been wrought on by any ancient or modern writer. This vein is no other than that of contrast, which runs through all the works of the creation, and may probably have a large share in constituting in us the idea of all beauty, as well natural as artificial: for what demonstrates the beauty and excellence of anything but its reverse? Thus the beauty of day, and that of summer, is set off

[9] "Sterne's *Tristram Shandy* and the Theory of the Novel" proceeded to be published in 1921, famously concluding that *Tristram Shandy* with its "crimes" against "the laws" of the novel is, paradoxically, the most *typical* novel in world literature. It has been observed that Shklovsky would have summed up his claim more effectively in a word like "essential" rather than "typical" (Rose 108)—but Shklovsky tended to prefer memorable aphorisms to exactness.

by the horrors of night and winter. And, I believe, if it was possible for a man to have seen only the two former, he would have a very imperfect idea of their beauty (Fielding; book V, Chapter I).[10]

[...]

Literature beyond Categories; Seeing like a Child

Image tropes consist in calling objects by unusual names. The goal of this device is to place an object into a new semantic field, among concepts of a different order—for instance, stars and eyes, girls and grey ducks[11]—whereby the image is usually expanded by the description of the substituted object.

Synesthetic epithets that, for instance, define auditory concepts through visual ones or vice versa, are comparable to images. For instance, crimson chimes, shining sounds. This device was popular among the Romantics.

Here, auditory representations intermix with visual ones, but I think there is no confusion here; what we have instead is the placement of an object into a new sphere, in short, its removal from a category.

Rozanov's images are interesting in this regard.

This is how Rozanov understands this phenomenon, citing Šperk:

Children differ from us in the force of their perception; they experience everything with a degree of realism that is impossible

[10] Andrei Kroneberg's 1849 translation used by Shklovsky is fairly exact; here, the original text is provided.
[11] Shklovsky is referring to the Russian fairy tale "The Grey Duck Tsarevna."

> for adults. For us, "the chair" is a detail of "furniture." But a child does not know the category of "furniture," and "the chair" is as huge and alive to him as it cannot be to us. This is why children enjoy the world much more than we do (Rozanov, *Uyedinennoye* 230).[12]

This is the work a writer does by violating categories, by wrenching the chair out of furniture.

[12] Rozanov presents this passage as something he was told by his friend Fedor Šperk, a philosopher.

Part Two

Autobiographic Hybrids

Part Two: Introduction

With their heady mixture of criticism, theory, fiction, and autobiography, the following texts are as Shklovskyan as Shklovsky gets. Most of them were written in Berlin, where he arrived in April 1922. At that time, the city was less-than-home to Nabokov, Gorky, Khodasevich, Remizov, Bely, and Pasternak, to name just a few; Tsvetaeva and Esenin were frequent visitors. The émigré community was vibrant. Shklovsky, however, returned to Russia in June 1923. (Both Bely and Pasternak followed a few months later, perhaps inspired by his example.) In private letters, Shklovsky confirmed what he wrote in *Zoo*: he felt out of place in Berlin. He also was in unrequited love. Most importantly, his wife was arrested and held hostage in Russia.

The Berlin year, though not happy, was extraordinarily productive for Shklovsky. In 1923, he published five books: apart from ***Zoo***, ***A Sentimental Journey*** and ***Knight's Move***,[13] there was also a volume on literature and cinema, and another on Pushkin and Sterne. Shklovsky was not the most productive member of the Berlin émigré community, though: in 1922, Remizov published seventeen books. A

[13] These three books are available in English. *Zoo* has been rendered into English in 1969 by Marjorie Ann Peech and in 2001 by Richard Sheldon, who also translated *Knight's Move*, *A Sentimental Journey* and *The Third Factory*. *Knight's Move* and *A Sentimental Journey* were finished in 1921 and 1922 respectively, but published in 1923.

writing fever was upon Russian Berlin, and much of this writing was personal. "At the time when I claimed that art was free of content and beyond emotion, I myself was writing books that were bleeding—*A Sentimental Journey* and *Zoo*. *Zoo* has the subtitle 'Letters not about Love,' because it was a book about love," Shklovsky would say almost fifty years later (*Tetiva*).

Shklovsky alternately denied and confirmed the love story behind *Zoo*. Apart from three prefaces to the book, which are all reproduced here, he frequently comments on it elsewhere, for instance, in "The Way I Write" (1930):

> I needed to write a book about people, something along the lines of Hundred Portraits of Russian Writers. But I was in love, or else in some sort of convergence, or perhaps I chose love the way a weakened organism chooses diseases.
>
> What I ended up with was a wrongly written book.

This last sentence is quite unidiomatic in Russian. It doesn't say "badly written," but suggests something akin to moral failure. In *On the Theory of Prose* (1983), Shklovsky is more direct:

> Roman Jakobson and I were in love with the same woman, but, as fate would have it, it was I who wrote a book about her.
>
> This book tells about a woman who doesn't hear me, but I'm all around her name like the surf, like an unfading garland.

The woman's name was Elsa Triolet (born Elsa Kagan in 1896; like her sister Lilya Brik, she became famous under her married name). To sum up complex and delicate matters with Hollywood simplicity: Shklovsky and Jakobson loved Elsa; Elsa loved Mayakovsky, who loved her elder sister Lilya, who was married to the artist Osip Brik. Elsa knew Shklovsky back in Petrograd; in Berlin, they met again. Lilya was married to, but separated from, a French officer; Shklovsky was married to Vasilisa Kordi, to whom he also wrote tender love letters, albeit without novelizing them. These were heady, revolutionary times; the 1920s are comparable to the American 1960s in terms of freedom of love. Still, Shklovsky's unpublished letters suggest a double standard: he both asks Elsa to marry him and asks Vasilisa to stay faithful, albeit semi-jocularly. The letters from Alya, which make up a large part of *Zoo*, are really written by Elsa Triolet,[14] though only Shklovsky's name graces the cover. Still, he did something important for her literary career: he showed her letters to Maxim Gorky, who urged Elsa to become a writer. She did. In 1944, Triolet was the first woman to be awarded the Prix Goncourt.

Nabokov, as it happens, also includes passages from a real lover's letters in his novel *Mashen'ka* /*Mary*, published in Berlin in 1926; he might well have borrowed the device from *Zoo*.

In translating *Zoo*, the lack of grammatical gender in English was a particular challenge. Shklovsky calls an ape *obezyan,*[15] a neologism (*obezyana* minus the final letter) which suggests not only masculinity but also, more subtly, humanity. Shklovsky readily explains that the zoo is "handy for parallelisms." The ape is a mock-autobiographical figure. "All day, this poor foreigner is suffering from ennui in his internal zoo." When Shklovsky proceeds to describe him

---

[14] A note on names might be opportune here: nonRussian readers of Russian literature never cease to be amazed at the variety of appellations bestowed on every character. Alya is a short form for many names, as witnessed by the present commentator (Alexandra, known as Alya to her friends). Elsa Triolet is Elya is Alya; Roman Jakobson is Roma is Romka (the diminutives are recreated as tokens of the close friendship between him and Shklovsky); Saint Petersburg is Petrograd is Leningrad (renamed first to get rid of German associations, and then of a tsar's name).

[15] The word *obezyana* can mean both "ape" and "monkey"; this particular *obezyan* is depicted in such human terms that he appears to be an ape.

masturbating, one wonders if this is a way to reproach Alya for her unavailability. Alya is repeatedly addressed as a masculine figure of authority, "dear guard commander, Sir."

Joseph Brodsky's poem "From Nowhere with Love" comes to mind, opening as it does with the words: "From nowhere with love the enth of Marchember sir / sweetie respected darling."

The ending of *Zoo*, in best Shklovsky fashion, claims fictionality while suggesting the opposite. Shklovsky lists items of clothing Alya requested him to buy, or shine, or crease: "Let me and all my simple luggage into Russia: six shirts (three at home, three at the laundry), a pair of yellow boots accidentally polished with black wax, and my old blue trousers on which I in vain attempted to make a crease." This final letter is addressed to the VTsIK, a Soviet organ Shklovsky was asking to let him return. Jangfeldt's brilliant biography of Mayakovsky records Osip Brik's reaction:

> "Vitya is a strange fellow," Brik commented ironically. "He hasn't studied grammar. He doesn't know that VTsIK is an inanimate object. Inanimate objects don't have a sense of humor, so one should not joke with them." But the Central Executive Committee proved to be a grammatical exception. (Jangfeldt 223)

Shklovsky was allowed to return to Soviet Russia, a country he describes in *A Sentimental Journey* thus: "The Bolsheviks had entered a Russia which was ill already, but they weren't neutral, no, they were special organizing bacilli, but out of another world, another dimension. This was like founding a state of fish and birds on the basis of double-entry bookkeeping." Considering his honesty in this and other books, the fact that he survived the regime, that he was never imprisoned, is amazing. In Berlin, Shklovsky felt out of place; in Soviet Russia, he felt

> like a man whose insides have been torn out by an explosion, still talking.
>
> Imagine a society of such people.
>
> There they sit, talking. It wouldn't do to be howling (ibid).

Again, one is reminded of Brodsky: "[I] munched the bread of exile: it's stale and warty. / Granted my lungs all sounds except the howl" ("May 24, 1980").

Not letting *them* (whoever they are) reduce you to a howl was a maxim of the intelligentsia. The image of people conversing with their bodies ripped open reappears in the reader's mind when Shklovsky says, later, "I didn't witness that October, I didn't see the explosion." In itself, the image of revolution as an explosion befits early communist rhetoric, but Shklovsky renders it terrifyingly tangible. Elsewhere in *A Sentimental Journey*, he uses a similar connective device, inverting the sequence. When he observes in an aside that "the most terrible thing about a shooting is that the executed must take off his boots and jacket," this might sound merely provocative. But much later in the book Shklovsky talks about a friend who is condemned to death. "I'm afraid of only one thing," his friend repeats, "I'm afraid that they'll tell me to take my boots off, and I've got knee-length lace-up boots, and I'm afraid to get tangled in the laces." Shklovsky concludes: "Citizens, stop killing! People do not fear death anymore." (On *ostranenie* of war and violence, see Berlina: "Faith and War", "Make it Strange".)

Not fearing death is arguably the apotheosis of automatization; "all life had to be turned into a formula and regulated." If Soviet life is formulaic, then *ostranenie* is what it needs, and Shklovsky uses it in the same socially critical function as Tolstoy. He describes murder and mutilation as something "the Kurd tribe did" only to subvert the image of Kurd barbarism by proceeding to depict the atrocities committed by "the Russian tribe." His own use of *ostranenie* shows that the content is not irrelevant, and he makes this abundantly clear: "The formal method is fundamentally simple. It's the return to craft. The most wonderful thing about it is that it doesn't deny the ideological content of art, but considers so-called content to be a phenomenon of form."

A Sentimental Journey would be important as a historical document even if it wasn't tremendously well written, both unflinchingly autobiographical and artistically constructed. (The fact that its title pays homage to Sterne is telling enough.) The events are described almost in real time. The part entitled "Revolution and the Front" was published on its own in 1921; Shklovsky says that he wrote the whole book in ten days while in Finland, fleeing from the Bolsheviks (*Gamburgskiy schet* [1990] 383). His honesty in describing his role in a socialist-revolutionary uprising is as stunning as the comparison he uses to describe its repeated postponement: "I think it would have been easier for a woman to go through half of a birth and stop than for us to do this." One attempt did take place on July 6, 1918, in Moscow. It failed, and Shklovsky had to flee and go into hiding: "I knew a doctor. He arranged a place at a mental hospital for me. He warned me: don't pretend anything, behave the way you always do. That's quite enough …"

A Sentimental Journey is, with all its horrors, a funny book. One could almost forget that, had Shklovsky been found out, his situation would have been no laughing matter. He certainly would be shot. The same is true for hiding in an archive, but still Shklovsky's friend (according to Berezin, it was Jakobson) is joking: "If there's a search in the night, rustle and claim you're paper." Shklovsky ends up with amusingly lilac hair when trying to disguise himself, perhaps inspiring Ilf and Petrov to put their protagonist in *The Twelve Chairs* in a similar predicament.

Fighting at the front, hiding in a mental hospital, and preparing a coup, Shklovsky proceeds with his philological work. He describes the death of his brother and mass executions with chilling laconism:

> He cried hard before he died.
>
> It was either the Whites or the Reds who killed him.
>
> [...]
>
> Lists of people executed by firing squad hung on the walls. Fifteen people a day. Batchwise.
>
> The last five names were always Jewish. This was a measure against anti-Semitism.

Despite all this, Shklovsky claims in *A Sentimental Journey*—for better or worse, this is one of his best-known lines:

> I never saw anything terrible. Life isn't dense.
>
> War consists of great mutual incapability.

After the revolution and the wars, life became calmer but hardly happier: "I live dimly, as if inside a condom," Shklovsky writes in ***The Third Factory***. One reason for this is that Shklovsky dedicates himself to cinematic work, most of which is to him senseless drudgery. Still, he neither sells out nor stops writing. "There are two ways now," he says, "there is no third way. This is the way to go." Quoted on its own, as it so often is, this might sound like an empty aphorism. But with the explanation that follows in *The Third Factory*, it becomes something more: "The third way is to work in newspapers, magazines, to work daily, to care not for oneself but only for the work, to change." This is the way Shklovsky chose, or at least believed himself to have chosen.

Mayakovsky (346) said that Shklovsky's "third way" was the way of "de-canonization and de-stereotypization."

The Third Factory, too, wrestles with this question of living and writing in a dictatorship. Shklovsky compares himself to "flax spread on the rettery." He knows about flax; for several years, he worked for the L'notrest (Flax Trust), writing technical manuals and articles on its planting and harvesting. As a leitmotif in *The Third Factory*, flax stands for submission. "Flax, if it had a voice, would be screaming while it is processed," writes Shklovsky, but goes on to say that "flax needs oppression." Shklovsky chooses words with care; the verb "need" (and its Russian equivalent) can be used not only to refer to internal necessity, but also in phrases like "needs a good thrashing"; it doesn't necessarily suggest an internal requirement. The second part of *The Third Factory* ends with the question "Have we been sawn for linen or for seed?"

Another leitmotif in *The Third Factory* is the red toy elephant. It, too, stands for censorship and oppression. Unlike flax, the elephant is discarded: "I wish to see life in earnest and to talk to it in my own voice, not through a squeaking hole." This, too, is very Shklovskyan: two images with very similar points of reference suggest opposing views. The red elephant is a toy belonging to Shklovsky's son; it makes sounds when pressed. In addition, Shklovsky's coinage "elephant's voice" might be an allusion to the popular ironic expression "Russia is the motherland of elephants," used to mock Soviet-style patriotism. According to Belinkov (163–4),[16] this phrase not only already existed in the 1920s, but also was one-upped (and simultaneously rendered true) by Shklovsky, who reacted to it by exclaiming "No, she's the motherland of mammoths!" The same passage in Belinkov criticizes

---

[16] Belinkov never states Shklovsky's name, but provides so many biographical details that the reference is clear. Shklovsky's grandson Nikita confirms the story.

Shklovsky's fatalism; in *The Third Factory*, "time can't be wrong" is a constant refrain.

Knight's Move also attempts to explain the way Shklovsky works under Soviet conditions:

> There are many reasons for the strangeness of the knight's move, the most important one being the conditional nature of art. I'm writing about the conditionality of art.
>
> The second reason consists in the fact that the knight is not free: it moves sideways because it's forbidden to move freely.

Shklovsky expresses the belief, be it quite sincere or not, that censorship can be beneficial to art, if only one doesn't bow to its dictate but slyly circumvents it. Art itself demands indirectness, he argues, and censorship intensifies this demand (on "Aesopian language" in Russian literature, cf. Loseff). Shklovsky tells all the truth, but tells it slanted.

The chess knight is literally a stallion (*kon'*) in Russian; Shklovsky's self-representation as this figure is not elevating but ironic. It also brings to mind the enstranging four-legged narrator of Tolstoy's "Strider." *The Knight's Move* is a collection of essays, most of which are dedicated to topics seemingly irrelevant for most contemporary readers, particularly Western ones—for instance, a Soviet sculpture entitled "The Great Metalworker." And yet, they are of great interest, touching as they do upon crucial questions of art. The essay on "The Great Metalworker," for instance, places *ostranenie* beyond literature, discussing the need for it in the visual arts. "A Thousand Herrings" argues that it is not the scope of the theme which defines artistic quality. "Driving Nails with a Samovar" discusses the relationship of art and propaganda, giving a twist to the argument by demanding (my italics): "*For the sake of propaganda*, remove propaganda from art." In a 1920 draft, the essay included this passage:

> You can go and find some revolutionary bits in Pushkin, or else you could find some counterrevolutionary ones, but neither matters.
>
> It's better to use poems to wrap up herring than to draw them into politics. (Shklovsky, *Gamburgskiy schet* [1990] 493)

Though Shklovsky doesn't want to draw poetry into politics, he doesn't refrain from political writing, as witnessed by "Teaser Stallions." The article appeared in a newspaper in 1924; an excerpt is included in *Zoo*, but the full text was only anthologized in Russian in 1990, in *Gamburgskiy schet*, and was never before published in English. "Teaser Stallions" was successful in stirring up a scandal; Shklovsky reiterated the comparison in his article "The Death of Russian Europe." Shklovsky first uses this image in a letter to Maxim Gorky in 1922, in which he bitterly refers to himself as a teaser stallion misused by the revolution: "My romance with the revolution is a deeply unhappy one. [...] The teaser stallion tries to mount the mare; first she flings and kicks, then gives in. At this point, the teaser is dragged down and a real studhorse takes his place. As for the teaser, he emigrates to practice masturbation in the émigré press. We right-wing socialists had the job of arousing Russia for the Bolsheviks" (Shklovsky, "Pochta veka" 393). In *The Third Factory*, he applies a similar image to formalism and literary scholarship: "Vegetables are sometimes cooked in soup, but not eaten. [...] Probably, it is us who were the vegetables" (Shklovsky, *Tretya Fabrika* 64).

When separated from his fellow "vegetables," Shklovsky wrote to them wistfully, combining scholarship and intimacy. Here are a few passages from letters written in the 1920s (quoted from *Gamburgskiy schet* [1990]):

to Lev Yakubinsky—

Lev, dear. I, too, live on the eighth floor. Every Young Komsomolets arrives at my apartment out of breath, and a cat, having looked down out of my window, fainted and fell onto the pavement. The curve of fatigue is a good thing; it drops at first, but after fatigue and before depletion, there is inspiration. I believe in your inspiration. I await your letters.

to Yury Tynyanov—

It's quite wrong to use diaries to study the genesis of works of art. There is a hidden lie here, as if a writer was creating and writing on his own—and not together with his genre, with the whole of literature, with all its conflicting movements. A writer's monograph is an impossible thing. Moreover, diaries lead us to the psychology of creativity and to the concept of the genius laboratory. What we need instead is the thing.

to Boris Eikhenbaum—

Boris. Our work was simple at first. We looked at the text as such in the belief that it begins with the title and ends with the author's signature, or else we analyzed a device, believing that it was the same no matter where it was encountered. I deliberately used examples from the works of the most diverse peoples and times, deliberately used examples that were not genetically related. It was important to establish the unity of devices. We argued for aesthetic isolation and aesthetic reproducibility. But theories exist in order to systematize facts, to find ways to predict these facts.

> The material made our work more complex. It turned out that a literary work is not experienced in isolation, that its form is perceived in comparison to other works.

The friendship with Roman Jakobson was particularly important to Shklovsky. They met in 1916 and quickly became friends. As a recent documentary film dedicated to their relations puts it, "their friendship was instant; their quarrel went on for half a century" (Nepevnyy). Jakobson, too, valued and missed Shklovsky, at least in the first decade after their separation. In 1928, he wrote: "I miss you so much that it hurts physically. [...] I understand what you mean by 'flax on the rettery,' but I fear the flax has been processed too intensely [...] The abandonment of formalism designates not a crisis of formalism but a crisis of the formalists." Shklovsky agreed, writing back: "You are absolutely right about the crisis of formalists. [...] If you came back, this would change the correlation of forces; there are too few of us, and your absence is destroying the system" (both letters are cited after *Gamburgskiy schet* [1990] 519). One of Shklovsky's letters to Jakobson reached its addressee through a magazine, *Knizhnyy ugol* (The Book Corner), in January 1922. This penchant for publishing epistolary nonfiction prefigures *Zoo*. "If I wished to write a love letter, I'd have to sell it to a publisher first," Shklovsky jokes, presumably not yet knowing that he'd do just that. Only a few months after his appeal to Jakobson to return from Prague, Shklovsky himself fled Russia. In the following, the letter is reproduced in full.

A Letter to Roman Jakobson (1922/1990)[1]

Dear Roma!

Nadya got married.[2]

I'm telling you this in a magazine, albeit not a large one, because life has become dense.

If I wished to write a love letter, I'd have to sell it to a publisher first and collect my advance payment.

If I go on a date, I have to take along some furnace tubes, to drop them off on my way.

During OPOYAZ lectures, I chop wood. I take a rest while stoking the stove and think while lugging bricks. This is why I have sold the letter to you to *The Book Corner*.

The Flood is finishing.

The beasts are leaving their arks; the unclean ones open cafes.

The remaining pairs of clean ones publish books.

Come back.

Without you, our zoo is missing a good, joyous beast.

We've experienced a great deal.

---

[1] Source: "Pis'mo Romanu Jakobsonu" in *Gamburgskiy schet*. Moscow: Sovetskiy Pisatel', 1990.

[2] Nadezhda Fridland, because of whom Shklovsky participated in a duel in 1920 (Galushkin, "Footnotes" 145, 164).

We've managed to give our own child to strangers so that it wouldn't be cut in half.

It remains with the strangers, unlike in the thick book which my father read from right to left, my mother read from left to right, and I do not read at all.

Yes, we must procure the straw for our bricks ourselves.

This is from that book again.

We do our own writing, our own printing, our own selling.

And we ourselves have contested our lives.

We know now how life is made, and how *Don Quixote* is made, and how a car is made, and what hard times are, and what true friendship is.

Come back.

You'll see how much we've done together—I'm speaking only of us, philologists. I'll tell you everything in the long queue to the House of Science. We'll have a lot of time to talk.

We'll install a stove for you.

Come back.

New times have come, and everyone must cultivate his garden well.

It's better to repair one's own leaky roof than to live under a stranger's.

As for milestones, we don't change them. Milestones are for carts, not for us.

Zoo, or Letters Not About Love (1923/1966)[1]

Author's Preface to the First Edition

Here is how this book was written.

My initial idea was to provide a series of sketches about Russian Berlin; then it seemed interesting to connect these sketches with a shared theme. I decided upon the theme "Zoo," and the book's title was born, but this didn't connect the parts. Then, I stumbled upon the idea of assembling them into something like an epistolary novel.

An epistolary novel needs motivation—why exactly should people be writing each other letters. Often, this motivation is provided by love and separation. I used this motivation in the following form: a man in love writes to a woman who has no time for him. Here, I needed another detail: as the main material of the book does not deal with love, I introduced the prohibition to write about love. What I ended up with is what I expressed in the subtitle: "Letters Not about Love."

At this point, the book started writing itself, it sought to connect the materials, namely the lyrical plot line and the descriptive plot line.

---

[1]Source: *Zoo. Pis'ma ne o lybvi, ili Tretya Eloiza.* in *Zhili-byli.* Moscow: Sovetskiy Pisatel', 1966.

Obedient to fate and the material, I connected these things with a comparison: all descriptions became metaphors for love.

This is a frequent device in erotic texts: real objects are negated, metaphorical ones are asserted.

See *Russian Censored Fairy Tales.*

Berlin, March 5, 1923

A Second Preface for an Old Book

My past, you were real.

There were the Berlin sidewalks in the mornings.

The markets showered with white apple blossoms.

Apple tree branches stood on long market tables in buckets.

Later, in summer, there were long branches of roses, probably climbers.

There were orchids at the florist's on Unter-den-Linden, and I never bought any. I was poor. I bought roses—instead of bread.

What was cut away from my heart is long gone. It's just that I feel sorry about that past, that man from the past.

I left him (my previous self) in this book the way guilty sailors were left on desert islands in old novels.

Live here, guiltily: it's warm here. I can't reform you. Sit here, look at the sunset. It really was you who wrote the letters which hadn't made it into the first publication, but you never mailed them.

Leningrad, 1924

A Third Preface

I'm seventy years old. My soul is lying in front of me.

It's worn out at the bends.

That book had bent it back then. I straightened it out again.

The deaths of friends bent my soul. The war. Arguments.

Mistakes. Injuries. Cinema. And old age, which has arrived, after all. It's easier for me not to know the places where you walk, the new friends you have, the old trees by your mill.

Memory became rings on the water. The rings reached the stony shore. There is no past.

The rings of love went off to the shore.

I won't sit down by the sea, I won't wait for good weather, I won't call my fish with its golden freckles.[2]

I won't sit down by the sea at night, ladling water into my old brown felt hat.

I won't say: "Sea, give me back the rings."

I've already waited long enough for night to come. Incomprehensible stars have been removed from the sky.

Only Venus, the title star of both evening and morning, is in the sky. I'm true to love: I love another woman.

In the morning, at the hour when you can already tell a white thread from a light-blue one, I'm saying this word: Love.

The sun has poured into the sky.

The morning of song never ends; it's only us who leave.

Let us see in the book, as if on water, what the heart had to cross and to pass, how much blood and pride—the things we call lyricism—remains from the past.

Moscow, 1963.

P.S. For several decades now, Alya has been a French writer, famed by her own prose and the poems that others dedicate to her.

---

[2] "Waiting for good weather by the sea" is a Russian saying denoting the expectation of something improbable; Shklovsky is also referencing Pushkin's *The Tale of the Fisherman and the Fish*, which is close to the folktale about the fisher and his wife.

Letter Four

On the cold, on Peter's betrayal, on Velimir Khlebnikov and his death. On the writing on his cross. Moreover: on Khlebnikov's love, on the cruelty of the unloving, on nails, on the cup, and on human culture built on the way toward love.

I won't be writing about love, I'll only be writing about the weather.

The weather in Berlin today is good.

Blue sky, the sun above the houses. The sun's looking directly into the Marzahn boardinghouse, into Eikhenwald's room.

I live on the other side of the apartment.

It's nice and fresh outside.

There was hardly any snow in Berlin this year.

Today is February the 5th ... Still not a word about love.

I wear an autumn coat; if it was cold, I'd have to call it a winter coat.

I don't like frost or even cold weather.

Apostle Peter renounced Jesus because of the cold. The night was fresh, so he came to the fire, and by the fire, there was the communal opinion; servants asked Peter about Christ, and Peter renounced him.

A rooster crowed.

It's not very cold in Palestine. It's probably even warmer than in Berlin.

Had that night been warm, Peter would have remained in the dark, the rooster would have cried uselessly, like all roosters, and the Gospel would contain no irony.

It's a good thing that Christ wasn't crucified in Russia: we have a continental climate, with frost and snowstorms; crowds of Jesus' disciples would have walked out onto the crossroads, toward the fires, queuing up to renounce.

Forgive me, Velimir Khlebnikov, for warming myself by the fires of other people's editorial offices. For publishing my own book, and not yours. Our climate is continental, teacher.

[…]

Letter Six

[…]

The llamas are very beautiful. They have warm woolen clothes and light heads. They look like you.

In winter, everything's closed up at the zoo.

From the perspective of the animals, this isn't a great change.

The aquarium remains.

Fish swim around in blue lemonade-like water, illuminated by electricity. Some plates of glass have terrible things behind them. A little tree is sitting there, quietly moving its white branches. Why does such anguish exist in the world? The ape wasn't sold off but placed in the upper floor of the aquarium. You're very busy, so busy that all my time is free now. I keep visiting the aquarium.

I don't need the aquarium. The zoo might have been handy for parallelisms.

Alya, the ape is about as big as I am, but with wider shoulders, an arched back and long arms. It doesn't look as if it was sitting in a cage.

Despite its fur and his nose, which appears broken, it looks like a prisoner.

Its cage is not a cage but a prison cell.

The cage has a double grate, I don't remember if a sentry is walking back and forth between bars. The ape is bored all day. At three, he (for it is a male) is fed. He eats from a plate. Sometimes, afterwards, he resorts to boring solitary monkey business. I feel offended and ashamed. There you are, regarding him as human, and he—he's indecent.

The rest of the time, the ape clambers about in his cage, throwing sideways looks at the spectators. I doubt that we have the right to keep this distant relative of ours imprisoned without charge or trial. Where is his consul?

He must be bored because he has nothing to do. People seem like evil spirits to him. All day, this poor foreigner is suffering from ennui in his internal zoo.

Nobody will even bring out a newspaper for him.

P.S. The ape has died.

[…]

Letter Eight

On the three tasks given me, on the question "do you love … ?," on my guard commander, on how Don Quixote is made; the letter then turns into a speech on a great Russian writer and ends with a thought on my service time.

You gave me two tasks:

1) not to call you, 2) not to see you.

This makes me a busy man.

There's also a third item: not to think about you. But you never asked me to.

Sometimes you ask me yourself: "Do you love?"

I know this is a post inspection. I answer with the diligence of an engineer troops soldier who doesn't know the post regulation too well:

"Post number three, but I don't know the number for sure, positioned at the telephone and on the streets from the Gedächtniskirche up to the Jorckstrasse bridges, not any further. Duties: to love, not to see, not to write. And to remember how *Don Quixote* was made."[3]

---

[3] The following paragraph is almost a summary of Shklovsky's "How *Don Quixote* is Made."

Don Quixote was made in prison by mistake. A mock protagonist was used by Cervantes not only to perform grotesque deeds but also to give wise speeches. You know yourself, guard commander, Sir, one needs to send one's letters somewhere. Don Quixote received his wisdom as a gift, there was nobody else in the novel to be wise; from the combination of wisdom and madness, the Don-Quixotic type was born.

I could tell you much more, but I see your slightly rounded back and the ends of a short sable tippet. You wear it so as to cover your throat.

I cannot go, I cannot leave my post.

The guard commander leaves quickly and lightly, only rarely stopping at the shop windows.

Through the glass, the guard commander looks at pointed shoes, at long ladies' gloves, at black silk chemises with white hems, the way children look through the glass of a store at a big beautiful doll.

This is how I look at Alya.

The sun is rising higher and higher, like in Cervantes: "it would have melted the poor hidalgo's brains had he had any."

The sun is right over my head.

But I'm not afraid; I know how to make [a] Don Quixote.

He's made to last.

[…]

Mankind invented method.

Method.

Method left home and began living on its own.

Ambrosia has been found, but we don't eat it.

Things, including the most complex things of all—sciences, are walking the earth.

How can we make them work for us?

And should we?

Instead, let's build things that are boundless and useless, but new.

In art, method is walking on its own, too.

An author writing something big is like a driver whose 300-horse-power car seems to be trying to dash him against the wall.

[…]

Letter Eleven

Written, it would seem, in response to a reprimand—apparently made by telephone, since there are no written traces in the file—on table manners, this letter also contains a refusal to accept as a fact that pants must be creased. Throughout, the letter is fitted out with Biblical parallels.

I swear, Alya, pants don't have to be creased.

Pants are worn against the cold.

You can ask the Serapion Brothers.[4]

As for hunching over food, maybe this really is indecent.

You're saying that we can't eat properly.

We lean down too far toward our plates instead of carrying the food to our mouths.

Well, let's go on being surprised at each other.

A great deal surprises me about this country, where pants have to be creased in front; poor people put their pants under the mattress overnight.

This method is known to Russian literature; it's used—in Kuprin—by professional beggars of noble origin.

---

[4]The Serapion Brotherhood was a technique-centered literary circle that consisted mostly of Zamyatin's and Shklovsky's students.

Life here annoys me!

Just as Levin in *Anna Karenina* was annoyed to see preserves made not his way but the way it was always done in Kitty's family.

When Judge Gideon was gathering a guerrilla detachment for an attack on the Philistines, he first of all sent home all the family men.

Then the Angel of the Lord told him to lead all remaining warriors to the river, and to take into battle only those who drank water from the palms of their hands, and not those who hunched over the water and lapped it like dogs.

Are we really bad warriors?

[...]

Letter Seventeen

On the unavoidability and predictability of a resolution. Awaiting it, the correspondent writes first about Hamburg, then about gray and striped Dresden, and finally about the city of ready-made houses—Berlin; further on, we read about the ring through which the author's every thought is threaded, about his nightly path under twelve iron bridges and about an encounter. Also about words being of no use.

I'm quite confused, Alya! You see, I'm writing these letters to you, and at the same time, I'm writing a book. The things in the book and the things in life got hopelessly entangled. Remember, I wrote to you about Andrey Bely and about method? Love has its own methods, its moves have their own logic, which have been determined without me, without us. I pronounced the word of love and started the whole thing. The game began. Where is love and where is the book, I don't know anymore. The game goes on. Somewhere on quire three or four, I'll be checkmated. The opening moves have been made. Nobody can change the outcome.

A tragic ending, at the very least a broken heart, is predicted by the epistolary genre.

Meanwhile, I'll be talking about the place where the action plays out, just for myself.

Berlin is difficult to describe.

Describing Hamburg, you can mention the seagulls above the canals, the shops and houses leaning down toward the canals, all the things that often get painted.

When you enter the free port of the city of Hamburg, the sluice gates open like a curtain. A theatric effect. The enormous field of water, the cranes bowing, black buckets drawing coal from ships into their maws. Their jaws, like crocodiles', open in both directions at once.

A tall, latticed port lift, as high as a revolver shot. Floating elevators, which can suck out up to 600 tons of grain a day.

To swim up to it and say: "Dear comrade, please suck out of me the 600 love devils which have infested my soul."

Or else to ask the biggest crane to grab me by the scruff of my neck and to show me the sluiced Elbe, all the iron, the steamers beside which cars are just fleas. And then, the steam crane would tell me: "Look, you sentimental pup, at the iron standing on end. Moaning and crying is no good; if you can't go on living, then stick your head into the iron coal bucket, to be bitten right off."

That's right!

Hamburg, then, is describable.

Describing Dresden takes more work, of course. But there is a solution, a popular one in contemporary Russian literature.

Let's take some detail of Dresden—for example, the fact that its cars are all nice and clean, and upholstered on the inside with gray striped material.

The rest is as easy as it is for a crane to lift a single ton.

One must claim that Dresden is gray and striped throughout, with Elbe a stripe against the gray, the houses gray, and the Sistine Madonna also gray and striped. This will hardly be true but very convincing and in very good taste.

In very good gray and striped taste.

Letter Twenty-Two

[...]

Initially, characters were only a means to connect parts of the novel. In the development of art, these connecting elements become the focus of interest. Psychological motivation and the verisimilitude of change begin to arouse more interest than the successful execution of the parts they connect. The psychological novel and drama emerge; old dramas and novels are perceived in psychological terms.

This can probably be explained by the worn-out state of the single parts.

At the next stage in art, psychological motivation wears out.

It needs change, *ostranenie*.

Stendhal's *The Red and the Black* is curious in this respect: here, the protagonist acts against his own will, as if to spite himself; the psychological motivation of the action is contrasted with the actual action.

The character acts according to the romantic adventure novel scheme, but his thoughts are his own.

In Lev Tolstoy, the characters make their own psychology conform to their actions.

Dostoyevsky contrasts the psychology of his characters with their moral and social significance.

His novels develop at the pace of a detective story, but their psychology has philosophical dimensions.

Finally, all contrasts are exhausted.

Then, there is only one thing to do—to return to the single parts, to sever the connections that have become scar tissue.

The most vital things in contemporary art are article collections and variety shows, which seek to make the single parts interesting, disregarding their connections. Something similar has been observed in vaudeville side shows.

But in theaters of this type, we already see a new aspect, new connections between the parts.

In a Czech theater of the same variety type as the Scala,[5] I witnessed another device, which seems to have been used for a long time in circuses. At the end of the show, an "eccentric" shows all the acts, parodying and exposing them. For example, he performs magic tricks standing with his back to the spectators, who then see where the disappearing card goes.

German theaters are at a very low stage of development in this respect.

The book which I'm currently writing represents a more interesting case. It's called *Zoo, Letters Not about Love* or *The Third Heloise*; in it, the single parts are connected by the story of a man's love for a woman. This book is an attempt to transgress the boundaries of the ordinary novel.

I'm writing this book for you, Alya, and it's physically painful for me to write it.

Letter Twenty-Eight

[…]

I swear to you, Alya, I'll finish my novel soon.

---

[5] A cabaret in Berlin, not La Scala.

Oh woman who doesn't answer me!

You've driven my love into the telephone receiver.

My grief comes to me and sits at my table.

We talk.

The doctor says that my blood pressure is normal and that my hallucination is a purely literary phenomenon.

My grief comes to me. I talk to it while inwardly counting the quires.

Only three, it seems.

What brief grief!

I should have gotten myself a different one, of international importance.

Things could have been different.

I didn't manage.

All I could manage was to follow your command and get six shirts.

"Three at home, three at the laundry."

I needed to be broken and I found a love that would break me: I'm almost finished, I already wrote this to you.

A man is sharpening a knife against a stone. He doesn't need the stone, though he bends toward it.

That's from Tolstoy.

[…]

Letter Thirty

The very last one. It is addressed to the All-Russian Central Executive Committee (VTsIK). The twelve iron bridges are mentioned again. This letter contains a request for permission to return to Russia.

Petition to the USSR VTsIK.

I cannot live in Berlin.

My entire way of life, all my skills bind me to today's Russia. I can only work for her.

It's not right for me to live in Berlin.

The revolution has transformed me, I cannot breathe without it. Here, I can only suffocate.

Bitter is the Berlin ennui, as bitter as carbide dust. Don't be surprised that I'm writing this letter after letters addressed to a woman.

I'm not involving a love affair in this matter.

The woman to whom I was writing never existed. Maybe there was another, a good comrade and friend to me, with whom I was unable to come to terms. Alya is the realization of a metaphor. I invented a woman and a love for a book about misunderstanding, about alien people, about an alien land. I want to return to Russia.

All that was has passed; my youth and self-assurance have been taken from me by twelve iron bridges. I raise my hand and surrender.

Let me and all my simple luggage into Russia: six shirts (three at home, three at the laundry), a pair of yellow boots accidentally polished with black wax, and my old blue trousers on which I in vain attempted to make a crease.

1922

A Sentimental Journey (1923)[1]

Memories of 1917–22: Petersburg—Galicia—Persia—Saratov—Kiev—Petersburg—Dnepr—Petersburg—Berlin

To Lusya[2]

Revolution and the Front

[...]

The sorrow and shame of pogroms are lying upon my soul, and "sadness, like a black army, has bloodied my heart" (this is the ending of a phrase from someone's translation of a Persian poem).

I don't want to cry on my own, and I will tell something which is too heavy to bear alone.

In our army committee, one soldier was energetically trying to prove that the population was starving, that it had nothing to give.

It must be said that our army, unlike some Caucasian corps, did not go hungry; we had at least 1½ pounds of bread, an abundance of mutton. Except for the posts at the passes.

From a requisitory mission, this soldier brought samples of what

---

[1] Source: *Sentimental'noye puteshestviye*. Berlin: Gelikon, 1923.

[2] Shklovsky's wife, Vasilisa Shklovskaya-Kordi.

the starving Kurds used for bread. This bread was made from coal and clay with a very small percentage of acorns.

Nobody listened to him.

One could imagine how the Kurds hated our requisitory detachments, particularly considering that many divisions stocked up on provisions independently, i.e. without any control.

One such division was surrounded by the Kurds. The leader, a certain Ivanov, defended himself with his sabre for a long time, until his head was torn off and given to the children to play with.

The children played with it for three weeks.

This is what the Kurd tribe did. The Russian tribe sent a punitive detachment and took a ransom in cattle per head killed, pillaging the guilty villages and some innocent ones.

People whom I know told me this: when our troops stormed into a village, the women there smeared their faces, breasts and bodies from the waist down to the knees with excrement, to save themselves from rape. The soldiers wiped the excrement off with rags, and raped.

[...]

About three weeks ago, on the train from Petrograd to Moscow, I met a soldier of the Persian army.

He told me another detail about the explosion.[3]

After the explosion, the soldiers, surrounded by enemies and waiting for the rolling stock, began to collect and put together the bodies of their friends that had been torn into pieces.

This took a long time.

Of course, many body parts got confused. An officer went up to a long row of corpses lying side by side.

The final corpse was assembled from leftover pieces.

---

[3] Several wagons of dynamite exploded by mistake: a bomb was thrown to blast fish.

He had the trunk of a big man. Attached to it was a small head, and on his breast, there were two small uneven arms, both of them left.

The officer looked at this for quite a while, then he sat down upon the earth, and roared, and roared, and roared with laughter …

[…]

The Writing Desk

I'm beginning to write this on May 20, 1922 in Raivola (Finland).[4]

Of course I don't regret kissing or eating, or seeing the sun; I regret trying to direct something that nevertheless rolled on along its rails. I regret fighting in Galicia, messing about with armored cars in Petersburg, fighting on the Dnepr. I changed nothing. And now, sitting by the window and watching the spring passing by without asking me what kind of weather it should make tomorrow, without asking for my permission, perhaps because I'm not from here, I believe that this is how I should have let the revolution pass by me.

When you are falling like a stone, you shouldn't be thinking; when you are thinking, you shouldn't be falling. I confused two crafts.

The causes that moved me were beyond me.

The causes that moved others were beyond them.

I'm but a falling stone.

A falling stone which can light a lantern to watch itself fall.

In mid-January 1918 I came to Petersburg from North Persia. What I was doing in Persia is described in book I, *Revolution and the Front*.

My first impression was how people hurled themselves upon the white bread I had brought.

Then, the city seemed deaf.

---

[4] Today's Roshchino, a village in the Leningrad Oblast, Russia.

As if after an explosion, when everything's over, when everything's torn apart.

Like a man whose insides have been torn out by an explosion, still talking.

Imagine a society of such people.

There they sit, talking. It wouldn't do to be howling.

This was my impression of Petersburg in 1918.

The All Russian Constituent Assembly was disbanded.[5]

There was no front. Everything was wide open.

There was no way of life, nothing but shards.

I didn't witness that October, I didn't see the explosion—if there was one.

I found myself directly in the shell hole.

[…]

We were waiting for the action to start; starting dates kept being fixed and abandoned; I remember one of those days—May 1, 1918, then another one: a supposed strike by the plenipotentiary council.

The strike fell through.

In the nights when the action was supposed to start, we met in our apartments, drank tea together, surveyed our revolvers and sent orderlies off to garages.

I think it would have been easier for a woman to go through half of a birth and stop than for us to do this.

It's very hard to keep people in such tension; they rot, they decay.

[…]

---

[5]The All Russian Constituent Assembly convened in Russia after the February Revolution of 1917. It was the first democratically elected legislative body in Russian history; its dissolution by the Bolsheviks marked the onset of Bolshevik dictatorship.

My arrested friends were shot. My brother was shot. He was not right-wing. He loved the revolution a thousand times more than three quarters of the "red commanders."

He just didn't believe that the Bolsheviks would resurrect burned-out Russia. Two children survived him. The volunteer army was inacceptable for him because it sought to turn Russia back.

Why did he fight?

I haven't told the most important thing yet.

There were heroes on our side.

Both we and you are human beings. I'm telling about the kind of human beings we were.

My brother was shot after the murder of [the Bolshevik leader] Uritsky.

My brother was executed on a firing ground near the Okhta.

He was executed by soldiers from his own regiment. I was told this by an officer who participated in killing him.

Later on, they had special people for killing.

That time, the regiment was on duty.

My brother was externally calm. He died bravely.

His name was Nikolai, he was 27 years old.

The most terrible thing about a shooting is that the executed must take off his boots and jacket. He is made to take them off before he dies.

[…]

It feels good to lose yourself. To forget your own name, to slip out of your habits. To invent a person and to believe that he is you. If it wasn't for the writing desk, for work, I'd never have become Viktor Shklovsky again. I was writing the book "The Plot as a Stylistic

Phenomenon."[6] I had separate scraps from the books I needed to cite, sewn together.

I had to do the writing on the windowsill.

Studying my false passport, I found, in the marital status column, a black stamp saying that so-and-so died on such-and-such date at the Obukhov hospital. A nice conversation I could have had with the Cheka:[7] "Are you So-and-So?"—"Yes, I am."—"Then why are you dead, please?"

[…]

I ventured to go to a place where I knew I could get a passport.

The one I had, I considered spoilt.

I came. Emptiness. A servant opened.

A big hedgehog was walking around, his heavy paws tapping on the floor. His master had been taken away. I don't know if he ever saw his pet hedgehog again.

I searched and found the passport, jumped on a tram and immediately left for Atkarsk on an oil train.

There, I collected the books which I needed in order to write the article "On the Connections between Plot Devices and General Stylistic Devices" (this article was to me like Kipling's tale about the whale: "you must *not* forget the suspenders!"), and mailed them to Petersburg.[8]

---

[6] Published in booklet form as *Rozanov. From "The Plot as a Stylistic Phenomenon"* in 1921 and later in several collections; the present one includes some excerpts under the title "Literature beyond 'Plot.'"

[7] The Cheka was the Soviet secret police in 1917–22.

[8] This article was published in *Poetika* in 1919. Throughout *A Sentimental Journey*, "On the Connections between Plot Devices and General Stylistic Devices" is mentioned in conjunction with Kipling's story. Shklovsky is quoting Kipling's tale "How the Whale Got its Throat." In Kipling, this phrase is a constant refrain, and it remains unclear why the suspenders should be important in the tale of a mariner swallowed by a whale until we

And left for Moscow.

I was wearing absurd clothes. A waterproof cloak, a sailor shirt and a Red Army cap.

My friends told me that I was asking to be arrested.

I was traveling in a heated goods van with sailors from Baku, and with fugitives carrying ten sacks of dried bread. That was all they had in life.

I came to Moscow, the news of failure was confirmed, and I decided to go to the Ukraine.

In Moscow, my money and documents were stolen while I was buying hair dye.

I came to a friend (who wasn't political), dyed my hair at his place, it turned out lilac. How we laughed. I had to shave. I couldn't stay at his place overnight.

I went to another friend; he brought me to an archive, locked me up there and said:

"If there's a search in the night, rustle and claim you're paper."

[...]

In Kharkov, I met my elder brother Evgeny Shklovsky, a doctor.[9]

He was killed a year later.

He was escorting a train with wounded people; the train was attacked, the wounded were being killed.

He started explaining that you couldn't do this. Before the revolution, he once managed to stop a cholera revolt in the city of Ostrov. Here, it was impossible. They beat him up, took his clothes off, locked him in an empty wagon and drove on.

---

learn that he used them to make a grate in the whale's mouth. Shklovsky might be implying that his scholarly pursuits, seemingly useless in times of crisis, was important after all—or else, he might be referring to a private joke.

[9] Actually, a half-brother.

The medical assistant gave him his coat.

He was brought to Kharkov, where he sent a note to his relatives.

For a long time, they searched for him, walking along the rails. They found him, begged to be allowed to take him away and brought him to a hospital where he died from the beating, fully conscious. He felt his own pulse stop.

He cried hard before he died.

It was either the Whites or the Reds who killed him.[10]

I don't remember. I really don't remember. He was killed unfairly.

[…]

The train carried several wagons of coffins with black inscriptions in tar, in quick cursive writing:

COFFINS BACK

If you die, they'll bring you to Kursk and bury you in a burned down forest. The coffin goes back. Recycling.

We came to a station and saw a passenger train packed with people, with compressed masses. They were climbing into the windows, which was dangerous: others could take your boots off while you were climbing in.

First, I was sitting on the buffer; an abundance of people was on the roofs; Russia flowing somewhere, slowly like black pitch.

[…]

I walked the Earth a lot and saw different wars, and still I seem to have spent all the time in a donut hole.

I never saw anything terrible. Life isn't dense.

War consists of great mutual incapability.

---

[10] When Shklovsky told this story to his friend Konetsky, the killers were neither Reds nor Whites but Greens (Konetsky 527). The Greens were armed peasant groups who fought against both Reds and Whites in the Russian Civil War.

Perhaps this is only true for Russia. I was suffering greatly from boredom and longing. I wrote a statement that I was no good as an infantry man, that I'd be of more use in the armored forces, at a pinch, in a demolition squad. Demolition specialists were needed, and I was called to Kherson.

I forgot to tell why I was of no earthly use in Teginka. I had no rifle. There weren't enough rifles.

Off we went; the cart in which I was put also carried two prisoners.

One was big, heavy, the head of the local militia. The other was a small, quiet deserter.

I was armed with a ramrod, but I wasn't alone; a short soldier traveled along as an escort for the prisoners, a prisoner of war himself. He had a rifle, and it was even loaded.

His legs hurt; he could neither sit in the cart nor walk beside it. He perched in the back of the cart, squatting.

The big prisoner was agitated; he'd been beaten badly in Teginka, accused of profiteering, perhaps even of treason. He kept telling us he was innocent.

He was big, and we were surrounded by the steppe. Beyond the steppe, there was a river, and behind the river, there were Whites; there were fewer Reds in the steppe than there were Kurgan stelae. You wouldn't find a Red if you were looking for one.

The steppe was not naked anymore, it was covered with shoots; a company, a regiment could hide in there.

The short escort soldier was telling the prisoner that they'd let him go in Kherson.

Saying this, he winked at me, throwing a look at his rifle: they'd shoot him. The steppe was all around. How easy it seemed for the prisoner to hit me and his disabled sentry and run—instead, he kept talking about his innocence, sitting there as if he was tied to the cart.

I couldn't understand him, the way I couldn't understand Russia.

We brought him to Kherson.

The other one was a boy; if they didn't shoot him on day two, they probably let him go on day three.

I arrived in Kherson.

In Kherson, the cannons kept firing, they became part of everyday life.

Only the bazaar was nervous and afraid.

Still, it kept trading; cannons don't spoil milk.

In the city, people lived and traded.

Lists of people executed by firing squad hung on the walls. Fifteen people a day. Batchwise.

The last five names were always Jewish. This was a measure against anti-Semitism.

[...]

In early 1919, I found myself in Petrograd. It was a cruel, savage time. Under my very eyes, the sled was invented.

Initially, people just dragged things and bags along the sidewalk, then they began to tie pieces of wood to the bags. By the end of the winter, they invented the sled.[11]

It was worse with housing. The city did not suit the new life. People could build no new houses. They did not have the skill of building ice huts, either.

Old-style stoves were first stoked with furniture, then not stoked at all. We moved into the kitchens. There were only two kinds of things:

---

[11] Throughout this excerpt, Shklovsky uses a verb form which can refer both to the first and third person plural (the English generic "you" is sometimes, but not always, applicable). Is it "they" or "we"? The text seems to move fluidly between the two, clearly saying "we" at one point, "they" at another, and remaining ambiguous most of the time.

those which burned and those which didn't. By 1920–2, the new type of home was established.

It was a smallish room that housed a makeshift stove with tins hanging from the joins of its iron pipes, for tar to drip into.

You cooked on that stove.

In the transition period, life was dreadful.

We slept in coats, covered ourselves with carpets; in homes with central heating, most people died.

Whole apartments of people froze to death.

Almost everyone was sitting around in coats at home; the coats were tied up with rope for warmth.

We didn't know that you need fat in order to live. We only had bread and potatoes; we ate potatoes, we devoured bread. Wounds do not heal without fat; you scratch your hand, and your hand begins rotting, and the cloth on the wound rots.

Inexorable axes wounded us. We had little interest in women. We were impotent, the women had no periods.

Later, the affairs began. Everything was bare and as open as open hours; women slept with men because they happened to be living in the same apartment. Girl with thick braids went to bed with you at 5.30 because the tram stopped running at six.

All in its time.

[…]

In Moscow, there was more food, but also more cold and more people.

One house in Moscow was taken up by a military unit; it was given two floors, but didn't use them. Instead, it first settled in the lower floor, burnt it out, then moved to the top, made a hole in the floor to the lower apartment, locked it, and used the hole as a latrine.

This went on for a year.

It's not so much piggishness as the use of things from a new perspective, and weakness.

No horseshoes on your feet, no spikes; it's hard to slide down the accursed earth, trodden slick.

There's noise in your ears, you become deaf with tension and you fall on your knees. And all the while, your head is thinking on its own "about the relation of plot-constructing devices and general stylistic devices." "You must *not* forget the suspenders." At the time, I was almost finished with my work, Boris [Eikhenbaum] with his. Osip Brik finished his work on repetition, and in 1919 we published the book *Poetika* with the IMO publishing house: 15 quires, 40,000 characters each.

We met. Once, we met in a room that was flooded. We sat on the backs of chairs. We met in darkness. Into the dark hallway, Sergey Bondi noisily entered with two linden cartons, tied up with a string. The string was cutting into his shoulder.

We lit a match. He had the face, the young and bearded face of Christ taken down from the cross.

We worked from 1917 to 1922; we created a school, we rolled a stone up a mountain.

[…]

Poetika was published on very thin paper, thinner than toilet paper. There wasn't any other.

The publication was handed over to the Narkompros, and we received our dues.

At the time, bookshops were not yet closed, but books were distributed via the Narkompros. This is how things stood for three years.

The print runs were very large, at least 10,000 and very often up to 200,000 copies; almost everything was printed by the Narkompros and then sent on to the Tsentropechat'.

The Tsentropechat' sent everything off to Gubpechat' and so on.[12]

As a result, there were no books at all in Russia. For instance, they'd send 900 copies of a star chart to Gomel. Nobody needs them, so they just lie around.

Our book was distributed in Red Army reading rooms in Saratov. A staggering number of issues was lost in warehouses. They simply disappeared. Most of propaganda literature ended up as rolling paper. There were cities—for instance, Zhitomir—in which no one saw a new book for three years.

What did get published, got published by chance, with the exception of propaganda.

Astonishing, how much more stupid a state is than single people! A publisher will find a reader, a reader will find a book. A single manuscript will find a publisher. But add Gosizdat and a printing section, and all you have are mountains of books like the Montblanc made from Lemke's *250 Days at the Tsar's Headquarters*, books distributed to foundling hospitals, literature stopped in its tracks.

What impossible tales I heard! Say, they are collecting milk. The order is to bring the milk to a certain point on a certain date. There are no vessels. They pour the milk right onto the earth. It happened near Tver. The man who told me this was the chairman of a food tax collecting committee, a communist. Finally, they found vessels: herring barrels. They poured milk in there, drove them to the

[12] Abbreviations were omnipresent in 1920s Russia, used even as names for newborns. The Narkompros was "The People's Commissariat for Education"; Tsentropechat' and Gubpechat' were central and local agencies for press distribution, Gosizdat stood for "state publishing house." Shklovsky's three-volume *Collected Works* published in 1973 had a print run of 100,000.

appointed place, and poured it out again. They felt sick from what they were doing.

Same thing with eggs. Just to imagine that for two or three years Petersburg was eating nothing but frozen potatoes.

All life had to be turned into a formula and regulated; the formula had been prepared beforehand. And us, we ate foul potatoes.

The Bolsheviks had entered a Russia which was ill already, but they weren't neutral, no, they were special organizing bacilli, but out of another world, another dimension. (This was like founding a state of fish and birds on the basis of double-entry bookkeeping.)

But the mechanism which came into Bolshevik hands, the mechanism they would enter, was so imperfect that it could work the other way around.

With lubrication instead of fuel.

The Bolsheviks persevered, are persevering and shall persevere because their control mechanism is imperfect.

I am being unfair, though. This is how a deaf man believes dancers to be crazy. The Bolsheviks had their own music.

[...]

And you, my friends of the final years, we've been raising—among the sea-smelling streets of a simple, touching Petersburg—our works, which no one seemed to need.[13]

I proceed with this longitudinal section of my life.

By the spring, I got sick with jaundice, probably because of the bad fat in the automobile squadron canteen (it wasn't free of charge, either).

---

[13] Or else, "which, as it appears, nobody needs"; the original grammar is ambiguous. The present translation chose the more optimistic version as Shklovsky was adamant in his belief in the relevance of literary studies.

I became greenish-yellow, bright as a canary. Yellow-eyed.

I didn't want to move, think, stir. But I had to get firewood, to carry this firewood by myself.

It was cold. My sister gave me some firewood, and also some rye bread with flax seeds.

The darkness in her apartment surprised me. It had no armored cables.

In the dark children's room, by the light of a petrol candle—a metal cylinder with an asbestos cord, like a big lighter—the children sat and waited quietly.

Two girls: Galya and Marina.

A few days later, my sister suddenly died. I was scared.

My sister Evgeniya was the closest person I had. We looked dreadfully similar, and I could guess her thoughts.

She differed from me in her patient and hopeless pessimism.

She was 27 when she died.

[...]

I don't like animals in a pit.

There is this fairy tale about animals that all fell into a pit. A bear, a fox, a wolf, maybe a ram. They didn't eat each other because they were in this pit together.

When hunger took its post at every street corner instead of policemen, the intelligentsia made peace.

Futurists and writers of the academic school, cadets and Mensheviks, the talented and the talentless sat around in World Literature studios and stood in line at the House of Literature.

They were broken.

I always tried to live without changing the tempo of life; I didn't want to live in a pit. I never made peace with anyone. I loved, I hated. All this, without bread.

[…]

I resurrected Sterne in Russia because I was able to read him.

When my friend Eikhenbaum, leaving Petersburg for Saratov, asked his friend, an Anglicist, to lend him *Tristram Shandy* to read on his way, the Anglicist replied: "Leave it be, it's such a bore." Now, he is interested in Sterne. I revived Sterne by understanding his structure. I showed his connection to Byron.

The formal method is fundamentally simple. It's the return to craft.[14] The most wonderful thing about it is that it doesn't deny the ideological content of art, but considers so-called content to be a phenomenon of form.

A thought is contrasted with a thought just like a word is contrasted with a word, an image with an image.

Art is, at its heart, ironic and destructive.[15] It animates the world. Its task consists in creating inequalities. It creates them through comparisons.

New forms of art are created by the canonization of low forms of art.

Pushkin is descended from album poetry, the novel from gothic stories and detective tales. Nekrasov is descended from vaudeville, Blok from Gypsy romance, Mayakovsky from humorous poetry.

Everything—the fate of the characters, the era in which the action takes place, everything—are motivations for form.

Motivations change quicker than form.

[…]

Mandelstam's walking around the house, his head thrown back. He

[14] *Masterstvo* can also be rendered as "skill," "mastery," "artistry," or "proficiency."

[15] In "Literature Beyond Plot," Shklovsky describes art as "harmless, self-contained, nonimperative."

writes poetry in public. Day by day, line by line. The poems are born heavy. Each line separately. And it all seems almost a joke with all these proper names and the archaic Russian. As if it was written by Kozma Prutkov. These poems border on the ridiculous.

Take from my palms some honey, if you please,
some honey and some sunshine for your pleasure,
the way Persephone has taught her bees.

You can't cast off a boat which is unmoored,
You can't perceive the fur-clad steps of shadows,
You cannot conquer fear in blackest life.

All that remains for us are little kisses,
as furry as a swarm of tiny bees
that die as soon as they give up their hive.[16]

Osip Mandelstam grazed like a sheep, wandered about the rooms like Homer.

He was a very intelligent person to talk to. The late Khlebnikov called him a "marble fly." Akhmatova says that he is the greatest poet.

Mandelstam was hysterically fond of sweets. He lived under very hard conditions; still, without any boots, in the cold, he managed to resemble a spoilt child.

His feminine lack of discipline and his bird-like flippancy were not without system. He had the manners of an artist, and artists lie in order to be free for their only task; they are like monkeys who, according to Hindu belief, refrain from talking so that they aren't made to work.

Down below, Nikolai Gumilev walked about with a straight back.

---

[16] Translation by Alexandra Berlina; for a version by Peter France, see *The Penguin Book of Russian Poetry* 284.

This man had willpower; he hypnotized himself. He was surrounded by young people. I don't like his school but I know that, in his way, he helped people grow. He forbade his disciples to write about spring, saying that there was no such season. You can't imagine what mountains of slime are contained in mass versification. Gumilev organized the versifiers. He made bad poets into not so bad poets. He had the pathos of skill and the confidence of an expert. He understood other people's poetry well, even if it was far beyond his orbit.

He was an alien man to me, and I find it hard to write about him. There was no need to kill him. No need whatsoever. I remember how he talked to me about proletarian poets in whose workshop he gave readings: "I respect them. They write poems; they eat potatoes and feel shy to take some salt at table, the way we are shy to take sugar."

Gumilev died calmly.

A friend of mine was imprisoned and condemned to death. We wrote letters. It was about three or four years ago. The guard smuggled letters in his holster. My friend wrote:

"I am fighting my will to live; I've forbidden myself to think about my family. I'm afraid of only one thing,—(this must have been his mania),—I'm afraid that they'll tell me to take my boots off, and I've got knee-length lace-up boots, and I'm afraid to get tangled in the laces."

Citizens!

Citizens, stop killing! People do not fear death anymore.

[…]

I declare that I have lived through the revolution honestly. I didn't drown anyone, I didn't trample anyone, I didn't make peace with anyone because of hunger. I worked all the time. And if I had my cross, I always wore it under my arm. My only guilt before the Russian revolution is this: I chopped wood in my room. This makes plaster crumble in the apartment below.

[…]

Knight's Move (1923)[1]

Preface One

[…]

There are many reasons for the strangeness of the knight's move, the most important one being the conditional nature of art. I'm writing about the conditionality of art.

The second reason consists in the fact that the knight is not free: it moves sideways because it's forbidden to move freely.

The articles and feuilletons in this book were all published in Russia between 1919 and 1921.

They were published in a tiny theater newspaper called *Life of Art*; this newspaper was a knight's move.

I am writing for Russians abroad.

Some people say: people are dying in the streets in Russia. People in Russia are eating, or could be eating, human flesh.

Others say: the universities in Russia are functioning; the theaters in Russia are full.

Choose what you will …

Don't choose. All this is true.

There is this in Russia, but also that.

Everything is so contradictory in Russia that we have all grown witty quite involuntarily.

---

[1] Source: *Khod konya*. Moscow/Berlin: Gelikon, 1923.

I've collected newspaper articles the way they were written. I've added very little.

One other thing: don't think the knight's move to be the move of a coward.

I'm not a coward.

Our broken way is the way of the brave, but what can we do if we have two eyes each and if we can see more than the honest pawns and the kings, who are duty-bound to have but one belief.

Driving Nails with a Samovar

If you take a samovar by the legs, you can use it to hammer nails, but this is not its intended purpose.

I have seen the war; I've stoked furnaces with a piano in Stanislav and burned oil-soaked carpets in fires, locked in the mountains of Kurdistan. Now I stoke my stove with books. I know the laws of war, and I understand that it reconstructs things in its own way, transforming a person into seventy kilograms of human meat, or a carpet into a wick surrogate.

But it won't do to judge a samovar by its usefulness in regard to the driving of nails, or to write books in such a way that they burn better. War—necessity—reconstructs things in its own way, it regards the old thing simply as material, and this is brutal and honest; but to change the purpose of a thing, to drill doors with spoons, to shave with an awl while assuring that all is well—this is dishonest.

Such thoughts have been plaguing me for a month, ever since I saw, in *Pravda*, the program (or a "program proposal") to organize a musical evening with the help of the Military Commissariat educational department.

This program is a program to use music for propaganda.

But how can one propagandize with music, whose essence, according to Kant, is pure form?

[...]

I won't defend art for art's sake; I will defend propaganda for propaganda's sake.

The tsarist government was good at putting its imperial stamp everywhere: every button, every institution had been stamped.

For ten years, in the morning—every morning—at school, I sang, in a herd of other children: "Lord, save Thy people ..." Today, and even long before, even the year I graduated from high school, I couldn't say this prayer without error. I can only sing it.

Propaganda filling the air, propaganda saturating the Neva's water, ceases to be felt. A vaccine develops against it, a form of immunity.

Propaganda in the opera, cinema, and exhibition hall is useless—it eats itself.

For the sake of propaganda, remove propaganda from art.

On "The Great Metalworker"

[...]

The perception of the human body left the sphere of seeing for the sphere of recognition; the body, at least as long as it is not altered, transfigured, mutilated, or decomposed, does not exist as an object of artistic perception. It is not by chance that language has next to no words for body parts. And our children, when they draw, always draw buttons, and hardly ever knees and elbows. You can mold humans out of habit and even make them very large and, for this reason, call them great, but simply measuring the work of an honest artisan, Ilya Ginzburg or Bloch, will show that these forms were sculptured by people who never saw a human being, who only knew by rote that a head, arms, and legs are usually required.

Those who don't want to search but cut coupons from old traditions think that they represent the old school.

They are wrong. You cannot create in forms made by other people, for creativity is change.

[...]

A Thousand Herrings

There are math books with problems arranged in a certain order. First come the equations with one unknown, then the quadratic equations ...

And at the back, there are the solutions, all neatly arranged in columns:

4835 5 sheep
4836 17 cranes
4837 13 days
4838 1000 herrings

Pity those who begin to learn math with the solutions, trying to find meaning in this neat column!

The problems matter, and so does the course of their solution, not the final numbers.

Art theorists who are interested in ideas and conclusions, not the way things are constructed, resemble one who wishes to study mathematics and ends up studying the columns of solutions.

Their heads look something like:

the Romantics = religious renunciation
Dostoyevsky = God-seeking
Rozanov = sexual issues
year 18 = religious renunciation

… 19 = God-seeking
… 20 = sexual issues
… 21 = relocation to North Siberia.

But art theorists have their fish curing plants at universities, and they are harmless.

Pity the writer who strives to increase the weight of his own work not by developing its moves, but by ensuring the magnitude of the solution.

As if the problem N 4837 was bigger, more important than N 4838 because one of them has 13 as its solution, and the other "1000 herrings."

These are simply two problems, both of them for the third grade.

[…]

The Tsar's Kitchen

I was sitting there, laughing.

You see, there's this fairy tale.

A certain tsar was a mighty man. A thousand camels carried his kitchen, another thousand carried the food for his kitchen, and yet another thousand carried the cooks.

There was a war, and the tsar was defeated.

There he was, in captivity, in shackles.

He was eating from a pot.

A dog was running past; it turned the pot over, got caught in the bail and carried away the pot.

The tsar laughed.

The guards asked: "Why are you laughing?"

The tsar said: "A thousand camels carried my kitchen, another thousand carried the food for my kitchen, and yet another thousand carried the cooks. Just now, a single dog carried away my kitchen on its tail."

* * *

I was sitting there, laughing.

In 1917, I wanted happiness for Russia. In 1918, I wanted happiness for the whole world, wouldn't accept less. Now I want only one thing: to return to Russia.

Teaser Stallions (1924/1990)[1]

Chaplin said that a man is most comical when he is in an incredible situation—and pretends that nothing is out of the ordinary.

A man is comical when he is trying to straighten his tie while hanging upside down.

There are very definite lists of things one may and may not write about.

In short, everyone writes while straightening his tie.

I'll write about teaser stallions. No one ever wrote about them; perhaps they are taking offense.

When horses are mated—this is terribly indecent, but otherwise there'd be no horses—the mare is often nervous, the defense reflex kicks in, and she doesn't let the stallion mount her. She might even kick him.

Now, a stud isn't made for passionate intrigues; his path must be strewn with roses, and nothing but exhaustion should be in the way of his romance.

So in such cases, they take a stallion of short stature (his soul might be most beautiful) and lead him to the mare.

---

[1] Source: "Probniki" in *Gamburgskiy schet*. Moscow: Sovetskiy Pisatel', 1990.

The two flirt, but as soon as they, so to speak, come to terms, the poor stallion is pulled away, and a big stud takes his place.

This first stallion is called a teaser.

A teaser stallion has a difficult job; I've heard that sometimes they even end up mad and suicidal.

I don't know if a teaser stallion straightens his tie.

In Russian history, the Russian intelligentsia has played the role of the teaser stallion.

This is the destiny of intermediate groups.

But even before, all of Russian literature was dedicated to describing the experiences of teaser stallions.

Writers described in great detail how their characters did not get what they wanted.

How they straightened their ties.

Alas, even Tolstoy's characters—favorite characters from *The Cossacks*, *War and Peace*, and *Anna Karenina*—are teaser stallions.

Today, the Russian émigré society is made up from organizations of political teaser stallions without any class consciousness.

As for myself, I'm tired.

Moreover, I'm not used to wearing ties.

Hereby I officially resign from the rank and title of a member of the Russian intelligentsia.

I am not responsible to anyone and do not know anything, except for a few tricks of my craft. I'm not serving anyone, but want to join the crowd of people who simply work; the profession of a writer does not give a greater right to control people's thoughts than that of a shoemaker. Down with teaser stallions.

The Third Factory (1926)[1]

The First Factory

On the Little Red Elephant

—Little red elephant, my son's toy, I'll let you walk into my book first so that the others don't get haughty.

The little red elephant is squeaking. All rubber toys squeak, why else would they let out air?

Thus, in defiance of Brehm, the little red elephant is squeaking while I write in my high nest above the Arbat Street.

Rare is the bird that reaches me without huffing and puffing. In my nest, I've lost the habit of breathing calmly.[2]

My son is laughing.

He laughed when he first saw a horse; he thought that it got itself that long face and the four legs for a joke.

We've been stamped with different forms, but we all have the same voice under pressure.

—Little red elephant, move away; I wish to see life in earnest and to talk to it in my own voice, not through a squeaking hole.

Here, the feuilleton ends.

---

[1] Source: *Tretya Fabrika*. Moscow: Krug, 1926.

[2] Shklovsky is alluding to Gogol's "it's a rare bird that can fly to the middle of the Dnieper."

I'm Writing about Being Determining Consciousness, and Conscience Remaining Unsettled

[...]

This book's title is going to be

The Third Factory.

First, I work at the Third Goskino [State Cinema] Factory.

Second, this title is easy to explain. My first factory was my family and school. My second was the OPOYAZ.

The third one is processing me now.

Do we know how humans are to be processed?

Perhaps it's right to make them queue at the cash register. Perhaps it's right to make them work outside of their profession.

I'm saying this in my own—not in the elephant's—voice.

Time can't be wrong, time can't be guilty before me.

It's wrong to say: "The whole company is marching out of step, only the ensign isn't." I want to talk to my time, to understand its voice. Right now, for instance, I'm finding it hard to write because I've almost reached the usual length of an article.

But art needs chance. The size of a book was always dictated to the author. The market gave the writer his voice.

A literary work lives on its material. *Don Quixote* and [Dostoyevsky's] *The Raw Youth* were not created by freedom.

The necessity of including any given material, all restrictions—they give rise to creativity. The freedom I need is constructive freedom. I need the freedom to find and reveal my material. What I don't want is to make Viennese chairs from stones. What I need now is time, and readers. I want to write about unfreedom, about Smirdin's accounts,[3] about the influence of magazines on literature,

[3]Smirdin was a Russian publisher credited with making books much cheaper and thus more widely read.

about the third factory that is life. We at the OPOYAZ are no cowards, we don't give in to wind pressure. We love the wind of the revolution. At 100 kilometers per hour, the air exists, it weighs upon you. When the car speeds down to 76, the pressure falls. This is unbearable. The emptiness sucks you in. Let me speed up.

Let me cultivate specialty crops. It's wrong to make everyone sow wheat. I cannot talk in the little elephant's squeaky voice.

[...]

The Second Factory

A Letter to Roman Jakobson, Translator for the Soviet Embassy in Czechoslovakia

Do you remember your typhus delirium?

You were raving that your head had disappeared. People with typhus always claim that. It seemed to you that you were being judged for betraying science. That I was condemning you to death.

You were hallucinating that Roman Jakobson had died, and in his stead there was only a boy on a god-forsaken station. The boy has no knowledge whatsoever, but still he is Roma. And Jakobson's manuscripts are being burned. The boy cannot get to Moscow and save them.

You live in Prague now, Roman Jakobson.

For two years, there've been no letters from you. And I am silent, as (if) this was my fault.[4]

My dear friend, *On the Theory of Prose* is published. I'm sending it to you.

It remained unfinished. That's how it was published. You and I,

---

[4] The original *kak vinovnyi* (lit. as/like guilty) is ambiguous: Shklovsky might or might not be saying that this really was his fault; the preceding comma suggests that he is.

we were like two pistons in one cylinder. These things happen to locomotives. You've been unscrewed, and are now being kept in Prague as a utensil.

Dear Roman! Why work when there is no one to tell? I miss you very much.

[...]

Tell me, why did we fall out? We had no fight.

Birds hold on to the branches even in their sleep. This is how we must hold on to each other.

Reply to me, and I'll answer you in a book. How is your family life? You know, Roman, family is like an old car that is still good and solid, still used because it would be a pity to get rid of—but it would make no sense to buy it.

The family doesn't work out. In a family, husband and wife have to make up for deficits every day.

The family fills up the home. One has to live between the windows, by the little glasses with sulfuric acid.

Roma, you are for real. You speak Czech well; you speak many other languages well. You don't sell science. You care for it.

You know what my delirium is like. I don't sell science, either, I dance it. You may judge me, Roma. But I don't feast on science, I don't wear it like a tie, and, Romka, I judge you.

Back then, when we met on Osya's [Mandelstam's] sofa, there were poems by Kuzmin hanging over it. Back then, you were younger than me, and I was trying to convert you to a new faith. With the inertia of your weight, you accepted it. Now, you're an Academy member again. There are few of us. I'm losing myself the way a merino sheep loses his wool on thistles.

Romka, the pain woke me up. I'm awake.

The shadow won't give me its hand.

I'm flax, flax spread out on the rettery. I look into the skies, and I feel pain.

And you're out for a walk, Romka.

A two-year-old girl called absence of all kinds "out for a walk." She had two categories: "here" and "out for a walk."

"Daddy's out for a walk, Mommy's out for a walk."

In winter, someone asked: "And where's the fly?"—"The fly's out for a walk."

The fly was lying, legs up, between the window frames.

[…]

The Third Factory

On Freedom of Art

[…]

Flax, if it had a voice, would be screaming while processed. It's grabbed by the head and pulled out of the ground. Roots and all. It's sown thickly for self-suppression, so that it grows stunted and does not branch out.

Flax needs oppression. It's pulled around. It's spread-eagled on the fields, and elsewhere soaked in pits and rivers.

Rivers used to wash flax are damned rivers—they have no fish anymore. Then, the flax is scutched and broken.

I want freedom.

But if I get it, I'll go look for bondage—by a woman, by a publisher.

Still, the writer does need a gap to take two steps, like a boxer for a strike, he needs the illusion of choice.

For the writer, illusion is a strong enough material.

[…]

There are two ways now. One is to leave, to dig yourself in, to make money with something other than literature and to write privately, at home.

The other way is to dedicate yourself to describing life, conscientiously looking for the new way of life and the right world view.

There is no third way. This is the way to go. The artist should not follow tram lines.

The third way is to work in newspapers, magazines, to work daily, to care not for yourself but only for the work, to change, to interbreed with the material, to change again, to interbreed with the material, to process it again, and then, there shall be literature.

Out of Pushkin's life, Dantes' bullet was probably the only thing the poet did not need.

But he did need the fear and oppression.

What strange work this is. Poor flax.

[…]

Change your biography. Make use of your life. Break yourself against the knee.

Leave only your stylistic composure untouched.

We, theorists, need to know the laws of chance in art.

Chance is non-aesthetical.

It has a non-causal connection to art.

But art lives on changes in material. On chance. On the writer's fate.

– Why did you need to go and hurt your foot?—Freud asked his son.

– What the hell did you idiot need syphilis for?—asked one man of another.

What I need my fate for is, of course, the third factory.

Plot devices are piled up at my door like copper springs from a burnt sofa. Bent, not worth repair.

[...]

What They're Making Me Into

I live badly. I live dimly, as if inside a condom. In Moscow, I don't work. At night, I have guilty dreams. I have no time for a book.

Sterne, whom I brought to life, confuses me. I make writers; I made myself into one.

I work for the Third Goskino Factory, remaking movies. My head is filled with scraps of film reels. Like the waste basket in the editing room. A life of chance.

A broken life, perhaps. I don't have the strength to resist time, and perhaps I shouldn't try.

Perhaps, time is right. It has processed me in its own way.

[...]

The difference between the OPOYAZ and Alexander Veselovsky's school is this: Veselovsky pictures literary evolution as the imperceptible accumulation of slow changes.

If Veselovsky sees that two points in plot history differ rather strongly, he looks for the missing link and, if he doesn't find one, assumes it to be lost.

I believe that plots develop dialectically, pushing off from themselves in self-parody. Veselovsky points out, sometimes almost correctly, that particular artistic devices could have developed from everyday life experience; I believe this solution to be insufficient.

Schematically, I envision the following: works of art can and do change for non-aesthetic reasons, for instance because a language is influenced by another language or because a new social mission emerges. Thus, a new art form arises unconsciously and without aesthetic consideration, and only then is judged aesthetically, at the same time losing its initial, pre-aesthetic meaning.

Simultaneously, the aesthetic construction which existed before ceases to be felt, loses its joints, coagulates into a single piece.

The Fields of Other Provinces

[…]

We're flax on the rettery. You know that.

My personal fate didn't fit into a book. My fate only went as far as childhood. My life was blown out through the cracks. The neighboring rooms were unheated.

Love, secret and concealed, didn't work out. What seems to have worked out is the right to be a specialty crop. I wish to be spread out on the rettery.

Childhood Two

He is a year and a half now. He's pink, round, and warm. His eyes are far apart and oval. Dark. He doesn't walk yet: he runs. His life is still continuous. It doesn't consist of single drops. It's experienced as a whole.

[…]

He plays with the window, with the heating pipe, and with me. He comes to me in the morning, to see how my room is doing and to tear up some books. He's growing all the time, quicker than spring grass.

I don't know how all that happens fits into him. He seems amazing to me.

What he likes about me is my shining cranium. Time will come …

When he grows up, he won't write, of course.

But he'll probably remember his father.[5]

[…]

[5] Shklovsky's only son died in World War II in 1944, aged twenty-one, forty years before Shklovsky's own death.

Part Three

Early Soviet Criticism and Advice to Young Writers

Part Three: Introduction

The texts in this chapter have never been translated into English before; some of them—for instance, *Technique of Writing Craft*—are difficult to get hold of in Russian. *Technique* is a curious book, a guide for proletarian writers. Shklovsky expects a certain kind of audience: he explains who Boccaccio was, what parallels and monologs are. When he speaks, say, of "the individual language of any single person," it is because his readers wouldn't understand the word "idiolect." Fond as Shklovsky was of images such as "to dedicate oneself only and exclusively to literature is not even a three field system, it's simply the exhaustion of soil," their abundance in *Technique* seems to be tailor-cut to the audience, to young authors who find themselves, without much education, "in a factory with abandoned tools."

An earlier draft defines the audience clearly. The first sentence reads "the VAPP—the All-Russian Association of Proletarian Writers—has three thousand members"; the description of their plight goes into more satirical detail than in the final version: "some live in the bathroom, say, 6 people or so, but no bathroom can accommodate everyone, because, as I said, there are three thousand people" (*Gamburgskiy schet* [1990] 393). Shklovsky's dry humor might have been invisible to the intended audience: "the contemporary writer does his best to become professional by the age of eighteen […] this is very inconvenient because he has nothing to live on"; a short story by Tolstoy "was written by an economic executive of his times and could have been read out loud at a production conference of the nobility, had there been such a thing." Forced to simplify, Shklovsky expresses some of his key ideas succinctly. "A literary work doesn't descend directly from another literary work, it needs a Dad on the side," for instance, is a key point in "Literature beyond 'Plot,'" but arguably phrased more memorably in *The Technique*.

When writers as diverse as Veniamin Kaverin and Danilo Kiš readily admit to have been influenced by Shklovsky, it is conceivable that the translation of an actual manual on technique might help others. The advice Shklovsky gives young writers might look banal to twenty-first-century eyes: one chapter, for instance, is entitled "Show, Don't Name." Shklovsky, however, wrote it ninety years ago; more to the point, he actually argues for *ostranenie* here: by not naming the thing directly, the writer can let the reader see it. Some of the instructions appear to contradict each other: "use not only the character traits you need but something extra," but "use only the descriptions you need." Often, it seems that the advice Shklovsky really wants to give his readers is to stop writing and start reading. One chapter bears the instructive title "On Poetry, and Why Not to Write Any." The warning is heart-felt: in *A Sentimental Journey*, Shklovsky observes, "you can't imagine what mountains of slime are contained in mass versification."

Sometimes, though, Shklovsky addresses not clueless wannabe-authors but fellow writers, those who could create "the kind of text that might replace the novel." For just a line or two, the manual becomes a manifesto: "great literature will turn up at the very place where we stand quietly, insisting that this is the most important place."

Technique of Writing Craft was published in 1927. Next year, the collection *Hamburg Score* appeared; in 1990, a posthumous volume appeared under the same title, including parts of the original and other material.[1] Both books also contain an essay entitled "Hamburg Score." While "Art as Device" is Shklovsky's most influential contribution to literary theory, this little vignette has played a great role in Russian culture. One doesn't need to have heard of Shklovsky to use "Hamburg Score" as a metaphor for the true value of things.

Shklovsky is usually regarded as the creator of the expression, but he once told his friend Konetsky that he had first heard it from the wrestler Ivan Poddubny. According to this account, Poddubny explained the concept as a fact; however, it seems that the decisive wrestling competition in Hamburg was a myth—or else, truly secret. At the beginning of the twentieth century, Hamburg was an important center for European wrestling (it was still second only to Berlin when Poddubny wrestled there with great success in 1927, a year before *Hamburg Score* was published). Public houses were the meeting point of choice in the early days of organized wrestling, as there were not many public areas or sports venues, and the problem of ungentlemanly agreements loomed large as soon as wrestling began drawing crowds.

While no concrete model for Shklovsky's tournament has been found, and a single, central tournament for the world's wrestlers seems unlikely, there is no doubt that fights intended for being exciting for a broad public and fights intended to compare the skills of the wrestlers in a more professional manner existed side by side. According to the North German Institute of Sports History, there have even been reports of nonpublic "proper" fights determining who would have to go down in a more spectacular way in the later exhibition match. Thus, while the particulars of Shklovsky's story are likely a fiction, it, like the wrestling matches of yore, is firmly footed in real life.

---

[1] The original titles are *Tekhnika pisatel'skogo remesla* and *Gamburgskiy schet.*

The ranking of writers has tradition in Russian literature; Shklovsky probably was familiar with Baratynsky's "Poets of the 15th Rank" and Chekhov's "Literary Table of Ranks." Talking to Konetsky, Shklovsky calls his "Hamburg Score," in which he managed to give offense to five writers on a single page, a cocky mistake of youth. Bulgakov felt particularly insulted by being placed "at the edge of the mat," which might suggest the role of a clown accompanying a wrestling show (Belozerskaya-Bulgakova 45). This phrase might actually be a compliment, describing Bulgakov preparing to participate in the real thing: in *Theory of Prose* (1983), Shklovsky writes: "if we don't see the thinking in this argument, the wrestling right at the edge of the mat, we'll never understand art." Shklovsky was critical of some of Bulgakov's texts, e.g. calling *The Fatal Eggs* "a quotation from Wells" (Shklovsky, *Gamburgskiy schet* [1990] 301), but he came to love others: "When I read, for example, *Master and Margarita* … I fall apart like clothes in the rain" (Vitale 146).

Serafimovich and Veresaev did indeed largely disappear from literary history, but Gorky and Babel were used to laudatory reviews from Shklovsky. The dismissal of Babel as a lightweight stands in contrast to the article "Babel: A Critical Romance" first published in 1924. It does contain some criticism, but first and foremost, Shklovsky is so charmed by Babel's style that he adopts it. "Babel wrote little, but persistently" alludes to one of his best-known phrases, "Benya speaks little, but he speaks with zest," from "How It Was Done in Odessa." When Shklovsky explains that "from [Babel] I learned that he had not been killed," the humor is also very much in Babel's vein. Moreover, "Babel: A Critical Romance" is full of unmarked quotations. The objects of comparison here are taken from Babel: "Boots polished so brilliantly that they resemble girls, the brightest breeches, bright as a banner in the sky, even a fire blazing like a Sunday—all these can't compete with Babel's style." Calling Babel "a foreigner with the right to wonder," Shklovsky admires his ability to "speak in the same voice about the stars and the clap."

Apart from criticism, *Hamburg Score* includes short stories and theoretical articles published in Petrograd newspapers and magazines. Perhaps the best-known one among these is "In Defense of the Sociological Method." Based on a lecture read in Leningrad in 1927, it has an ironic or, depending on the audience, slyly misleading title. Far from defending the conventional sociological approach to literature, Shklovsky argues for aesthetics as a social category.

The final text in this chapter, "The Way I Write," was written in 1928 and published in a 1930 anthology entitled *The Way We Write* (*Kak my pishem*); the present translation follows a reprint in *Gamburgskiy schet* (1990: 422–5). The anthology participants were supposed to answer a series of questions. Explaining how he works, Shklovsky says that he tries "to connect facts that stand far apart." This process bears resemblance to such concepts as "bisociation" (Koestler) and "conceptual blending" (Fauconnier and Turner), which have become crucial to cognitive studies and other fields. Shklovsky's regret that writing fiction "hinders [him] from smoothing out the instrument's traces in [his] scholarly work," from replacing wittiness with greater clarity, seems genuine. But it is precisely this mixture which makes up not only his style but his way of thinking.

Technique of Writing Craft (1927)[1]

Introduction: Don't Hurry to Become a Professional Writer

Three Thousand Writers

There are several thousand writers today. This is a very large number.

The contemporary writer does his best to become professional by the age of 18 and not to have a profession other than literature. This is very inconvenient because he has nothing to live on; in Moscow, he lives at his friends' place or in the stairway of the Herzen House. This wouldn't be so bad in itself because we could build special barracks for writers—we do find space for new military recruits, after all—the thing is that the writers in these barracks won't have anything to write about. You need a profession other than literature in order to write, for the professional—a person with a profession—describes things in terms of a professional relation. Gogol's blacksmith Vakula examines Catherine's Palace from the perspective of a blacksmith and a house painter, and this is how he might describe the palace. Bunin, describing the Roman Forum, does so in terms of a Russian villager.

[1] Source: *Tekhnika pisatel'skogo remesla*. Moscow/Leningrad: Molodaya Gvardia, 1927.

On Lev Tolstoy's Closeness to the People

Lev Nikolayevich Tolstoy wrote as a professional artillerist as well as a professional landowner; he followed his professional and class interests in creating works of art. The short story "Master and Man," for instance, was written by an economic executive of his times and could have been read out loud at a production conference of the nobility, had there been such a thing. If you take the letters exchanged by Tolstoy and Fet, you can see even more clearly that Tolstoy is a small landowner interested in his small estate (though he was no good at being a landowner, and his pigs kept dying). This estate made him change the forms of his art. If Lev Nikolayevich Tolstoy had gone to live at the Herzen House aged 18, he would have never become Tolstoy as he'd have nothing to write about.

Tolstoy began to feel like a professional writer when he was forty, after having written several volumes. Here is an excerpt from his letter to Fet:

> Let me tell you something surprising about myself: when the horse dropped me on the floor and broke my arm, or rather, when I woke up from the narcotics, I said to myself that I was a man of letters. I am a man of letters, albeit in my slow and lonely way. The first half of the first part of *1805* [*War and Peace*] is about to be published.
>
> Yasnaya Polyana, Jan 23, 1865

He advises Fet to make literature his main source of income and to leave farming alone—but only because Fet had no success as farmer.

> What unkind fate. I always knew from our conversations that there was only one aspect to farming which you loved and which required everything from you, namely horse breeding—which now has suffered a disaster. You'll need to reharness your chariot,

to make farming your trace horse instead of your head horse: thought and art have done an immense lot of carrying for you. I've reharnessed mine and am now much calmer on my way.

Yasnaya Polyana, May 16, 1860

Before becoming a professional writer, you need to acquire different skills and knowledge, and then you need to succeed in bringing them into your literary work.

Pushkin was a more professional writer, he lived on his literary earnings; but he moved forward by departing from literature—toward history, for instance.

To dedicate oneself only and exclusively to literature is not even a three field system, it's simply the exhaustion of soil. A literary work doesn't descend directly from another literary work, it needs a Dad on the side. The pressure of time is a progressive fact; without it, no new artistic forms can be created.

Dickens' novel *The Pickwick Papers* was written to order for a newspaper, just like some funny captions for "Flops in Sports" pictures. The chapter lengths depended on the space in newspaper issues. Michelangelo similarly used the pressure of material restrictions: he liked using what were considered bad pieces of marble as these provided his sculptures with unexpected poses; this is how his David is made.

Theater technology puts pressure upon the playwright; you cannot understand Shakespeare's technique without knowing how the stage was constructed at his time. It might seem that you could film anything, but cinema, too, requires a tight squeeze in order to create works of art.

A writer needs a second profession not just to avoid starvation but also to be able to create literary texts. This second profession must never be forgotten, it must remain a real place of work: the writer must be a blacksmith, or a doctor, or an astronomer. When entering literature, you cannot leave your other profession in the hallway like a pair of galoshes.

I knew a blacksmith who brought me some poems; in these poems, he "splintered the *iron* of rails with his hammer." I told him the following: first, rails are not forged but welded; second, they are made not from iron but from steel; third, a hammer does not splinter metal; fourth, it was him who was the smith, certainly he must have known all this better than I did. To which he replied: "Well yeah—but this is poetry."

In order to become a poet you must drag your profession into your poetry because a work of art begins with a unique perspective.

When creating a work of art you must not try to avoid the pressure of your time but to use it the way a sailing boat uses the wind.

As long as contemporary writers try to join the literary milieu as soon as they can, as long as they seek to leave all other work behind them, we'll be engaging in astrakhan fur production: astrakhan furs are made by beating a pregnant sheep until she miscarries; then, the lamb is skinned.

It is only possible and indeed necessary to become a professional writer—to make literature your head horse, as Lev Tolstoy puts it—after several years of writing, when you've already learned to write. Dickens, for instance, had been a packer, a stenographer, and a journalist before he finally became a novelist. And even after having become an author, you must keep in mind that prose writers and poets alike sometimes remain silent for *years*. Alexander Blok, Fet, Gogol, Maxim Gorky—all of them had such dead periods in their work. You need to build your life in such a way that you can live without writing when you are unable to write.

A Writer's Reading

How should a writer read?

We read quickly, inattentively, almost as inattentively as we eat.

Eating quickly and inattentively is bad for you.

So is reading.

There are only very few good books, books that absolutely must be read; we read them much too quickly and are left with a false impression of familiarity. We spoil our reading. One must read slowly, calmly, making pauses, not leaving anything out.

If you want to become a writer you need to study a book as closely as a watchmaker studies a watch or a driver studies a car.

There are different ways to look at a car. The silliest people walk up to a car and press the claxon—this is the stage of utmost stupidity. Others, people who know a bit about cars but who overestimate their knowledge, walk up to a car and shift the speed-change lever. This is both silly and harmful: they are touching another person's thing, a machine for which another worker is responsible.

A person with understanding takes a calm look at a car and comprehends what's what, why the car has many cylinders and big wheels, how the transmission works, and why the car has a pointed back and an unpolished radiator.

This is how one should read.

To begin with, you must learn to take texts apart. First, you can simply separate nature descriptions from the characterization of characters; then a writer should study the way these characters talk—in monologues (i.e. one person speaking for a long time) or exchanging short phrases—and also the way they are characterized by their talk. You need to see how the plot is entangled, how the story begins, how its development drives the whole novel like a spring. How soon does the story get disentangled? Are any additional stories inserted? How is the denouement—the disentanglement—constructed? Studying other people's work is very important for writers who want to preserve their independence. Some young writers avoid reading others for fear of unwittingly imitating them; this, of course, is quite wrong, for you cannot write without any form.

Every way to begin a literary work results from the experience of a thousand people before us.

There is a legend about a king who wanted to learn what the most ancient language was. He took two babies and kept them apart from all people, except for a shepherd who brought them bread. When these children grew older, they greeted the shepherd with the shouts of "Begos, begos!" which meant "bread" in Phrygian. Thus it was decided that Phrygian was the most ancient language. However, if a shepherd was visiting these children, then goats might have been nearby, and perhaps the children were not really saying "begos" but merely imitating their bleating.[2]

A writer who wants to separate himself from other writers in order to write independently ends up imitating the bleating of goats; he does not avoid imitation, he merely imitates what's worst.

If you read the work of other writers without making sense of it, without taking it apart, you won't be able to avoid imitation; moreover, you won't even notice it. The manuscripts that the editor throws into the paper basket resemble other people's work more than the manuscripts that achieve publication.

Bicycles are produced in series, and each one is identical. Literary works are multiplied by printing, but each single one must be an invention—a new bicycle, a new type of bicycle. While inventing this bicycle, we must picture the reasons why it needs wheels and

---

[2] Shklovsky provides no source, but this version of the anecdote along with the explanation seems to be taken (perhaps indirectly) from Herodotus' *Histories*, which describe the Egyptian pharaoh Psamtik I conducting a language deprivation experiment.

handlebars. A clear idea of another writer's work allows you not to copy from him, which is called plagiarism and is prohibited in literature, but to use his methods to work on new material.

Young writers, including those who go on to become good writers, are strongly inclined to plagiarize, i.e. to borrow descriptive forms from others. The first childish attempts by Lermontov plagiarize Pushkin's long poem "Prisoner of the Caucasus." Young provincial writers keep submitting only slightly reworked versions of well-known works to publishers. They aren't being dishonest; rather, they experience a literary work as a whole, and, wishing to write something of their own, end up repeating it, changing only the names. To conclude: to preserve your writerly originality, you should read not less but more; however, you need to dissect and study what you read, trying to understand why every given line was written and how it's supposed to affect the reader.

On the Ability to Write Finding the Characteristic Traits of the Thing Described

The most important thing for a novice writer is to have a personal relation to things, to see things as if they hadn't been described before, to place them into a previously undescribed relation.

Literary works very often deal with a naïve man or foreigner who enters a town and understands nothing. A writer doesn't need to be this innocent but he does need to see thing afresh. What really happens is quite different: people are unable to see what's around them; our average contemporary novice writer is unable to compose a simple newspaper report. He writes as if his source of news was the newspaper itself rather than his own village: he reads the newspaper and uses it like a questionnaire to be filled with events from his own village; if the questionnaire doesn't feature certain kinds of events, these events remain unmentioned.

Often, reports from sawmills, clothes factories and the Donbass region look identical: "We must improve our standards; we need a ventilator, and the roof is leaking." Sometimes, though, the reporter gives away an interesting detail. Once, looking through newspaper correspondence, I read the following item from Ussuriland: "Tigers hinder the collection of labor union fees; once, the correspondent spent over twenty-four hours in a watch box until the tiger decided to call it a day and take his leave." I'm not saying that reports should be anecdotal, but reporters should not all be describing the same things, hinting at the real situation only in slips of the pen.

On Writers Learning How to Write from Newspaper Work

In today's America, they debate whether newspaper work is good for fiction writers. In our country, many authors started out at newspapers. Leonid Andreev, for instance, worked as a court reporter for many years. Chekhov, too, had been a court reporter, Gorky worked for a newspaper under the pseudonym Iegudiil Khalamida; Dickens had many years of newspaper work behind him. Many contemporary writers have worked for newspapers or small women's magazines, or as composers in print shops. Formerly, journalists began their work for magazines as critics, which was quite wrong: you cannot judge another's work if you cannot write yourself. Still, this is how people traditionally started out, and this is how I began my apprenticeship at *Letopis'*, the journal published by Gorky.[3] Only after having gained experience, after having learned to tell about things just as they happened—only then can one proceed, via short stories, to novels. This is, if

---

[3] *Letopis'* is where Shklovsky first encountered the excerpts from Tolstoy's diary that became crucial for his idea of *ostranenie*, as well as several short stories by Babel discussed in "Babel: a Critical Romance."

one is able to write a novel at all. Real literary schooling consists in learning to describe things, processes; for instance, it's very difficult to explain in words, using no pictures, how to tie a knot. One needs to describe things exactly, so that they can be imagined, imagined exactly the way they are described. You don't need to try and make your way into "great literature": great literature will turn up at the very place where we stand, quietly insisting that this is the most important place. Imagine what would happen if Budyonny had the goal of making a career in the tsarist army—he would have ended up a warrant officer. Instead, he participated in the revolution and changed combat tactics; he became Budyonny. It often happens that a writer working in what seem the lowest branches of literature doesn't know that he is creating something great. Boccaccio—the Italian Renaissance writer who wrote the *Decameron*, a collection of short stories—was ashamed of it and didn't even mention it to his friend Petrarch, so that *Decameron* was not included in the list of his works.

Boccaccio dedicated himself to Latin poems which no one remembers now.

Dostoyevsky didn't respect the novels he wrote, he wanted to write differently, it seemed to him that his novels were newspaper stuff; in letters, he said: "If I was paid as much as Turgenev, I'd write as well as him."

But he wasn't paid that much, and he wrote better.[4]

Great literature is not the kind of literature that gets published in thick journals;[5] it is the kind of literature that makes use of its time, that employs the material of its time.

---

[4]The passage on Dostoyevsky and Boccaccio appears particularly important to Shklovsky; he uses versions of it in several other essays.

[5]"Thick journals" is shorthand for high-brow, respectable publications.

The position of a contemporary writer is more difficult than that of a writer in former times because back then, writers learned from each other. Gorky learned from Korolenko, and he also very attentively studied Chekhov; Maupassant learned from Flaubert.

Learning to Write is Not About Learning Rules but About Learning to See Things Independently

Our contemporaries have no one to learn from; they've arrived in a factory with abandoned tools, they don't know which tool is used for shaving wood and which for drilling. This is why they often imitate rather than learn, wishing to write a text that has already been written, only about a topic of their own. This attitude is wrong: every work of art is only written once, and all great ones—such as *Dead Souls, War and Peace, The Brothers Karamazov*—are written "incorrectly," not the way people wrote before them, because their mission was different from the mission of previous writers. These missions have been completed, and the people whom they concerned are long dead, but the texts remain. What had been a complaint about contemporaries, an accusation, be it Dante's *Divine Comedy* or Dostoyevsky's *Demons*,[6] has become a literary work that can be read by people quite uninterested in the relations which had originally created it. We must remember that literary works are not created by budding, like the lower lifeforms—with one novel dividing into two novels—but by the interbreeding of different specimens, like the higher animals.[7] There are many writers who attempt to seize old texts, tossing out names and events in order to replace them with names and events of their own; in poetry, they use other people's

---

[6] Dostoyevsky's novel is also known as *The Possessed* and *The Devils*.

[7] In a 1920 article "On King Lear", included in *The Knight's Move*, Shklovsky writes: "Sometimes, books can be created by budding, like the lower lifeforms, without fertilization. Most scholarly work on Shakespeare belongs to this category."

phrase constructions, other people's rhyming patterns. Nothing ever comes of this; this is a dead end.

Thus, if you want to learn how to write, you must first of all be good at your own profession. You must also learn to look at another's profession with the eyes of a master, to realize how things are made.

Don't believe in the usual attitude to things, don't believe in the usual use of things, don't accept other people's inventories of the ocean. This comes first.

To Learn How to Write, You Must Learn How to Read

Second—you must learn to read, to read an author's works slowly and to realize what serves which function, how the phrases are connected and what the separate parts are for. Then, try and throw out a part of a page; Tolstoy, for instance, describes a scene between Princess Mary and her old father [in *War and Peace*]; during this scene, a wheel is creaking; try crossing out this wheel and see what happens. Think about what could replace this wheel: would the description of the landscape in the window make sense here, a description of rain, say, or maybe the mention of someone passing through the corridor?

Become a conscious reader.

Literature badly needs conscious readers.

In Pushkin's times, the nobility was mostly able to write poetry, i.e. almost every school friend of Pushkin wrote poems of his own, competing with him in albums. Back then, people could write poetry just as people today can read. But these were no professional poets. In this environment of people who understood the techniques of writing, Pushkin was created. Today, we need conscious readers, readers who can appraise a text and understand how it is made. There should be hundreds of thousands of such readers, and a group of hobby writers will crystallize from these hundreds of thousands, and from such a group of unprofessional writers, a single writer can arise—a writer of genius.

This is why learning to write too quickly is a great danger for contemporary writers; merely training oneself to write short stories and articles is bad training. You only need a couple of weeks to teach an intelligent person how to use ready-made templates. In one small editorial office, I taught the accountant to write articles because he needed some extra money, but, of course, he wrote badly, the way most newspaper journalists do nowadays.

A literary worker shouldn't avoid work in different professions, be it newspaper reporting or any trade at all; you must keep in mind that the production technique is always the same. You need to learn how to write reports, chronicles, then articles and feuilletons, short stories, theater critiques, sketches, and finally the kind of text that might replace the novel. You need to work for the future, for the form which you must create yourself. Simply teaching people how to use literary forms means teaching them how do sums rather than teaching them math—it means stealing from the future and creating vulgarians.

Newspaper Work

Show, Don't Name

One should try to write in such a way that the reader immediately remembers and understands even more than the narrator.

Let me give two examples: a book describes a soldier returning from the front and riding on the roof of a train; the soldier is so cold that he even wraps himself in a newspaper.

Gorky read through this passage and changed it as follows (it was first person narration, a man telling about himself): "I was very cold even though I had wrapped myself in newspapers."

The thing he creates here is this: a man wrapped in newspapers seems to consider himself lucky; it's only the reader who sees his grievous state.

You need to learn how to describe things as if you didn't know them: for instance, you can get used to walking along a street and stop noticing that it's dirty, or else that the tram is crowded, but you need to describe these very details which seem familiar to everyone, to describe them not directly but by showing things.

Let me give another example.

A literary workshop had among its participants a lady, who turned up there by chance, and a boy who worked in a factory. The lady wrote a short story in which she listed, at great length, all the things in a worker's room. She had entered that room for some sort of inspection. All the things were listed, and still she didn't manage to create an impression of a crowded space. The boy said: "It doesn't seem crowded." She turned to him and said quickly: "But can't you see—I couldn't even enter that room with my muff." "That's what you should write," said the boy.

Write for Newspapers; Don't Copy from Them

[...]

If you are describing a theater performance, don't begin by saying "I came in and sat down, and the curtains rose"; this is how a performance always begins for the spectator. If you had to sit on the floor, on the other hand, this is worth mentioning. If you are describing a village, don't begin by saying that it stretches away along a meandering path among golden fields: everyone knows this one. But if it doesn't "stretch away" but is very narrow, or else it hangs over a cliff, or there is no village but only single huts scattered far apart, and the windows of these huts are nailed shut because there is no glass, and the straw on the roofs is bound together with ropes also made from straw, so as not to fly away in a storm—this is worth describing. Such details, be they about good or bad things, are always worthwhile. Don't think that these are trifles: the small things often let you guess at the big ones.

Whether you want to praise or criticize, the most important thing is not to use general phrases. "Getting better," "getting on," "getting out of hand"—all these aren't getting anywhere. *Show* what is getting "better," "on" or "out of hand"; that will be the real thing. Don't try to prettify your article by mentioning that the rye is growing, or by describing the sky and informing the reader that it is blue, while the ground is black. Have a closer look: is the ground really black, or is it perhaps brown or gray; does the sky, in this particular case, have any relation to the ground? It might make sense, though, to mention that the water is murky if the river has shoals.

An ancient Russian pilgrim once described the holy land near Jerusalem as follows: "I came to the Navel of the World, and I saw the Navel of the World." Now, there is no such thing as a navel of the world, but he was a simple and religious man. He did not see a navel, but he described it anyway. This is the way newspapers often write.

You need to look at a thing as if you didn't know whether it was the navel of the world, or else a pit, or a hillock.

[...]

How to Begin Writing an Article

As a practical rule I can tell you a thing I often heard from experienced writers and journalists.

If you write, my readers, you probably know how difficult it is to begin.

You sit there, and it just won't work out, and all you want is to walk away, and you don't know how to start.

Here's some advice we, professional writers, often give each other: begin with the middle, with the part you're good at, where you know what to say.

Once you're done with the middle, you'll find the beginning and the end, or else the middle will turn out to be the beginning.

[...]

Narrative Prose

On the Absence of Clear Demarcations between "Fiction" and "Non-Fiction"

There are no clear demarcations between imaginative literature and what we call non-fiction. Many texts that we ascribe to so-called belles-lettres were originally written as articles. The well-known satirist Saltykov-Shchedrin, for instance, always considered his works as articles; he was surprised and argued when Nekrasov called them short stories. Lev Nikolayevich Tolstoy learned how to write from war reports, and war reports are what he apparently meant his "Sevastopol Sketches" to be.

[...]

The Purpose of the Plot

Let's take a description of the crime committed in Chubarov Lane. In itself, the description of this terrible event [a gang rape] will have the character of an indictment. But if, for instance, one of the rapists suddenly recognized the victim as a woman he had once loved, or else as a relative, the insertion of this motif into the text would have provided it with a plot, a narrative—albeit a banal one. This device is very wide-spread: there are hundreds of folk songs about fathers killing their sons by accident and then recognizing them; there are dozens of stories about men possessing women who turn out to be their daughters or sisters. This is not a suggestion to use this particular motivation to create a narrative; rather, the matter lies in understanding the essence of the device: thanks to the changed situation, the attitude toward things changes in the midst of the story, and the whole text is suddenly interpreted in an entirely different way.

[...]

Sometimes, the meaning of a phenomenon remains unchanged throughout a fragment of prose and then is compared to some other phenomenon; in this case, the plot emerges not in the fragment itself but between two fragments with which we work. This is called a parallelism. This is, for instance, how Lev Tolstoy's story "Two Hussars" is built.

It describes two hussars. They do more or less the same in different epochs, but they do it differently. The writer compares them, and this comparison constitutes the irony of the text. Another story by Tolstoy, "Three Deaths," describes the death of a gentlewoman, the death of a coachman, and the death of a tree. The connection is motivated—the three descriptions are justified in appearing together—by the fact that the coachman had driven the gentlewoman, and the tree was felled for the coachman's cross.

The author's artistic intention consists in showing these three deaths in their dissimilarity.

[...]

The Novella and the Mystery Novel

There are two ways to tell a story: either we can tell everything in succession, with each new point explained by the preceding one, or else we can make temporal transpositions, i.e. describe the consequence before describing the cause. For instance, we can show vehement enmity between people and only tell about its reasons at the end. This is how Pushkin's "The Shot" is made.

The novella and the mystery novel are based on a riddle that is only resolved at the end of the text. This device is most often used and easiest to trace in detective stories: they usually begin with a crime, proceed with a false solution, and then accumulate facts and evidence until someone finally finds the real answer.

Contemporary Russian literature rarely uses the mystery device, but in Western European literature it forms the basis of whole series of novels. Many of these are so-called classic works. Dickens, a well-known English writer, uses the technique of the mystery novel extensively. In the mystery novel, the solution is usually only revealed at the very end. Some characteristics of the mystery novel have made their way into classic Russian literature. In Gogol's *Dead Souls*, for instance, we first see the protagonist buying "dead souls," i.e. doing something entirely mysterious, and only later learn where he comes from and how he had conceived this plan. It was the Western European mystery novel which inspired Gogol to this. We see that the effect of mysteriousness can be achieved by introducing a real mystery (we don't know who has murdered the victim, or who has stolen the documents), but also by transposing parts of the novel.

What do we achieve in using the device of mystery?

The reader is waiting for the denouement, and we delay it.

[...]

Unfolding a Text

Creating Characters

During its development, a text can assume an altogether new form. The characters do not merely act out a plot, but change it. Whatever plot scheme we consider, the text will change depending on which characters "perform" it. Very often, during the process of writing, characters turn out to be quite different from the original plan. Dostoyevsky's letters, for instance, express his amazement at the fact that Verkhovensky became a semi-comical figure in *Demons*. In Turgenev's *Fathers and Sons*, Bazarov was intended as a negative character but implemented as a positive one.

Thus we see that the material used to develop the plot does not simply help it unfold but also enters a certain relationship with it, and sometimes fights against it.

The analysis of writers' notebooks shows how initial plot ideas, enriched by descriptions, give rise to stories, how living characters are created. Discussing any artistic work, one must keep in mind that people sought to achieve different goals in different kinds of literature and at different times; they concentrated on different techniques and aspects of the text.

There had been a time when people weren't interested in the protagonists of literary texts. A character was like a chip of wood on the wave, a chip of wood thrown into the water in order to see how the water moves.

In *One Thousand and One Nights* and in the novellas of the *Decameron*, the princes, merchants, and knights have no faces of their own. Then, the time came, and, for complex historical reasons, literature began developing types, trying to depict human personalities.

Not only the action, but also the actor now became a point of interest.

Later still, there emerged the psychological novel with its detailed development of the characters' psychologies. Today, these genres coexist, though they are not all equally vital. What you must learn is not how to follow any of these genres but simply how to write and finally how to create what might be called a genre of your own.

[...]

When describing a character, you should not only provide the traits immediately needed in your particular text but also add something unnecessary, something characterizing him in a seemingly irrelevant way. Then, the reader will stand a better chance of believing into the character's authenticity; the reader doesn't like to be kept on a short leash. Try not to explain your character to your readers but to make the readers understand him on their own. Lev Tolstoy provided a great account of how sometimes, when he was describing a villain or a dislikeable character, he took pity on him and gave him some nice little trait. This is not human pity speaking but the craft of an artist.

[...]

Working Out Details

Every literary text constitutes a closed unit built according to its own laws.

Consider this example: in most writers' work, we can find descriptions of nature, of the setting in which people live—but Dostoyevsky hardly ever describes landscapes. He is rarely interested in the setting. What he cares for are people, their actions, thoughts, and conversations. Tolstoy seems to have more interest for settings than Dostoyevsky but he, too, mainly focuses on the human as such. While Turgenev describes settings in detail, in *War and Peace* we find no descriptions of the chairs on which the characters sit or the rooms in which they live—and we don't notice this omission.[8]

The thing is not to describe everything but to describe only what works in this particular text. When you write, don't try to remember the rules, thinking that, say, other writers usually mention the skies at

---

[8] In *War and Peace*, chairs are described only half a dozen of times.

this point, and so you should. You should proceed from your text, from your own task, and then you'll know if you're going to need the skies.

There is a whole series of beginnings which authors are used to, particularly authors who land in the waste paper baskets of editorial offices. For instance, village stories usually begin with a village "stretching away freely on both sides of the road," or else with the weather, with a description of rain.

All these texts are copied from each other, and their rainy villages stretch away to no avail.

If you do use a detail, you must think it out fully.

Here is a conversation that took place between Lev Nikolayevich Tolstoy and Alexey Maximovich Peshkov (Gorky), when Gorky first visited Tolstoy. The first thing Tolstoy asked was: "In your short story 'Twenty-six and one,' how many steps away is the table from the stove?"

Gorky gave an answer. "And what about the opening of the stove, how wide is it?" Gorky showed the width with his hands; then Tolstoy grew angry. "Well then, what business do you have saying that the people are illuminated by the fire in the stove? It's not wide enough!"

[…]

Selecting a characteristic detail, looking for a precise feature, for a good comparison, it's best to connect this detail to the overall theme of the text. Let us look at a detail used by Chekhov. In his notebook, he describes a bedroom: "The moon shines into the windows so strongly that you can see every button on the nightshirt."

Why is this description good?

Because the brightness of the light is shown by a detail typical of a bedroom.

On Literary Language

Every kind of production needs technical language. It's almost impossible to present a textbook in mechanics or physics without specialized terminology; to study these subjects, you need to become familiar with it.

Literary language is a cultural achievement; first and foremost, it is a language shared by different provinces and towns.

Moreover, it is a language whose concepts are relatively exact.

Technically, it is better developed than the individual language of a single person or village. It has been better cultivated and worked out. Of course, you cannot use literary language entirely on its own; it's constantly renewed by local languages, languages from other areas, slang, foreign expressions etc. Still, literary language needs to be cared for; it can be good to break its rules, but its basis should remain unbroken as the very beauty of non-standard expressions and local color can only emerge against the background of literary language.

On *Skaz* and its Meaning for the Plot

[...]

A good text containing *skaz* contains a plot device which motivates its use.[9]

Let's take a tale about a flea [Leskov's "The Tale of Cross-eyed Lefty from Tula and the Steel Flea"]. Its content is this: the English gave Alexander I a wind-up flea made of steel. This flea could dance. [His successor] Nikolas I decided to outdo the English and gave the flea to Lefty, a master from Tula. He managed to shoe it. This was a feat but simultaneously an act of technical nonsense: the flea couldn't dance anymore. This is the main plot of the story. The whole text is written

---

[9]The term *skaz* was coined by Boris Eikhenbaum who used it to describe unmediated, folk-like speech. The word *skaz* also means "tale"; it appears in this meaning in the title of Leskov's short story discussed here. "Proleterian writers" tended to overuse *skaz*. Indeed, sometimes, the only language they could use had the unintended effect of *skaz*.

in a boastful style: the Russians boast of their inventiveness and rail against the English any old way.

The technical nonsensicality is presented as secondary, masked by the boastful tone.

The narrator doesn't seem to understand the meaning of what he is telling; the reader guesses it on his own. Thus, a good text contains *skaz*, this special coloring of speech, not only in order to ornament the verbal material but as a plot device that changes the meaning of the whole.

A Few Words on Poetry

On Poetry, and Why Not to Write Any

A great many people write poems. Hardly any literate person can avoid this servitude; almost everyone has written a couple of lines.

All editorial offices are snowed under with poems. Hundreds of them are technically sound, well-made.

There are thousands of poets who can write and could be published; but there are very few or hardly any consumers of the ware thus produced.

I've warned against prematurely making writing your profession; poets need to be warned with particular severity.

Nobody can or should live on poetry in our country today because no poet can guarantee to publish poems every month.

Pushkin and Blok experienced years of silence; had they lived on poetry alone, they would have been forced either to write badly or to starve.

The novice writer needs to be warned against yet another danger.

The first book is comparatively easy to write.

The first book can be created not by skill but by one's stock of knowledge and experience—particularly if one has lived through a revolution.

This is like a river breaking the ice, carrying away stacks of hay, destroying bridges—but then, the writer must go on flowing for years, and the second, the third book turn out to be much harder to write, all the more so because we tend to be wasteful in the first one.

We spend our material, shove it everywhere, not sparing ourselves; there is less simple biographical material for the second book, and still not enough literary experience, technique, and skill for doing new things.

A young writer's second or third book usually disappoints.

Because of many cultural conditions, our country is not very attentive toward young writers. First, young writers are lauded too highly, praised to high heaven, expected to be the next Tolstoy tomorrow; the second book is then criticized as bitterly as if by publishing the first one the author had borrowed money and now fails to return it.

This cessation of compliments needs to be endured.

One must be able to go on working after the first success passes, one must know that not the first or second book is decisive for a writer, but perhaps the third one.

Conclusion

Final Advice

Reread what you write as often as you can.

When you add a new detail or technical particularity, when you enrich the language or expand a description, reread the whole text from start to finish and look: is there perhaps a discrepancy between the old material and the new part? If there is none, ask yourself if the new material enriches the text; does it perhaps give you a chance to reinterpret the whole? Working helps you think: when you place different materials side by side, new thoughts and new opportunities arise, ideas that couldn't be foreseen in the initial plan.

Don't consider different parts of your text in isolation; in every single moment, you are working on the whole.

But this isn't simply a matter of adjusting and compressing the material so that everything fits together, so that no detail contradicts the character of the whole.

Take a closer look at the contradictions: perhaps the text is wiser than you are.

This doesn't mean leaving the work to chance, it means leaving it to the material: a writer can never consider all the possibilities when beginning a text.

Very often, and at the hands of the greatest writers, texts develop into something much more complex, more necessary and richer in meaning than originally intended.

This is why we are able to read texts from preceding epochs: their authors wrote not only what they wanted to write but also what the material made them write.

Hamburg Score (1928)[1]

Babel: A Critical Romance (1924)

[...]

Babel wrote little, but persistently. He kept writing one and the same tale about two Chinese in a brothel.

He loved this story as much as he loved Storitsyn.[2] The Chinese and the woman changed. They grew younger and older, broke windows and bones, did this and that.

What he ended up with were many stories, not one. One sunny autumn day, with the Chinese still unsettled, Babel left, leaving me his gray sweater and a leather travelling bag. The bag was later borrowed for life by Yuri Annenkov. From Babel, there was not a whisper, as if he had left for Kamchatka, to chat about the prosecutor's daughters with their father.[3]

Once, a visitor from Odessa, having played cards all night with our shared acquaintances, told me—out of gratitude, while borrowing his

---

[1] Source: *Gamburgskiy schet.* Leningrad: Izdatel'stvo pisateley, 1928.

[2] Petr Storitsyn, a close friend of Babel's, was a chemist turned poet and critic; Shklovsky might be playing with the "story" (*istoriya* in Russian) in his name.

[3] Earlier in the essay, Shklovsky mentions a short story by Babel "about two girls who did not know how to have an abortion. Their father was a prosecutor on Kamchatka." The text in question is "*Mama, Rimma i Alla,*" the story to make the twenty-two-year-old Babel famous in St. Petersburg when it was published in 1916. An English translation of the story is included in *Isaac Babel's Selected Writings* (2009) but not *in The Collected Stories of Isaac Babel* (2002).

loss in the morning—that Babel was either translating from French or making a book of short stories from a book of jokes.

Then, when I was passing through Kharkov, injured, I heard that Babel had been killed in the Cavalry.

Fate, slowly, made a hundred permutations with all of us.

In 1924, I met Babel again. From him I learned that he had not been killed, though he had been beaten within an inch of his life.

He remained the same. The stories he told became even more interesting.

He brought two books from Odessa and from the front. The Chinese had been forgotten and settled in some story all by themselves.[4]

The new things are written masterfully. It's unlikely that we have anyone writing better now.

Babel is often compared to Maupassant, because the French influence is tangible, and critics are in a hurry to name a commendable enough parallel.

I propose a different name—Flaubert. To be precise, Flaubert in "Salammbô."

In that wonderful opera libretto.

Boots polished so brilliantly that they resemble girls, the brightest breeches, bright as a banner in the sky, even a fire blazing like a Sunday—all these can't compete with Babel's style.

A foreigner from Paris—Paris only, not London—Babel saw Russia as it might have been seen by a French writer assigned to Napoleon's army.

He didn't need the Chinese anymore; they were replaced by Cossacks drawn from French illustrations.

Connoisseurs of endearments say that swear words can be used to caress.

---

[4] Perhaps in "*Ty promorgal, kapitan!*" ("You've missed it, captain!") in *Odessa Tales*.

"The effect and force of using words whose lexical meaning opposes their intonation coloring lies precisely in this sense of a mismatch" (Tynyanov, *Problema stikhotvornogo yazyka*).

The essence of Babel's device is that he speaks in the same voice about the stars and the clap.

[…]

Babel uses two contradictions to replace the plot: 1) the style and the everyday, 2) the everyday and the author.

He is a stranger in the army; he's a foreigner with the right to wonder. When describing everyday life in the military, he stresses the viewer's "weakness and despair."

[…]

Babel pretends to be a foreigner because this device—just like irony—makes writing easier. Not even Babel dares to present pathos without irony.

Babel's writing conceals the music in the description of a dance while presenting the text in a high register. His device of responses that repeat questions is probably borrowed from epics.[5]

He uses this device again and again.

Benya Krik in "Odessa Tales" speaks this way:

Grach asked him:

—Who are you, where are you coming from, and what are you breathing?

---

[5]While epics might play a role, Shklovsky, whose father was Jewish, could have hardly been unfamiliar with the old joke (making the rounds in early twentieth-century Russia, as it still is) that a Jew answers a question with a question. The device used by Babel is not identical but related. When Babel goes on to use this device with non-Jewish protagonists, it is arguably "liberated from its initial motivation," as Shklovsky puts it elsewhere.

—Try me, Froim,—said Benya,—let us not smear the white gruel all over the clean table.

—Let us not smear the gruel,—Grach replied,—I will try you.

The Cossacks in "The Letter" speak this way, too.

And Senka asked Timofey Rodionych:

—Are you happy in my hands, grandpa?

—No,—said grandpa,—I'm in pain.

Then Senka asked:

—And Fedya, was he happy in your hands when you were putting a knife in him?

—No,—said grandpa,—Fedya was in pain.

Then Senka asked:

—Well then, grandpa, have you thought that you, too, might find yourself in pain?

—No,—said grandpa,—I didn't think that I'd find myself in pain.

Babel's books are good books.

Russian literature is gray as a siskin, it needs crimson breeches and leather boots the color of an azure sky.

It also needs what Babel had realized when he left his Chinese to their own devices and joined the Red Cavalry.

Fictional characters—girls, old people, young men—and all their situations are worn out. Literature need concreteness, it needs hybridization with the new everyday life to create new form.

In Defense of the Sociological Method (1927)

A writer uses the contradictory planes of his work but he doesn't always create them. More often, the different planes and their conflicts are created by the unequal genetics of the work's formal aspects. The writer uses devices whose genesis varies. He sees their collision. He modifies the functions of devices. He realizes a device in a different kind of material. This is how Derzhavin presented the ode in a low style. And Gogol used devices of [Ukrainian] songs first with themes connected to the Ukraine but qualitatively different, and then with non-Ukrainian themes.

This is where one of Gogol's humorous devices comes from.

[...]

The Crusaders

During the first crusade, they mistook every city for Jerusalem. On closer inspection, every city turned out to not to be Jerusalem.

Then, every time, the crusaders would start a pogrom.

Out of resentment.

However, Jerusalem does exist.

However, facts do exist.

The formalists (OPOYAZ) don't want to fight scientific facts.

If facts destroy the theory, all the better for the theory.

It was created by us, not given to us for safekeeping.

The change of aesthetic material is a social fact—observable, for instance, in *The Captain's Daughter*.

Ten Years (1927)

[...]

If you ask villagers about the name of the neighboring village, particularly if you ask women, they often won't know.

Their fate had bound them to their hut by the cow's mooing.

Before the revolution, we were bound to our fate the way sad sponges are bound to the bottom of the sea.

You get born; you get attached. You enter a profession by chance, and you live it. Great poets lived as synod officials and insurance agents.

In capitalist society, this fascinating thing which is human fate was terribly misorganized.

And then, during the revolution, there was no fate.

If you don't bother about mittens and such, you get a lot of time to anticipate the realm of freedom—weightless, but already three-dimensional.

Go whenever you want to, open a school of theater prompters for the Red Fleet, lecture on the theory of rhythm in a hospital—you'll find an audience. People had attention then.

The world set sail, unmoored.

I'm thirty-four years old, and many of these years I remember.

And I'd like to rearrange the memory of two or three years of my life and to relive the times we call military communism.

Even with the night passes and patrols on the streets, the city was hungry but free.

We owe our inventions to that time; that wind was enough for all the sails.

Dostoyevsky, Jerome K. Jerome, who rests in peace, and Merezhkovsky, still restless, all said that socialism was boredom.

As an eyewitness, I'll refute this.

We had abandoned the bitterness of setting up a life and fixing it; we were happy, it seems.

Carbohydrates and proteins were the only things missing to secure this realm of intellectual freedom under the guns of the *Aurora*.[6]

Hamburg Score (1928)

The Hamburg score is a very important concept.

All wrestlers cheat when they wrestle, they allow themselves to be pinned to the ground when the matchmaker says so.

Once a year, wrestlers gather in a public house in Hamburg.

They fight with the doors closed and the windows veiled.

Their fight is long, hard, ugly.

This is where the wrestlers establish their real rank—so as not to succumb to shoddiness.

Literature needs a Hamburg score.

Reckoned this way, Serafimovich and Veresayev don't exist.

They don't even arrive in town.

In Hamburg, Bulgakov is at the edge of the mat.

Babel is a lightweight.

Gorky is dubious (often in bad form).

Khlebnikov was the champion.

---

[6] A blank shot from the cruiser *Aurora* signaled the start of the assault on the Winter Palace, which began the October Revolution. In 1917—ten years before this article was first published.

The Way I Write (1930/1990)[1]

I've been writing for fifteen years, and, of course, in this time my style and manner of writing changed a lot.

Fifteen years ago, I found writing very hard; I didn't know where to begin. When I wrote, it seemed to me that everything had already been said. Separate parts didn't merge. Examples had a will of their own. Actually, this hasn't changed. It's still hard to write, though in a different way now. Single parts unfold into independent works, and the main thing, just as in cinema, is between the parts.

Inventions in general, and the invention of a literary style in particular, are often born from a chance mutation, a chance alteration becoming fixed. This works more or less like breeding a new sort of cattle.

General literary style, which was itself created on the basis of individual style, cannot be used for writing; it is unable to move things; it does not exist, it isn't experienced.

Mayakovsky consolidated errors against syllabo-tonic poetry.

Gogol consolidated dialect, half-language. He probably wrote in one language and thought in another, and the Ukrainian element whirled up his style. This is how distant stars perturb the ellipses of planets.

---

[1] Source: "Kak ya pishu" in *Gamburgskiy schet.* Moscow: Sovetskiy Pisatel', 1990.

When I write, I proceed from facts. I try not to change facts. I try to connect facts that stand far apart. This might be coming from Lomonosov's idea of bringing together "rather-far-removed ideas" or else from Anatole France who mentioned butting epithets against each other.[2]

As for me, I try to butt not epithets but things, facts.

I begin to write differently now, particularly when I work on a scholarly book. But even so, I begin with the material. Before the "what" and the "how" are solved, I'm not interested in the question "why." I don't look for the reasons of things unknown.

I begin work with reading. I read, trying to avoid tension. Or rather, not trying to remember. Tension, suspiciousness—they do no good. One must read calmly, looking the book in the eye.

I read a lot. As you can see, this turns out to be an article not on how I write but on how I work.

I proceed.

I read, relaxed. I use colored bookmarks, or bookmarks of different widths. It would be sensible to note the page numbers on the bookmarks in case they fall out, which I fail to do. Then, I look through the bookmarks. I make notes. The typist—the one that is typing this article right now—types up excerpts with their page numbers. These excerpts, and there are usually lots and lots of them, I hang on the walls of the room. Unfortunately, my room is small, and there isn't enough space.

It is crucial to understand the quotation, to turn it this way and that, to connect it to others.

---

[2] What Lomonosov actually says is: "one should not always discard ideas which seem rather far removed from the theme, for sometimes [...] they can produce considerable and appropriate ideas" (Lomonosov § 27). This is yet another case of Shklovsky referring to an intermediate rather than a direct source: the unidiomatic adjectivized form he uses comes from an article published two years previously by a friend (Tynyanov, *Poetika* 236).

The excerpts hang on the wall for a long time. I group them together, hang them side by side; by and by, very short connecting passages arise. Then I write down relatively detailed sketches of single chapters and put the connected excerpts into different folders.

Then I begin to dictate the text, referring to insertions by number.

This technique accelerates work speed considerably and simplifies matters. It's like using a typewriter with visible print.[3]

Almost always, the plan changes in the work process, and often even the very theme does. Your work turns out to be meaningless, and then, on the ruins of your future text, you experience that possibility of new composition, that unification and unconscious algebraic tightening of the material that is called inspiration.

The work grows and changes. I think that I don't really finish my books, that I break off too early, that, rewritten two or three times more, they would have become better, clearer, that readers—and not only friends—would begin to understand me, that I would have freed it of wittiness.

This wittiness of mine, for which I'm often reproached, is the trace of the instrument, a certain crudeness.

I don't proof-read corrections because I can't read my own texts. Other thoughts come to mind, and I become distracted.

Listening to myself would have been torture for me.

The manner of my work and its crudeness are not a mistake. When I master the technique fully, I won't make any mistakes even when working very fast, the way a glassblower works. I won't end up producing more end results than others, though, for this pace of work is tiring.

---

[3] In early typewriters, the typist could not see the text as it was typed; it only scrolled into view later. First open-print models were introduced in the late nineteenth century, but the closed type continued to be used for many decades.

I need to rest.

I tell a lot to others, I don't think that people should write everything down by themselves. I'm convinced that you need to write in groups, that friends should live in the same city and meet, that work is only possible in a team.

The best year of my life was the one when I spent an hour, two hours every day talking to Lev Yakubinsky on the phone. We set up little tables by the phones.

I am convinced, Lev Petrovich, that you were wrong to leave that phone and to dedicate yourself to organizing.

I am convinced that I'm wrong not to live in Leningrad.

I am convinced that Roman Jakobson's departure to Prague is a great loss for his work and mine.

I am convinced that people from one literary group should consider each other in their work, that they must change their personal fate for each other's sake.

What confuses me is that I'm not only a scholar but also a journalist and even a fiction writer. Facts are different there, the relation to the object is different, the work is device-oriented. This hinders me from smoothing out the instrument's traces in my scholarly work, from writing books that would be understandable to other people's followers, books that would be unconditional, that would not require a reconstruction of your head.

[…]

The OPOYAZ has a hymn. It's long, for we are rather well-spoken and not very young. It features the following lines:

> And passion, from a formal viewpoint,
> is the convergence of devices.

This might well be true.

Passion is drawn in by the inertia of skills and habits, in particular by the literary inertia of passion.

The way this happens in books is this.

I needed to write a book about people, something along the lines of *One Hundred Portraits of Russian Writers*. But I was in love, or else in some sort of convergence, or perhaps I chose love the way a weakened organism chooses diseases.

What I ended up with was a wrongly written book.

I have a strong urge to write fiction. I'm waiting. Waiting for convergence. Waiting for invention. Waiting for material and inspiration.

[…]

Part Four

After the Freeze

Part Four: Introduction

There is a gap in the present collection. Following texts from the late 1920s, this chapter begins with the 1960s. Its working title was "After a Long Silence," but it would have been wrong. In 1930, when Stalin's power became absolute, Shklovsky published "A Monument to a Scholarly Mistake," a self-accusatory antiformalist article—but it was not followed by silence. In 1931, Shklovsky wrote *Poiski optimizma* (in Shushan Avagyan's translation, *A Hunt for Optimism*), a hybrid text with a considerable proportion of fiction. Between 1930 and 1960, he did not only work as a screen writer and film editor, but also published a dozen books, mostly historical fiction and studies of Russian writers—Pushkin, Dostoyevsky, Mayakovsky. This last one is a palpably personal work, though subject to censorship. The rest is, to put it bluntly, tame, with rare glimpses of recognizably Shklovskyan writing. Even scholars specializing in Pushkin and Dostoyevsky hardly use it now.

There were only a couple of years in which Shklovsky's work was not published at all, namely in the aftermath of a 1949 article penned by the writer Konstantin Simonov that denounced "antipatriotic," "anti-Soviet" critics—headed, he asserted, by Shklovsky. According to Shklovsky's grandson Nikita, his grandfather never wrote "for the drawer," as so many others did; it wasn't in his nature to work without hope for publication. (Instead, he slept: luckily for Shklovsky, he reacted to stress by sleeping for inordinate amounts of time.) Still, apart from the period from 1949 to the early 1950s, Shklovsky was never quite silenced; rather, as Nina Berberova (230) puts it, "the Soviet Union froze him for thirty years (to be unfrozen in the late fifties)." The verb she uses, *zamorozit'*, literally means "to freeze" and can be used in the sense of "to put on ice," "to tie up," "to block"; it is particularly appropriate considering that de-stalinization is also known as Khrushchev's Thaw. One of the first books Shklovsky wrote when "unfrozen" was the autobiographical *Zhili-byli*. Its title, which literally translates as "they were and lived," is a fairy-tale formula, hence *Once Upon a Time*.

Like Shklovsky's early books, this one has several metaphorical leitmotifs. One of them is the Russian fairy tale "The Swan-Geese." To Shklovsky, the magic birds signify the victory of freedom and imagination, like Gogol's "horses rising into the air and flying over the world," an image he grew to love as an older boy. This boy "is not offered up for reform: he is almost seventy" and "unreformable." Shklovsky describes his childhood and youth not at all pastorally but still with a touch of lyricism, telling about his dreams of becoming a wrestler (hence, perhaps, "Hamburg Score") or a sculptor.

Then, he returns to the themes of *The Third Factory*: the wars and the OPOYAZ, "a research institute without financing, without personnel, without assistance." Shklovsky still feels the need to recant "formalist fallacies," but at the same time, he lauds his OPOYAZ friends, addressing Eikhenbaum: "I am talking to you as if you were alive. Our forty-five-year-old friendship is not dead." *Once Upon a Time* makes it very clear that Shklovsky's early books "weren't written with the quiet consistency of academic works." Instead, they were part of a passionate discussion among friends, and simultaneously a way to stay human in inhuman times.

Once Upon a Time touches upon some intriguing questions of art, for instance, “why the fifty-year-old invention of Russian leftist artists became almost official art in today’s United States.” Shklovsky’s conclusions in this regard are reminiscent of Borges’ “Pierre Menard, Author of the Quixote”: “the thing being canonized in the United States is not the same as the one created fifty years ago,” even if it looks the same. First and foremost, though, *Once Upon a Time* is a fascinating memoir. Here are some quotations which didn’t make it into the translation:

> “I’m writing this knowing what happens next; instead, I’d like to remember the way a fat boy saw life, looking at it sullenly, scowling.”
>
> “All I had instead of a sculptor’s talent was quiet rage and three minutes of inspiration.”
>
> “We grew up in Petersburg. Petersburg was full of water, mist, palaces, factories, and glory.”
>
> “Petersburg is the city of poets, and it is built like a poem.
>
> Petersburg has been designed; it is superior to the flower of an old city, for even a nail is superior to a flower: a nail is created consciously. This is what Belinsky said.”
>
> “It’s difficult to take leave of your own childhood.
>
> You feel as if you had entered your old apartment: you see the familiar sun-bleached wallpaper, the familiar round stove in the corner, its door unpainted, and the stucco with holes poked in it, all the way to the wooden planks. There is no furniture, and you’d rather not sit on the windowsill, but you linger. You cannot live here, but how can you leave your past, on what kind of transport?”

Shklovsky returns to Belinsky’s statement in his *Tales about Prose* (*Povesti o proze*), for instance, when discussing the stream of consciousness technique. In general, a harsh critic might call Shklovsky's later work repetitive and even suspect the repetitions to be a matter of age (by 1966, when *Tales about Prose* was published, Shklovsky was seventy-three; he went on writing until his death in 1984). However, most people who knew him as an old man stress how young his mind stayed. According to Shklovsky himself, his work benefits rather than suffers from repetition: his work tends to circle certain motifs, quotations, texts, and ideas, contemplating them again and again from different angles.

Tales about Prose partly consists of revised versions of two books, the 1961 *Literary Prose. Reflections and Readings* (which became part I, "On Western Prose") and the 1953 *Notes on the Prose of Russian Classics* (Part Two, "On Russian Prose"). In the present selection, everything but "Concept Renewal" is taken from part I. "Concept Renewal," as well as "On the Sense of Wonder," returns to the question of *ostranenie*, the former drawing connections to Brecht's *Verfremdung*. At the time of writing, Brecht was *the* Western communist playwright; still, Shklovsky dares to argue that epic theater sometimes "actually prevents the spectator from seeing the new in the usual." As it happens, Shklovsky had criticized that kind of theater long before Brecht gave it a name. In 1920, in the essay "On the Psychological Ramp," he argued that the illusion of reality is necessary, if only to be broken (*Khod konya* 76–9).

"A Note From the Author" is a later addition to a 1983 reissue (*Izbrannoe v dvuhk tomakh*). When, in this note, Shklovsky says that "Viktor Shklovsky made a mistake," the third person singular is more than a mannerism. An eighty-eight-year-old man is writing about a twenty-year-old: it might well be truer to self-perception to say "he" rather than "I." (Christopher Isherwood used the same device when writing about his younger self in *Christopher and His Kind*.)

The mistake Shklovsky claims to regret is his alleged earlier belief in the "immobility" of art, in its independence from the material and historic circumstance. He seems to be talking to the censors here, rather than misremembering his own writings. Some of his beliefs did change; as a very young man, he had hoped for literary scholarship to become a hard science, but went on to realize that "literary terms will never be as exact as mathematical definitions." However, many of his retractions are to be taken with a large pinch of salt. Phrases such as the following, be they playfully ironic or bitterly sarcastic, are typical of the late Shklovsky: "I must apologize to the professors of many Western universities for suggesting to them a wrong interpretation, and also to thank them for the fact that they do not mention my name when repeating my idea thirty-five years later."

By quoting Marx and Lenin, too, Shklovsky seems to be merely making the obligatory nod to Soviet mores. On the other hand, during the same period Shklovsky wrote to his grandson Nikita, "I think it a great pity that I failed to read Hegel and Marx when I was young, that I only read Lenin 20 years ago." These letters were not intended for publication; the regret appears to be honest. However, Nikita himself comments: "I'll always remember how he, very tired and in a bad mood, asked me to get him a volume of the Brockhaus encyclopedia, any one, and, opening it at random with a loud sigh of contentment, began to read an article on pigs, immersed into the text, free from everything. Now, Lenin and Marx can serve just as well as pigs, right?" (personal communication).

A selection of *Shklovsky's letters to his grandson*, private letters addressed to a teenage boy, was published in a magazine in 2002 ("Pis'ma vnuku"). The letter from July 20, 1969 is arguably Shklovsky's shortest and sincerest autobiography. Neither *Once Upon a Time* nor *Tales about Prose* (not to speak of the letters) have ever been translated into English. *Bowstring* (*Tetiva)* and *Energy of Delusion* (*Energiya *zabluzhdeniya*), on the other hand, have been recently published, with prefaces and translators' notes providing a background.[1] Here, only a few short excerpts are provided to give a taste of the books. One observation on *Energy of Delusion* seems worth making: it happened to be published in the same year in which it was suggested by clinical psychologists that a heightened mood creates an illusion of control and opportunity (Alloy), an observation that soon developed into the hypothesis of depressive realism (Alloy and Abramson). According to this idea, which is supported by a number of empirical studies, people suffering from depression have a more accurate and realistic perception of reality. It is the energy of delusion which allows us to be happy and to create.

[1] The books were published in Shushan Avagyan's translation by the Dalkey Archive Press in 2007 and 2011 respectively (*Energy of Delusion*; *Bowstring*).

Once Upon A Time (1964)[1]

Childhood

Why Begin with Childhood?

[…]

Don't be surprised: you will now be reading about a small boy, about grown-ups who aren't famous, and about simple events.

To see the flow of a river, you throw a bundle of grass on the water and try to guess at the stream by the blades of grass which swim away, sometimes slowly and sometimes quickly, straightforwardly or aslant.

I want to show you the movement of time. The people about whom I will tell you in this first part are simple people from the old times, and the boy whom I describe is not offered up for reform: he is almost seventy. He is unreformable.

The willful biblical god created the world in his own image, they say, but even this is only said of Adam.

There are also ants, elephants, giraffes in the world: they do not resemble each other. They are not to be edited—they are simply different kinds of animals. No reason to be annoyed about this.

People, too, are different.

---

[1] Source: *Zhili-byli*. Moscow: Sovetskiy Pisatel', 1966.

There are many memoirs out there, but the past in them is too pretty. My past isn't pretty.

Pomyalovsky, a good writer, has a character asking himself: "Where are the linden trees under which I grew up?" And he replies to his own question: "There are no such trees, nor have there ever been."

There are many memoirs out there now, but people like their own past and decorate it with flowers and traditional linden trees.

My writing will be linden-free.[2]

The Very Beginning

[...]

On the Nevsky Prospect, on high poles, electricity buzzes and trembles with a violet glow.

Electricity is still young and walking on all fours.

The city is quiet. In winter, the city is white-haired with snow. There are no automobiles in the city, and it seems there will never be any.

In summer, the city becomes grey with dust and noisy with the wheels of heavy carts.

All this happened on the other side of a mountain of time, with another climate and other solutions for everything.

Life proceeded along different markings.

I was born in a city that back then was called St. Petersburg, in the family of a district teacher who had a four-class-school without higher examination rights on *Znamenskaya Ulitsa* [Street-of-the-Sign]. Back then, it was called after the white church of Our Lady of the Sign at the corner of Nevsky.

---

[2] The Russian for "linden," *lipa*, has the slang meaning of "falsification," already in use by the time of Shklovsky's writing.

Today, the city is called Leningrad, the street is called *Ulitsa Vosstaniya* [Revolt Street], and my father, as a very old man, finished the pedagogical academy and died a professor of the Artillery college.

Instead of the church, there is a big metro building—white, with a great dome.

Don't worry, I won't be going on like this and describing all changes in detail: after all, everything has changed.

[…]

Our nanny never told us any fairy tales: she was a city woman, daughter of the bankrupt merchant Bakalov.

The one who read out fairy tales, from Afanasiev's frayed collection, was our sister Zhenya [Evgeniya]. She was two years older than me. She had soft golden curls.

We chose fairy tales with many devils in them, but we feared those devils. Zhenya took a blue pencil and struck out all mentions of devils. I can still see this book in front of me, with all its blue blots; when we arrived at a blue word, my sister showed me two fingers, which meant horns, which meant devil. Zhenya was the first editor in my life.

[…]

Fences and Money

Life was lived in fear, in hiding. Aunt Nadya used to say, raising her grey head in pride:

"I had lived my life needing nobody, was never involved in anything and never attracted any attention."

All life was surrounded by fences.

Everything was locked up because everything was expensive. Everything was counted and measured. Chipped sugar cost fourteen kopek, granulated sugar eleven; when servants were engaged, special agreements were made about tea and sugar.

For a long time, I didn't know the names of trees, grasses, and stars. I knew the names of animals only from lotto. But I did know all the kopek costs.

Life was very quiet. War existed only in strange countries far away—China, Africa.

The XIXth century was almost over. Once, I saw a picture in a magazine: a man with wings; neck-high flat wings, and long legs sticking out below. Later I learned that the man was called Lilienthal. He wanted to fly and broke his legs.

Never try to fly.

If I try and remember how I saw myself back then, what comes to mind is this: I am made of glass, transparent, I swim along without overtaking the stream or falling behind; there is no me, and everything around keeps changing.

I am sad and curious.

[...]

Near the dacha, on the hillside near the river, there is a cemetery. The graves are fenced in. This is a rich cemetery. The spiked rods of the metallic lattice represent spears. Everything is coated with white enamel. The monuments, too. They feature oval lacquered photos on china. The earth between the stones of the monument and the iron of the lattice is embroidered with little crosses and circles of flowers in many colors.

Oval boxes with glass roofs are standing aslant; under the glass, there are wreaths of artificial flowers with black and white bands. They are packed up very cozily.

A dead man is also laid into a cozy box. He gets to wear his own picture in an oval frame. On the picture, he has a necktie and a collar. No legs, no arms.

His fate is not to be feared: he has a new room with a carpet of little flowers by the grave-bed.

There are little vaults, too—tiny apartments made of glass, resembling canary cages. Bars above, glass below. Bird cages used to have glass plates like this, for birds not to splash water on the floor when they bathed in their white little jars.

I never liked canaries; I had a big red bird of my own—a pine grosbeak. He sang a clear and very short song in the early morning. I woke up to listen to it. The cage was standing by my bed.

Then, a rat ate my grosbeak.

[…]

Father

My father, Boris Vladimirovich, a district math teacher, and later an instructor at the Artillery college, was a Jew converted to Christianity. He loved the cinema and watched two films every Sunday: one in the morning and one in the evening.

Father was born in 1863 in Elizavetgrad, a mid-sized and very dusty town, poetic only in spring when its high white acacias were in bloom. The town had sixty thousand people, windmills, distilleries, a factory for agricultural machinery, and four fairs.

Elizavetgrad was standing among wheat fields, by the upper reaches of the Ingul river, whose banks were trampled and covered in garbage from the market. Elizavetgrad dealt in bread and wool. The steppe around it is so wide that in the XXth century, thirty years ago or so, I myself saw all the cars of an international rally get lost in it. Wheat and watermelons ripened in the fields, the streets were covered in straw just like the Milky Way is covered in stars, and you could look right at the horizon without seeing a single human being.

The streets of Elizavetgrad are dusty, flanked by two- and three-story houses, but also by log huts—by *izbas*. The empty spaces between the izbas were meant to show that this was a proper town: they were supposed to be streets. My paternal grandfather, a woodyard guard, lived in one of such streets. My grandmother divided his fourteen children into three detachments: when one ate, the other studied, and the third one went out to play.

Thrice a day, white acacia blossoms fell on the traditional herring dish. The girls grew up. They were married into neighboring families.

The boys were sent to a Russian school.[3] My father finished secondary school, moved to Petersburg, was accepted at the Technological Institute, married and had a son. His first wife left with a friend from the institute.

Father transferred to the Institute of Forestry, converted to Christianity, stopped writing to Elizavetgrad, never saw his first wife or son, and suffered greatly. He took a dirk, planted its hilt into a tree stump and threw himself upon the blade. The dirk went through his breast and missed his heart.

[…]

My [maternal] grandfather wanted one of his younger daughters, Nadya, to pass an exam to become a home teacher. He placed an ad for a tutor, and my father came.

He came wearing a tartan plaid, longhaired, undersized, his boots high-topped and high-heeled.

---

[3] As opposed to Cheder: the herring dish signals that Shklovsky is talking about the Jewish part of his family.

In my grandfather's house, my father was disliked because of his height, his hair, his stern manners.

He did his tutoring, though. Then, one day, he took a skiff on the Neva, accompanying my mother, Varvara Bundel, to the Okhtinsky graveyard, talked to her about inconsequential things, carried her umbrella, than jabbed the umbrella into the earth, looked at his companion with his large brown eyes and said: "Would you marry me?"

Varvara Bundel told Boris Shklovsky, student and baptized Jew:

"I am not in love with you."

Then she warned that there would be no dowry.

They went home. Mother told grandfather that she had received a proposal.

Karl Ivanovich replied, with displeasure and a seeming lack of interest:

"We don't know who he is or where he's from. It's your choice. I don't advise it."

This is what mother told me many times.

Varvara Bundel married Boris Shklovsky.

It was a long time before they began to love each other, and it was even longer, thirty years or so, until they admitted to this love.

[…]

It's difficult to take leave of your own childhood.

You feel as if you had entered your old apartment: you see the familiar sun-bleached wallpaper, the familiar round stove in the corner, its door unpainted, and the stucco with holes poked in it, all the way to the wooden planks. There is no furniture, and you'd rather not sit on the windowsill, but you linger. You cannot live here, but how can you leave your past, on what kind of transport?

My Parents' Dacha

[...]

We tried to live in the dacha in winter, too. It was a very cold year. You step out, and the sea is lying in front of you, striped with ice hummocks, like broken asphalt. Toward the evening, on the left, the sky above Petersburg pinkens slightly.

I forgot, there was hardly any asphalt back then: this is a modern comparison. The ice, then, was like a broken layer of fat on yesterday's soup.

It was so cold that you felt, separately, every single item of clothing you were wearing. The rooms were cold, too.

We always had to pay out debts. We've been auctioned off: this is the main memory of my youth. As a child, I didn't have ice skates, much less a bicycle.

[...]

The Shapovalenko Gymnasium on the Kamennoostrovsky

Nikolai Petrovich Shapovalenko, a student of Ivan Pavlov, turned from an experimental physiologist into a practicing doctor, a specialist in infant diseases.

He became the protégé of some influential person whose infant had been healed. Back then, there were private gymnasiums and secondary schools with exam rights. They provided their pupils with full certificates.

Doctors used to receive strange gifts: mother-of-pearl cigarette cases, old bronzes of the kind that couldn't be sold, bad artists' paintings, or sometimes bronze ashtrays.

Our gymnasium was such a bronze ashtray, the present of an influential patient.

In this ashtray, we lay like cigarette stubs. The gymnasium was filled with pupils expelled elsewhere; now, that it has turned into a mirage, I remember it tenderly.

[…]

The Swan-Geese

I'm writing out of order. It's a good way to test things. I compare how the passages fit together, passages that were written with the equal desire to tell the truth but that use different details and change the point of view.

Let me try to pick out what people of my generation read.

There is this tale, "The Swan-Geese." The little boy Ivan ran away from the witch and her oven in which he was about to be baked. The witch gave chase. Little Ivan climbed upon an oak, but the witch started gnawing the oak with her iron teeth.

Little Ivan doesn't know what to do. But look, there is a flock of swan-geese flying. Ivan asks them: Ye swans, ye geese, take me upon your wings!

"Let the middle ones take you," say the birds. Another flock is coming. Little Ivan asks again: Ye swans, ye geese, take me upon your wings!

"Let the last ones take you."

A third flock came.

Little Ivan asked again.

The swan-geese came, picked him up, brought him home and set him down in the attic.

The rest is of no interest: everyone was happy, and little Ivan got a pancake.

Why am I telling this?

A person cannot rise on his own; he asks people who had thought, dreamt, reproached, protested before him; it is to them he talks when reading:

—Take me along!

—I can't!—says the book.—Ask another!

White-winged, white-paged books don't always take a straight path to carry you away. Away from fear, from the chase.

Don Quixote's dreams carried him up and sideward. Before, he had only been kind; the reading made him a great dreamer.

Books carried people out of their poor flats, their huts, their prisons.

I can give another example, a contemporary one. Myself, my heartache.

When I sleep, my heart, pierced with many wrongs, begins to hurt, but the hand of mankind lies down upon it, turns it like the disc of a telephone, and far-away long-ago voices become alive. My heart, connected to the great gateway of human consciousness, stops hurting.

What am I talking about?

About you.

We don't think on our own, we think using words created back when mammoths and elks were leaving the woods for the steppes and approaching the Black Sea. The animals disappeared, the words changed, but the great cybernetic machine of human self-awareness keeps thinking, keeps rocking the skies with its many wings, and the individual human connects to it.

The writer is mankind's apprentice. You cannot write without working, without reading, without watching the flocks of swan-geese that fly above you, a people after another, a school after another, until they finally take you and carry you on their wings.

Art is free from injury, from selfishness, because all of it is shared.

Trees need the mushrooms growing on the earth. You are not a tree in a field, you are a tree in a wood; you are the wood itself.

Koltsov compared Pushkin not to a tree, but to a wood.

A single writer is a union revealing panhuman thought.

I'll try to tell now what we read, and how.

Help me, ye swan-geese!

A Boy with a Book

The quiet start of a century. A deaf, frightened, self-contented time. The past is ticking away briskly, like the clock in a dead man's room.

The time is expressed in a lady; this lady represents the time: she sits in Great Britain and has gray hair; her name is Queen Victoria.

I remember that mother had a book by Elena Molochovets, *A Gift to Young Housewives*. Among other things, it featured the carving up of carcasses: the meat was carved in straight but fanciful lines.

That is how the world was divided: Africa, islands in the Pacific Ocean, India, Indo-China. The world was being carved up. Tsar Nicholas is sitting in Gatchina or perhaps Tsarskoe Selo, wearing a small beard and a colonel's uniform, surrounded by guards who protect him from Russia. The Trans-Siberian Railway is being built; steamboats with many-colored flags brave the sea on their way to faraway colonies.

The sails have drooped, there's smoke above the steamboats, and the faraway countries, too, are abloom with smoke and fire.

In a room devoid of all things but the barest necessities, under an unreachably high light bulb with a yellow-red carbon filament, there is a rather plump gray-eyed boy in a worn-out jacket and rust-colored boots that peek out from under his trousers. He's kneeling on a chair. His elbows are on the table. Silence.

The room is looking out on the triangle of the yard. The telephone is not ringing—it does not exist yet, and neither does the tram, the car, the TU-104 plane. The South and North poles are big white spots.

The room is quiet like a trunk.

Putting your elbows on the table is not allowed.

Life is full of "nots."

No walking on the grass, no dogs—this applies to nature in the garden.

Along the city's embankments, big letters written directly on the granite proclaim there should be "No breaking of fences" and "No casting of anchors."

The homework isn't done yet. I need to do it; then I could drink some cold tea, prepared beforehand. Instead, I begin to read—not the textbook. A book I need to return to another boy at school. The homework is learning a poem by Pleshcheev by heart; back then he was considered a great poet. I have a good memory, but it doesn't help. The poem is easy to read and impossible to remember, as impossible as crunching jelly.

That same school reader has excerpts by Aksakov, Turgenev; the swan-geese fly over my head and don't take me along. But now, overtaking the sound of the shot, tearing through the space of zero gravity, its steely sides shining, a cannonball with three talkative foreigners is flying through empty space to the Moon. There are pictures, too. The book overcomes the drabness of life; it carries me out of the poorly lit room into the incredible future.

Jules Verne again.

[…]

An Adolescent Reading

I didn't yet like Pushkin. Gogol astonished me with the final monologue from "Diary of a Madman." I can still feel the words in my head—alive, real: "Save me! take me away! give me a troika of horses, as quick as a whirlwind!"

I didn't understand Poprishchin's tragedy, but these horses rising into the air and flying over the world, back to their homeland, and the single string ringing out in the mist, all this was very close to me.

[…]

Youth

A Young Man Reading

A sixteen-year-old, his chestnut-brown hair curly but thin, his breast wide and his shoulders sloping, dreaming about the fame of a wrestler and the fame of a sculptor.

I had been expelled from different gymnasiums by people who wondered at my character and my rash speech.

So there I was, at home, studying by myself, preparing for the career of a loser: in my presence, I was talked about as if I was dangerously ill.

Tolstoy is like the morning. The sun has risen, the snow is shining, pigeons are flying, Levin, in love, is walking to see Kitty, trying not to run.

As a young man, I looked around and saw that our world existed, but without joy. All the "nots" were hard like thrones, quays, and fences.

I didn't believe that they could be broken. I remember, back when I was a teenager, gymnasium pupils and students didn't dance. The revolution was on the way,[4] and dancing was morally prohibited.

---

[4] Shklovsky is talking of the 1905 revolution, a wave of social unrest and military mutinies that led to reforms including the establishment of the State Duma and the Russian Constitution of 1906.

Then, the dancing started. Artsybashev's *Sanin* was published.[5] It was a strange time when clocks were ticking but time was standing still, when the train had reached a dead end, its lights off, the timetable torn into pieces.

Books saved from despair.

It was then that I read Tolstoy, reread Gogol. Then, too, Pushkin gradually emerged for me like a faraway island in a sea.

I Proceed Without Hurrying or Looking Back

[...]

Poets came to the [Stray Dog Café]. Osip Mandelstam was walking around, throwing back the narrow head of a youth grown old; he pronounced the lines of poems as if he was an apprentice studying a powerful spell. The poem broke off; then, another line appeared.

He was writing his book *The Stone* at the time.

Seldom, Anna Andreevna Akhmatova came here—young, wearing a black skirt, she with her very own movement of the shoulders, the special turn of the head.

Georgy Ivanov came often, his head beautifully sculptured, his face as if drawn on a pinkish-yellow, not yet dirtied hen egg.

The Futurists

[...]

I remember walking with Mayakovsky, whom even now in my mind I must call Vladimir Vladimirovich and not Volodya, along the paved streets of Petersburg, the sun-speckled avenues of the Summer

---

[5] The scandalous and, by the standards of the time, "pornographic" novel was published in 1907.

Garden, the Neva embankments, the Zhukovskaya Street, where the woman lived whom the poet loved.

Bits of landscape melted into—burned themselves into—Mayakovsky's poems.

The poet was quiet, sad, ironic, calm. He was sure—he knew—that the revolution would happen soon. He looked at the things around him the way one does when the thing is about to disappear.

Baudouin de Courtenay, Member of the Krakow Academy

[…]

I wanted to explain everything because I was young. I wrote the book *Resurrecting the Word*—a tiny brochure, printed with corpus (foliant) type. It dealt with glossolalia—words, exclamations, sound gestures which have no meaning but sometimes seem to anticipate it.

Cubo-futurists were keen on this kind of thing; they advanced "the word as such," the word as its own end.

The brochure featured many quotations from poets, examples of word games played by children, examples from sayings, and the use of nonsense in religious cults.

Baudouin de Courtenay's students—the one-armed Evgeny Dmitriyevich Polivanov, a specialist in Korean language, a man of immense linguistic learning and a mad lifestyle, and the quiet handsome Lev Petrovich Yakubinsky, back then Baudouin's favorite pupil—became interested in the little book.

Baudouin de Courtenay himself challenged me by publishing, in 1914, the articles "The Word and 'The Word'" and "On the Theory of 'The Word as Such' and 'The Letter as Such.'"[6]

---

[6]Baudouin de Courtenay was a linguist and Slavist best known for his phonetic theories. Shklovsky was particularly excited by the maître's attention as he himself had no formal linguistic education.

I went to see Baudouin de Courtenay and gave the professor my brochure, had a look at his poor, book-filled apartment. An army of books, ruffled and constantly restructuring, filled the badly painted shelves; my own thin booklet bound in blue wrapping paper took its place here.

A lecture on "The Living Word," followed by a dispute, was announced.

At the Tenishevsky School, of course.

The school's small hall sympathized with the student who gave his lecture in a long frock-coat made for somebody else. This frock-coat—indestructible, like iron armor—was my version of Don Quixote's chamois-leather doublet.

[...]

More on the Futurists

[...]

The group took on the name *budetlyane* (from *budu*: "I will") and published the book *A Slap in the Face of Public Taste*. It featured the first printing of Khlebnikov's list of dates. They were printed in columns, with intervals of 317 or its multiples. The final line looked thus: "Someone 1917."

I met Velimir Khlebnikov, quiet and wearing a buttoned-up black frock-coat, at a reading.

"The dates in the book,—I said,—are years when great empires were destroyed. Do you believe that our empire will be destroyed in 1917"? (*A Slap in the Face* was published in 1912.)

Khlebnikov replied, hardly moving his lips:

"You are the first to understand me."

Old things were being destroyed. In poetry, too.

A change of genre was on its way: after symbolism, some poets turned to the simplest themes, which had not been exterminated because they hadn't been poetic before; they were headed by Mikhail Kuzmin and Anna Andreevna Akhmatova. Others tried to do science or else to work with things that had been aesthetically rejected.

[...]

Velimir Khlebnikov wanted to understand the rhythm of history.

David Burliuk was a sensationalist; he tried to make Velimir Khlebnikov not better understood, but more surprising.

Khlebnikov was unhappy about this. In order not to depend on anyone and not to be bound by the self-interest of friendship, he turned into a wanderer.

When he came to Persia, they called him a dervish.

People wondered at him more than they read him; he explained quietly that many of his words are not *zaum*, not transrational language—*zenziver*, for instance, is the name of a bird.[7] He talked about words that could be divided, shared, renewed. Instead, the snobs wanted him to produce words against which they could scratch themselves.

[...]

Sergey Esenin had a big sowing basket. Peasants store seeds in such baskets. The sower would throw the sash over his shoulder, take handfuls of seeds and strew them upon the plowed field.

Esenin used the basket to store cards with words written on them. Sometimes the poet laid out the cards on the table.

A poet searches for his own self on the way of the word, which consolidates the thinking of mankind.

---

[7] It is indeed a rare Russian regionalism for "titmouse."

We live in order to learn to see things truly, but we mustn't lose contact with others so as not to get lost in the dusty labyrinth of selfhood.

We need to know ourselves not in order to talk to ourselves, and not merely in order to talk about ourselves, but in order to talk to others. This is the only way to self-knowledge.

The change of literary schools is connected to changing tasks art sets itself. At the same time, every literary form, using language shared by all to think, sets itself a program of using human thought; it redefines the meaning of the beautiful, the touching, the necessary, the horrible; it reconsiders the mutual relationships of meanings—i.e., the form of artworks.

There was an old academic painter, a teacher of great artists—P. Chistyakov. He used to say that, when drawing a body, it was useful to understand its form via geometric figures—spheres, cones, cylinders—to build a form in space, to feel one's way toward it through geometry.

Chistyakov didn't "invent" cubism, but different painters in different countries consolidated the transitional understanding of form, the moment in which the laws of construction were being comprehended, the moment in which form was being contemplated from all sides.

Picasso's drawings consolidate the sculptor's progressing sensations while he contemplates a model, decomposing nature in order to recompose it.

Cubists were trying to consolidate the progressing construction of an artwork.

During the construction process, an artist can see a painting as a relation of color quantities.

If we reject the material of life, we arrive at abstract painting. It appeared in Russia in 1912–13, created by hungry, selfless artists who never sold any of their paintings. There was no element of speculation here—they were only carving their way through, as directly as they could. In fifty years, much has changed; the way didn't lead to victory and is now covered in potholes left by the wheels of epigones.

Here, I need to express—or rather, to explore—my doubts: why the fifty-year-old invention of Russian leftist artists became almost official art in today's United States.

Now, first of all, the thing canonized in the United States is not the same as the one created fifty years ago. At the start of the century, abstract art existed against the background of bourgeois art, of sweetened depiction—which it rejected. It understood itself as a protest against that kind of art. Early left art was not realist, but its theorists are not to be confused with today's abstractionists, either.

Another time—another meaning.

In Russia, many theorists in the first quarter of the XX century were feeling their way from the abstract to the real, from trans-rational language to plot theory, to history, to an understanding of meaning, to meaning as the dominator of all constructional elements.

Now, the most important thing, the reason of all art—the study of the world—is being left behind. All signs are nonsensical if they send no signals about human life in the universe.

[...]

We Publish Books

I was a bad university student because I was busy with other things. We had the Society for the Study of the Theory of Poetic Language [*Obshchestvo izucheniya teorii poeticheskogo yazyka*], which we called OPOYAZ, following the style of military abbreviations.

As a part of the movement, I do not know the magnitude of its mistakes or successes.

As a living being, I understand more now, forty years later, than I understood then. It was a research institute without financing, without personnel, without assistance, without conflicts about "You said that, I said this." We worked together, we shared our findings. We believed that poetic language differed from prosaic language in its function and its orientation toward the mode of expression.

The OPOYAZ united people connected to Mayakovsky's and Khlebnikov's poetry—to put it bluntly, futurists—and young philologists who were deeply familiar with the poetry of that time.

What could possibly get the academically minded students of Baudouin de Courtenay interested in the futurists, in people who were sometimes strangely dressed and always strangely spoken?

It was word analysis and untraditional thinking.

Baudouin's students were, so to speak, superacademic: they left the university, setting sail for distant lands, in the belief that they were already well-supplied with instruments for orientation. No royalties were paid at first; the authors received a third of the copies. The print runs of the books were six hundred. After the revolution, things got easier.

The revolution's magnetic field involuntary changed people's thoughts even if the revolution wasn't on their agenda. Even so, they said "no" to the past. What was needed was an opportunity to publish.

The OPOYAZ was created during the war, before the revolution. Two collections were published in 1916 and 1918.[8] We had no publisher. We self-published: we had acquaintances in a small print shop specializing in business cards.

[…]

---

[8] Actually, three collections appeared in 1916, 1917, and 1919.

Our understanding of literature was opposed to the theories of symbolists such as Bryusov, Vyacheslav Ivanov, Andrey Bely. In their view, literature mattered because it transfigured the form of life into a swarm of analogies.[9] The symbolists wanted to paint not nature but whatever seemed hidden behind it. Shifting the source of light, the symbolist mistook the swarm of shadows and reflections for a mystic revelation. The symbolist believed "mystery" to be not only the solution to the world, but the world itself, its very entrance. The swarm of symbols was supposed to reveal the hidden, transcendent, secret, mystical meaning of life.

The acmeists, though not all of them, beckoned back to life—to real, exotic, rough, or intimate life; the intimate was least worn out.

When Akhmatova said "I fumbled the glove for my left hand onto my right,"[10] it was a stylistic discovery, for the symbolists made love appear in a scarlet circle, transforming the world, revealing its deepest wisdom or its international vulgarity. The symbolists claimed that another world existed, not as a way to study this world but as a kind of counter-world.

[…]

The OPOYAZ people were trying to find common laws in different phenomena of developing art. They did not call themselves "formalists." But they ignored what was beyond the image. They

---

[9] The original *stroy* could be rendered as "form," "formation," "arrayal," "structure," "harmony," "order," or "system." The rhyming juxtaposition *stroy / roy* (swarm) was coined by Andrey Bely; "form" was chosen here to recreate the effect. As Shklovsky observes elsewhere (Gamburgskiy schet [1990] 227), it was Andrey Bely who coined the terms "roy" (for collection of metaphors) and "stroy" (for their object).

[10] Akhmatova is considered an acmeist; the line is quoted in A. S. Kline's translation; the full text is available at www.poetryintranslation.com/PITBR/Russian/Akhmatova.htm.

didn't claim the existence of lilac worlds but they seemed to be claiming that only the poem itself existed.[11]

Futurists marched in a motley formation and wanted different things. Khlebnikov had a foreboding of great perturbations and kept trying to substantiate his presentiment with numbers. He wanted to find the rhythm of history. At the same time, he was fighting against Fedor Sologub in the name of life.

Alexey Kruchenykh was looking for words that were not merely "as simple as mooing" but that really were mooing, a replacement of speech with sound gestures.

Mayakovsky walked among the others, looking into the future over our heads and reinterpreting our words for the future.[12]

Symbolist poetics produced a number of highly technological observations, but this poetics kept trying to turn into a course in esoteric arts.

The acmeists created no poetics of their own.

The OPOYAZ was most closely connected to futurism, or rather, this was the case first, but soon it began studying general questions of style, attempting at the same time to find the laws of stylistic change proceeding from the needs of the form itself.

Do not think that we, the members of the OPOYAZ, which existed at a time filled with belief in and expectation of the revolution, were conservative—that we were consciously conservative, that we tried to fence ourselves off from life. Most of all, we wanted to see the new essence of life. To see the unusual in the usual, not to replace the usual with the contrived.

---

[11] "Lilac worlds" appear in a poem by Alexander Blok, and so does the "scarlet circle" from the previous paragraph—or, rather, a "scarlet-gray circle" and, in another poem, a "halo of red fire." Shklovsky is mocking both the symbolist (over)use of color imagery and the school's esoteric bent.

[12] Mayakovsky's collection *Simple As Mooing* was published in 1916. His tall stature made him quite literally look over others' heads.

[…]

The War

[…]

The muses and erinyes of the February revolution were rushing about in the city—trucks beset and behung with soldiers, going the devil knew where, receiving fuel from the devil knew whom, doing something the devil knew to what end. A bourgeois revolution is a light, dazzling, unreliable, joyful thing. All attempts at resistance soon stopped.

I don't remember why I was spending that night at the Technological Institute. A woman came running to me in the early morning; I was still sleeping on my fur coat. She woke me up and said:

"Divorce me from my husband."

"I'm a non-commissioned officer in charge of an armored car and five men. How can I divorce anyone?"

"But it's the revolution,"—the woman replied.—"I've been pleading for so long."

We discussed this together and decided to divorce that woman; we gave her a divorce certificate in the name of the revolution. We stamped it with the stamp of the chemical laboratory: we had no other, and the supplicant absolutely insisted on a stamp.

The city was crunching: cars kept colliding and turning over.

What a day it was! What potholes under the cars! What belief! What joy!

[…]

The Ending of Youth

On Time, not on Myself[13]

[...]

Flamingos are flying into the air over a lake. They appear white. But the undersides of their wings are pink, and they seem to cheer up when they take wing.

A little cutter was dragging barges along a sea that was saltier than tears.

On the other side, I was met by a soldier who began complaining that he had been sent there to work as a telegrapher, that he was dying with boredom.

"Why have you been sent here?" I asked.

"I killed someone. They had no time for a process."

He believed that working as a telegrapher and temporary commandant at the Lake Urmia was too cruel a punishment for killing someone. The killing he did was not in battle.

Beyond Lake Urmia lie the worn-out Persian roads. The rivers hiss over the stones like a primus stove. A mad moon shines at night.

The steep arcs of bridges destroyed a thousand years ago throw shadows which seem like quotation marks around the word "Persia."

It was in late autumn that I came to the Persian front. Replenishments, in great detachments, came from hard labor prisons. They had their own traditions. Life became very hard.

It was hard to defend the Kurds, the Kurd villages. I saw a colonial war, which I'm not going to write about here. I keep seeing it in my sleep.

---

[13] An allusion to the phrase "on time and on myself" from Mayakovsky's "Out Loud."

[...]

I have done little in Urmia. I have done no harm, perhaps. My heart has been abraded in that country the way a hard road is abraded under the furry feet of camels. Camels, it then seemed to me, walk reluctantly, shuffling their heavy feet. Their bells jingle. Camels walk on, bound together by woolen ropes, and carry their load. I felt like both the camel and the road.

I came home. The army was already in retreat. It was sliding down the steep slope of Persia toward the Caucasus. The trains were running so quickly that the rocks seemed hatched.

We drove past Baku. Barriers were built from provisions to stop us from entering the city. We drove past Dagestan. Cossacks came out of their villages, approached the train asking us to help in their civil war against the highlanders or to sell them arms.

Every man has his measure of grief, his measure of weariness, and if he is filled with grief, you can pour another bucket of it over him—he won't absorb more. I had lost all my papers and all my friends. I came back cowering on the roof of a train, wrapping myself in a newspaper. This is how I arrived in Russia. The rest is easier. I can speak about it.

In Petersburg, I met Gorky and my OPOYAZ friends.

OPOYAZ after the October revolution

I returned from the Persian front in early December.

After the October revolution, the OPOYAZ received a stamp and a seal, and was registered as a scholarly association.

The publishing was done by Osip Brik and myself.

We had many students—at the Art History Institute at Saint Isaac's Square, at the Living Word Institute near the Public Library, and partly also at the University. We worked more academically now, encountering no administrative obstacles and constantly arguing about the foundations of literary creation. It was always I who led the arguments to escalation, trying to solve general questions, building bridges from one fact to another, missing what was most important, making wrong claims. This period ended two or three years later when the leadership was transferred to the LEF [Left Front of the Arts] group, i.e. mostly to Mayakovsky.

The LEF had a burning passion—the desire to participate in creating a new way of life.

The strange thing was that the magazine headed by Mayakovsky was trying to deny the importance of art in general and poetry in particular.

Mayakovsky, Aseev, Pasternak, Tretyakov, Kirsanov, and other well-known poets published in the magazine which negated poetry and painting, and proclaimed the importance of newspapers and textile patterns instead.

The magazine which disclaimed art printed not only poems but also articles on poetry; it was connected to [the theater director] Meyerhold, to Eisenstein and to new architecture.

The LEF was also connected to the OPOYAZ, whose work was entirely dedicated to art.

One of the old OPOYAZ members was Lev Yakubinsky. I am not a linguist and will not attempt to survey his scientific work, but I was connected to him for a few years that went by in a state of high inspiration.

[…]

I met Boris Mikhailovich Eikhenbaum over fifty years ago in the Saperny Lane.

This handsome and elegant lecturer didn't know back then how difficult his life would be.

Many things we've experienced together. Many things he thought through clearly. Many others I confused for him. He wrote a study on Gogol's "The Overcoat," showing the semantic load of *skaz*.

[...]

Eikhenbaum's study "How 'The Overcoat' is Made" was published in 1919. In its own way, it elucidated much about Gogol's style and, probably, about the construction of many literary works by Gogol's contemporaries. This study cannot be torn out of Soviet literary scholarship, and if we look at the very important work by V. Vinogradov, member of the Academy, I find it important to point out that it not only appeared after Eikhenbaum's study chronologically but is also connected to it in its form of analysis. However, in Eikhenbaum's work the character is only fuzzily visible through *skaz*; the sound signals and the whole sound construction do not express the essence of a human being and his attitude to the world around him. Meanwhile, Akaky Akakievich's way of expression is not an end in itself, and not a plot substitute—it's a plot device.

A man is so crushed that he can only mumble, he stops thinking; this *skaz* is repeatedly refreshed by the appearance of literary, authorial speech; the author is constantly present in the text, thus preserving for the reader, so to speak, a plot-driven attitude to the *skaz*, preserving the [reader's] way of analyzing *skaz*.

In Eikhenbaum's reading, the titular counsellor Akaky Akakievich is imprisoned in *skaz* as if it was the Peter and Paul Fortress.

However, the titular counsellor Akaky Akakievich changes his way of expressing himself before his death—he swears.[14] Truth be

---

[14] Shklovsky puns on the verb *vyrazhat'sya* which usually means "to express oneself" but can be used as a euphemism for swearing.

told, Gogol merely mentions this, but then, tsar Nicolas' censorship wouldn't allow to cite Akaky Akakievich swearing. The young and quick-tempered study by Eikhenbaum is wider than its task; it has taught us all to analyze—its conclusions were not inserted from without but born in the analysis, and if these conclusions were often mistaken, then these mistakes can be traced, with analysis helping the reader to separate right from wrong.

If we break up the path of an arrow into infinitely small segments, we can provide illusory proof that in each moment the arrow can only be in one particular place and thus try to prove that the arrow does not move at all, for movement is a change of places. If we break up a literary work into closed stylistic segments, we can try to prove that the work does not move—but this would be wrong.

The plot of "The Overcoat" consists, from the very beginning, not only in showing a crushed man by imitating his *skaz*, but also in the revolt of the crushed man.

The earliest handwritten draft of "The Overcoat" is entitled "The Tale of a Clerk Who Steals Overcoats." It was written in 1839. This is how that text began; this is what it was written for.

The path from a downtrodden state to aggression against the rich and noble is the opposition on which the plot is built.

Similarly, in Dostoyevsky's "Poor Folk," Makar Devushkin changes, and so does his style. He says so himself in a letter: "See, my manner of writing, too, is forming now."

Boris Eikhenbaum wrote an immensely interesting text, he saw things that hadn't been seen before, but because of the mistakes of the OPOYAZ he misplaced his observations on the map.

His work didn't reach the stage of self-negation, i.e. the reassertion of the unity of form and content.

When analyzing a man's mistakes, the bitterest thing is to see not that his path was wrong but that he had stopped halfway.

I had stopped halfway because my attitude toward the world was wrong; the things which time, youth, and talent had placed directly in our hands remained unfinished because of philosophical mistakes.

We buried Boris Mikhailovich Eikhenbaum on the remote Vyborgsky graveyard, among naked birches beset with winter-worried crows.

[…]

Farewell, my friend! Forgive me, my friend! We have thought about many things together; many things have I freighted your life with. I am talking to you as if you were alive. Our forty-five-year-old friendship is not dead.

I walked left and right, searching the fields. I walked up and down, trampling the hillsides, wearing down the heels of my shoes.

My steps are not light anymore; my calves hurt; my veins have turned blue, my aorta is covered in hoarfrost, my heart has burned itself out beating.

Like trees remaining in a chopped down forest, we saw each other from afar.

The trees are falling, rustling with their needles, saying farewell to each other with this bow, seeing the unreached horizon for the final time. I pity my friend and myself.

[…]

Yury Tynyanov was a knight of Soviet literary studies.

As a literary historian, he has done a lot; what he did not finish in his field, was never finished without him.

In the book *Archaists and Innovators*, he raised the question of literary forms' changing meaning, of their different uses within different ideologies. Thus, in a way, he was refuting formalism, which was trailing "the literary device."

When studying the importance of literary schools, you cannot follow the similarity of literary form. The dialectics of history shift these forms.

It's a pity about the books which haven't been written, which still exist only as drafts. But life had gaps which necessitated catching up. We left much unfinished, we wrote many wrong things, and wrongly rejected many others. Now, having read Shaw's opinion on Tolstoy, and Brecht's articles on drama, I believe that my ideas on *ostranenie* in general and Tolstoy's use of it in particular were right, but wrongly generalized.

Ostranenie means showing an object outside the usual patterns, describing a phenomenon with new words, taken from a different field of relations.

Tolstoy described the life of his circle—landowners, nobility—introducing the attitude of a patriarchal peasant who doesn't know the meanings of words and events, and who argues against the legality of things which are habitual to old literature.

The solution to Tolstoy is not that he was a holy man leaving his milieu, or that he was a landowner; it was Lenin who resolved his phenomenon as that of a man expressing the revolution—the demolition of relations. This is why Tolstoy needed to look around the way a man who just woke up looks around.

Old life seemed like a dream to him.

My contemporaries in the West want to abandon the awakening for the sake of dreaming, for the illogic of sleep, and my fault consists in not placing the charts of art on the map of world history.

[…]

In his youth [Evgeny Polivanov] believed that everything was possible for him. Once, he placed his hand on the rails while a train was approaching: his goal was to outdo Kolya Krasotkin from *The Brothers Karamazov*—that boy only lay down between the rails.

Polivanov did not jerk his hand away; the wheel cut it off; the boys ran away. He stood up, took the cutaway hand by the fingers and started walking, carrying it. He told me how all cabmen were driving away in horror from the sight of him, whipping their horses wildly.

This occurrence made an impression on Polivanov; he became quiet for a time and good at school; he finished the gymnasium and became a regular listener of Baudouin de Courtenay's lectures. He told me later that he had once dozed off during one of these contradictory, brilliant, and confusing lectures and, awaking a second later, he had realized something which was, for him, the most important thing of all.

What this thing was he never told me, but I saw how easily he worked.

[...]

Bernstein said that he couldn't write a book without solving all the questions once and for all, without having it out with all the books published before him. I think he was wrong in this: you can write a book on botany, but you cannot call it *The Absolute and Final Truth about Flowers*.

Sergey Bondi dealt with poetry, lectured. He had long left OPOYAZ ideas behind; what he wanted to write was not simply an inspired book containing precise knowledge in poetry scholarship but a book worthy of its time, a book containing the experience of the age. This is a good thing to do, but it's also good to live like a tree, changing leaves. Even the evergreen trees somewhere in the native land of Horace inaudibly change and renew their leaves.

[...]

In those years, we met in different apartments, burned books on stoves, put our feet into the oven to get warmer. It was still cold, and still we kept working.

What we wanted was not so much to find previously undescribed phenomena as to clarify the relations between phenomena.

Later, of course, we came by habits, disciples, and patterns.

Let's write down our debts.

Literature was not the only thing bourgeois theorists regarded as the self-development of ideas. The history of state form, law history etc. were also analyzed this way.

The OPOYAZ explained the change of literary forms with the forms becoming obsolete and automatic, ceasing to be experienced.

At the time, OPOYAZ members believed that new forms arose from old but non-canonical artistic phenomena. Art was placed in a wave conductor of sorts. This work separated form from content, producing an idealistic image of development.

However, the theory of the OPOYAZ is not to be confused with its practice.

OPOYAZ was created by life, and its work constantly violated its theory.

[…]

A Few Words on the Ukraine

Blood drops look very red on grass when the sun is shining. This makes sense: red and green are complementary colors, after all.

I was blown up in Kherson, in the moat of an old fortress [while unscrewing a projectile]. […]

The little cylinder exploded in my hand. This is when I saw the red on green. Horses were galloping in a nearby field; it seemed to me that no time had yet passed, that the dust raised by the explosion had not yet fallen, when I suddenly heard myself squealing, when I saw my legs thrown apart by the explosion, my shirt black with blood, my left hand smashed, my right hand tearing out handfuls of grass.

Some people from our detachment came, lifted me up, got hold of a cart, brought me to a hospital; there, my body was shaved, my leg and arm were about to be amputated, but then an old doctor came and said: "Why the hurry?" I could see my body quivering on its bones—not trembling, but quivering, as if it was about to boil.

I lay there. They couldn't take out the splinters—there were too many. They came out by themselves. There you are, walking—and suddenly your underwear is creaking, a splinter is coming out. You can pull it out with your fingers.

Almost forty years have passed. Nothing but little black dots remain from those multiple wounds—there were eighteen main splinters—and my left wrist is slightly thinner than the right one, and the wounds hurt when the weather changes.

But everyone is like this.

I returned to Petrograd, fell ill with jaundice, walked around all yellow—not like a canary, but with a reddish tint, shading into orange, and with yellow eyeballs. Jaundice has a depressing effect; with jaundice, you don't feel like joking and talking.

It was at this time that Gorky and I became close friends. I told him about the slow trains, the front lines suddenly building around villages and disintegrating again, about wounded men who cross the Dnepr and cannot move anymore when they arrive, about the markets. Thread was sold there by the meter. Glasses were made from beer bottles, shirts from sacks.

Telling about it calms you down.

After I was wounded, I kept waking up seeing a red light in the middle of the night. A scarlet light. This passed. I'm writing this down to show, by the example of some of my life's events, that my books of those times weren't written with the quiet consistency of academic works.

On an Apartment on the Kronwerk Prospect, on Humanism and Hate

In 1920, Petersburg was under siege; the city was cut off from both sea and land. Petrograd's factories had always worked with external coal: it had been either shipped in as ballast by steamers when they came to get wood and flax from Petrograd, or else it had been brought by rail.

Now, Petersburg-Petrograd was cut off, and only a single factory chimney was smoking over it: the chimney of the water-pump station. We still had water.

At the outskirts, trams were running; the coaches were filled to bursting. Children on sleighs, children on ice skates hooked onto the trams, sometimes whole trains of them. All this happened without laughter. They were not doing it for fun.

The plumbing froze in one house after another: people brought up bucketfuls of water from the basement. The stairs iced over.

Petrograd was going through its first siege.

There were no little cast-iron stoves back then; they were only about to be made, made from everything that was handy, including iron signboards.

We used what we could to stoke the stoves: I burned my shelves, my modeling stand, and innumerable books.

Boris Eikhenbaum got hold of a trench stove; he sat in front of it, leafing through journals, tearing out what he needed most, burning the rest. He couldn't burn an unread book.

I burned everything. If my arms and legs were made of wood, I would have burned them that year.

Little wooden houses were devoured by big stone houses. Man-made ruins appeared. Frost bit into house walls, freezing them through right to the wallpaper; people slept fully clothed. They sat in their rooms wearing tightly belted coats.

Everyone shared the same fate, everything came in streaks. There was the month of falling horses, when dying horses lay on every street, every day.

There was the month of saccharin, when every store sold nothing but little bags of sweetener. There had been months of eating potato peels, and in autumn, when Yudenich was attacking, everybody ate cabbage.

The horses were dead. I will never forget the creaking and the weariness of the sledge you are dragging behind you.

The great city lived with many souls, it was not extinguished—the way a heap of coal, once it catches fire, can remain unextinguished under rain and snow.

People emerged from dark apartments, in which only night lamps burned feebly, and went to theaters to watch a play; new plays were being put on. Writers wrote, scientists worked.

Young literary scholars met in apartments. Once, we had to walk upon chairs because the first story floor was flooded by burst plumbing.

The city was empty; the streets grew so wide it seemed that a river of cobbles had washed away the shores of houses. The city was alive, burning with the red fire of the revolution.

This city never became provincial and was never taken because its heat melted—its fire burned—everyone who rose against it.

The potatoes and carrots presented like flowers, the poems and the day of tomorrow were holy.

I greet you, friends with whom I wrote, with whom I hungered, with whom I made mistakes.

[...]

Tales about Prose (1966/1983)[1]

A Note From the Author

[...]

Try to imagine Dostoyevsky or Tolstoy without content, i.e. without the insistence on certain moral—or, which is the same, prophetic—ideas, without thoughts about future morals: these books are unimaginable without their context.

Tolstoy's drama was that he couldn't follow his own texts.

He kept changing their very question.

Or rather: the question kept changing before him of its own accord.

The immobility of art, its independence—this was my mistake. Viktor Shklovsky made a mistake.

He didn't consider that Don Quixote leaves his home not only because he reads knightly romances but also because a new world is opening up before him in its greatness.

The heroes and heroines in Shakespeare's tragedies change their fates and begin new lives even while dying.

The characters of the tragedy themselves call their old life a prison.

[...]

---

[1] Source: *Povesti o proze*. Moscow: Khudozhestvennaya Literatura, 1983.

I'm not yet ninety.

Measured against time and its events, I'm almost a young man; or rather, I'm a man rich in years, as old books say.

Greetings, reader.

Read this book at home; read it in the garden if you don't get dizzy from the specks of sunshine on the trees.

But don't forget this book with the old thoughts of a man who longs for the future, don't forget this book on the bench when you leave.

Viktor Shklovsky
November 1981

On the Novella

We can say that the Volga is the river which flows through Yaroslavl, Kostroma, Kineshma, and Gorky; this definition contains no lies or mistakes.

The Volga really passes through all these cities; moreover, no other river does.

However, if we characterize the Volga according to the location just defined, we'll be describing a flow of water which resembles the Volga neither upstream nor downstream.

In the same way, if we say that the Volga is a river passing through Volgograd and Astrakhan', we cannot apply what we learn about this rivers' banks and its width to the Volga as a whole.

The same is true for historical definitions.

For instance, the term "realism."

First of all, a reasonable doubt arises. "Realism" is a rather late term. Can we apply it to epochs before its existence? This doubt extends far: the term didn't exist at the time of Belinsky.[2]

[2] Belinsky, Pushkin's contemporary, was considered *the* realist critic *par excellence.*

But we need to be consequent: we never analyze historical phenomena in the terms which coexisted with the phenomena—for instance, no one in Egypt or Rome called their state a "slaveholding society."

We can know more, and often do know more about a historical event than its contemporaries did.

This is why we can't fully avoid using such terms as "the Greek novel," or, more generally, "the antique novel," though this is a late term and we must use it carefully so as to not couple it with anachronistic notions.

Literature isn't mathematics, and literary terms will never be as precise as mathematical definitions. What we have is a terminology for continuing processes and phenomena, which can be never fully grasped by a definition.

Let us now turn to the definition of the genre called "novella."

The word was created after the phenomenon; the phenomenon is changing.

It was changing before the term arose, and kept changing thereafter. There are many definitions, and all of them correspond to different stages and kinds of the same artistic phenomenon.

Things are complicated; the Volga, you can at least visit and judge for yourself that it really is one unified river.

The Volga is a physical unity, a geographic continuity.

The novella is a stylistic notion created by us and depending on many phenomena that keep creating and, in a way, replacing it.

[...]

Spielhagen separated the novella from the novel, believing that the former deals with ready-made characters.

This definition applies to the novella midstream, so to speak. In early examples, by Apuleius, for instance, the protagonists are quite uncharacterized. These novellas describe events rather than show human characters through events.

In Chekhov's novellas, people change; they grow disappointed, embittered, sometimes mellow.

Some scholars of the novella claim that it always needs a special kind of condensed, intense plot telling about a single event.

This definition suits O. Henry's novellas—after all, they are the material it was built on. But we shall see that it doesn't suit Chekhov's; he never sought to make the plot "intense."

Chekhov's novellas are not always dedicated to a single event, either. They rarely have an exposition, but they do often feature a backstory: they deal with several events.

The situations used by Chekhov are always taken from his own time. The conflicts are grounded in looking for work, in poverty, in the closed nature of life, in the failure to understand it.

Novellas are built to reveal the new in the known more often than to make an old, traditional conflict escalate using new social material.

This kind of novella is clearly new, not borrowed.

Without denying the existence of so-called "wandering plots," we must keep in mind that stories whose plots coincide are not always connected in their origin and can have different meanings.

[…]

Some Empirical Remarks on the Methods of Connecting Novellas

[…]

In India, in the jungle, behind the swamps, there are the white marble cities that I remember from children's books.

Lianas rise from the windows of abandoned palaces like green smoke, they coil like smoke when making their way into the wood.

The palace has become "pure architecture." The old reality of the house—the connections between the rooms, the logic of their arrangement—is lost.

Monkeys run up and down the stairs in the belief that these are merely a construction; they perceive the stairs as pure form.

But people had been living in this house, though their ways were different from ours. The reality of faraway countries is as authentic as the reality of a quiet crossing in a little town we know well.

Novels and collections of novellas were created in the search for new artistic unity, born from new production relations, from new consciousness. Fragments of knowledge, inventions, and jokes came together and, under the influence of the magnetic field of a new life, were transformed, entering into new connections.

On the Different Meanings of "Character" when Applied to Literary Works of Different Epochs

[…]

In the fairy tales of *A Thousand and One Nights*, the protagonists often have talismans but they rarely have personal character traits. They have adventures, but they don't experience them. The plot moves ready-made protagonists along its way.

Their body language, their emotions, and poses show very little variation.

People faint; when they are afraid, their knees shake, their teeth chatter, and their mouths grow dry; when they laugh, their canines show.

Concrete, individualized descriptions are rare; they do occur, but without becoming a method of looking at a protagonist closely.

The sequence of events is organized in the same way; the parts don't interact.

Episodes and whole novellas are strung together according to the order in which they are told, without taking into consideration the situation of telling: a wheel might be turning on a person's head, and still he tells a story.

In fairy tales, even enraged spirits listen patiently.

[…]

Fairy tales don't bring the protagonists' traits together to create a "character."

This is not only true for Arab tales. The appearance of character traits is usually constructed as a contrast between the protagonist and the events.

A lucky fool, a tailor who conquers giants, a woman who defeats men, a boy who turns out to be wiser than all wise men—it is the sensation of difference which begins creating character here.

I'd even put it like this: a character as we understand it appears in the fairy tale when a simple person is contrasted with a "hero." It is the simple person who needs to be described in his usualness.

[…]

On the True Unity of Works of Art[3]

[…]

In my early youth, in one of my first books, I expressed the supposition that the form of *Eugene Onegin* is mainly defined by Onegin first refusing Tatyana, and then Tatyana refusing Onegin.

[3] The chapter is originally entitled "On the True Unity of Works of Art in General and on the Unity of the *Decameron* in Particular," but the discussion of the *Decameron* is not included in the present excerpt.

I compared this construction with Ariosto's novels, in which such a mismatch was explained by a miracle: the water of a magic spring transformed every feeling into its opposite; having quenched their thirst, the man and the woman swapped their feelings for each other.

But such an interpretation throws overboard the whole connective apparatus, i.e. the very form of the text, the sensation of renewed experience.[4]

Such an interpretation projects the laws of one kind of connection on all others.

You can compare anything to anything, and who knows where your comparison ends up.

Once, I compared the story of Tatyana Larina and Onegin to the unlucky attempt of a heron to wed a crane.[5] It was a joke, but a joke should never be served warmed up.

Ariosto's construction is to a large degree defined by the text's parodic nature. With Pushkin, such analysis only takes into consideration the main events of *Eugene Onegin*, not the background in whose light the characters are presented, and not the way they make us enter their world.

The characters appear in the light of their surroundings. In terms of painting, this text has colored shadows; in the scheme I offered, there are only outlines and rough shadings.

The form of the novel consists in showing Onegin lonely among his surroundings, and showing Tatyana lonely, too.

In his quarrel with Lensky, Onegin follows not his internal laws but the laws of high society.

---

[4] In the original, "the sensation of the renewal of renewed experience," probably a mistake made in dictation; Shklovsky never read the proofs of his works.

[5] Shklovsky is alluding to a Russian fairy tale. First, the heron asks the crane to marry him; the crane refuses but then asks the heron, who refuses in his turn, and thus ad infinitum.

He is lonely but not free; Tatyana, too, is lonely but not free. You cannot cut her out of what we could call the landscape.

Without her family, Tatyana Larina doesn't exist.

Without his books and his arguments with Lensky, Onegin doesn't exist.

Thus, the form of *Eugene Onegin* depends on many semantic and rhythmic connections.

The rhyme and the strophic structure also contribute to the construction of meaning.

Each form is only comprehensible in connection, and incomprehensible in itself. For instance, Pushkin uses the word *morozy* [frosts] and then jokes that the reader must be expecting the rhyme word *rozy* [roses]. And indeed, rhyming the word with *rozy* is what he seems to be doing. However, in reality he's doing something else, namely rhyming *morozy* with the compound *rifmy "rozy"* [rhyme "rose"]—and the traditional rhyme which seems to be offered here is immediately subverted. The old form exists in the very act of its own destruction.

The interconnection of meanings is very complex and cannot be reduced to, so to speak, two duets: Onegin and Tatyana, Tatyana and Onegin.

I must apologize to the professors of many Western universities for suggesting to them a wrong interpretation, and also to thank them for the fact that they do not mention my name when repeating my idea thirty-five years later.

[…]

What Happened after the Plague of 1348?

[…]

[In the *Decameron*], seven women meet three men named Panfilo, Filostrato, and Dioneo. All three names are Boccaccio's pseudonyms: names he had given to himself in earlier works.

Thus, there are three Boccaccios in the book, along with seven women whose names are the names of women he once loved and never quite forgot.

The essence of the plot contrast, of the semantic shift that defines the construction of the *Decameron* as a whole, is the plague, which enabled new relationships to crystallize quicker.

Everything became different, grew sharper with fear and the desire to live.

In his conclusion, Boccaccio says that the book was set at a time "when even the most respectable people thought nothing of walking around with their trousers on their heads in order to save themselves."

The pest had lifted prohibitions, had unleashed wit, had made it possible to express a new attitude toward the old in laughter.

Almost all plots in the *Decameron* are old, and the narrative form is also old in many respects, but the attitude is new, the revelation of contradictions is new; this is why the style is also partly, though not fully, changed.

[…]

On the Sense of Wonder

When the young Gorky was reading French dime novels, constantly surprised at the characters' cheerfulness and spirit of enterprise, he not only recognized the old but also saw the old in a new way, against the background of his own being; conscious of the difference, he then constructed the new.

Topoi—plot devices, some of which we've discussed—exist not in isolation, but in certain couplings; they analyze reality, but they change slowly, sometimes belatedly.

Not only the phenomena themselves change; their meanings do, too.

On the Taman peninsula, there were sheds made from debris. Gravestones, fragments of statues, bits of old brickwork—all this was used for new walls.

Architecture doesn't always consist in the combination of old fragments. The new can arise not only from new couplings but also from the use of new material.

[...]

The inhabitants of Coketown [in *Hard Times*]—a place distilled from other towns' characteristics by Dickens, a disciple of Fielding—were forbidden to wonder.

Let us now, somewhat prematurely, visit Coketown, a mid-nineteenth-century industrial town built from bricks that have already grown black, on the bank of a river that has already begun to stink and acquired a purple sheen, a town full of machines whose pistons rise and fall with a deadly monotony, like the heads of elephants gone melancholically mad. The rulers of this real town forbid, first and foremost, to wonder. Wonder is forbidden, just like love.

Louisa Gradgrind is raised as a woman without a sense of wonder.

Wondering means discovering the distance between oneself and a phenomenon, it means criticizing, judging.

The sense of wonder is one of the goals achieved by the construction of events, their sequence, and their contradictory relations.

Fielding, Smollett, and Dickens are Cervantes' disciples, and this is how they see themselves, but they are his disciples because of their ability to look at life, to see the new—and not because of a knack for copying old forms and relations.

[...]

Scenes of Recognition in Dickens

[...]

Apart from his great success with Pickwick, we can say that Dickens wasn't very good at creating main characters. Pickwick, childishly naïve, constantly surprised, good-natured and steadfast, and his friend Samuel [Sam Weller], with all his life experience, turned out to be the true heroes of the Pickwick story. In other novels, secondary characters, of which Dickens had hundreds, always were the authors' real successes, while the main ones were merely nominal threads sewing together the plot—or, rather, the nominal skeleton of the plot, empty, transparent, and unlikely. The main character, a virtuous hero, must achieve victory and happiness, but happiness is impossible for such a hero, as Hegel has pointed out with great clarity. The kind of wellbeing which can be granted to such a hero doesn't much resemble happiness.

We mentioned Walter Scott's irony toward happy endings, which he nevertheless constantly used: Ivanhoe needs to be happy with Lady Rowena, but he himself is boring in all his valorous glory. Ivanhoe is in love with Rebecca, a Jewess, who is much more interesting—but all Walter Scott can offer her in terms of justice is that the knight remembers her.

In his book on Dickens, Chesterton claims that Dickens' novels prove that being poor is interesting and entertaining.

No, they prove something else: that it isn't interesting to be victorious in a bourgeois world. If a bourgeois in *Hard Times* asserts that the poor want to eat turtle soup with silver spoons, then Dickens' lucky, successful characters end up supping on a broth of pink clouds with spoons of silver and gold in the epilogue.

Tom Jones loses his daring; Nicholas Nickleby is both strong and brave but he doesn't dare see Madeleine, whom he loves, because she is richer than him, and his sister Kate doesn't dare love Frank because he is the nephew of her benefactors.

Apart from the usual perspective, old paintings use the perspective of a horseman: of a man looking down. There's also the perspective of a frog, when the painters' eyes are looking up.

Cervantes' and Fielding's novels are written from the perspective of a horseman. Dickens' happy endings are written from the perspective of a frog.

The poor are interesting because their conflicts are real, because they live in a real world and overcome real challenges.

But Dickens can only help the poor with miracles, such as his scenes of recognition.

[...]

Concept Renewal

Creating the new "epic" theater, Bertolt Brecht attempts to teach the spectator to perceive and analyze complex phenomena of life in new ways, rendering him class-conscious. This leads Brecht to a kind of theater that could be called conceptual.[6] In this theater, an

[6] The word *uslovnyi*, which appears several times in the article, is difficult to translate: deriving from *uslovie* (convention, condition), it means neither "conventional" nor "conditional" in the usual sense here. Rather, it suggests that a work of art is transparently based on certain conditions or conventions, rather than attempting realism. Another possible translation is "notional."

emphasized remove is created between the spectator and the stage. The spectator is, so to speak, moved away from the theater.

Brecht introduces into his theater practice what he calls "the device of alienation,"[7] showing phenomena of life and human types not in their usual form, but from a new, unexpected perspective, forcing one to actively take position toward them. "The sense of this technique known as 'the device of alienation,'" explains Brecht, "consists in inspiring the spectator to perceive the depicted events in an analytical, critical fashion."

Brecht's principle of alienation is, of course, not the only dramatic principle there is; sometimes it not only fails to remove the spectator from the spectacle so as to provide him with a new perspective but also actually prevents the spectator from seeing the new in the usual—still, this principle is real; it is frequently encountered in realistic art, and has frequently been pointed out by very different artists.

In a literary work, everything is connected, and when we try to isolate the character from the plot, this is already a conceptual condition; the isolated element of the whole is placed in an unnatural situation.

Take Tolstoy's story "Strider."

The gelding, nicknamed for his long stride, is the work's protagonist.

He looks at human life from the stable. Life appears to him outside of normal relations. But this gelding is not a mere abstraction, he has a character of his own; he is selfless, affectionate, proud, he remembers his old master.

---

[7] Shklovsky calls *Verfremdung*, as was usual in Russian at the time, *otchuzhdeniye*, which is closest to "alienation" in English. This is a problematic translation, as *Verfremdung* is the opposite of what Marx called *Entfremdung*, alienation (cf. Brooker 193). Moreover, Shklovsky speaks of a device (a key formalist term), though Brecht calls *Verfremdung* an effect.

The thing is, of course, entirely conceptual, and its most conceptual part is the breadth of Strider's interests. Strider does not exist in isolation; his useful, selfless life is opposed to the filthy, futile life of his owner—a bankrupt descendant of the Rurik dynasty, rendered a useless sponger.

[…]

The artist's conscious act of creation consists in transferring a phenomenon from one system into another, a seemingly simplified one, testing the connections with the help of a new character (a horse).

"Strider" begins a new phase in the ideological development of Tolstoy. Tolstoy says "no" to the usual world.

[…]

When movable type is taken from its case, sometimes it turns out to be glued together with ink; the letters must be washed clean in order to be combined in new ways.

In life, this happens to words, relations, relationships: they stick together, they slide by in one piece, unseparated by new analysis, devoid of new sensations.

Art brings the word closer to the phenomena.[8]

The easiest way to do this is by taking the word out of its usual context.

[…]

Tolstoy wrote: "Therefore, life is only life if it is illuminated by

---

[8] In "Art as Device," Shklovsky wrote: "The goal of an image is *not* to bring its meaning closer to our understanding, but to create a special way of experiencing an object" (my italics). However, Shklovsky is not really reversing his position here; rather, he seems to be using a different definition of "understanding."

consciousness. So what is consciousness? What actions are illuminated by consciousness? Actions illuminated by consciousness are actions that we take deliberately, i.e. in the awareness that we could also do otherwise. Therefore, consciousness is freedom. There is no freedom without consciousness, and no consciousness is possible without freedom. (If we are subjected to violence without the slightest choice as to how we shall endure it, we will not experience this violence.) Memory is nothing but consciousness of the past—of past freedom. If I had no choice between dusting or failing to do so, I couldn't be aware of dusting; if I was not aware of dusting, I couldn't have a choice between dusting and refraining from doing so. If I had no consciousness and no freedom, I would not remember my past, would not see it as a unity. Thus, consciousness and freedom—the awareness of freedom—are the very basis of life. (All this seemed clearer when I was thinking it.)"

[…]

Over forty years ago, I introduced—for the first time, as I then believed—the concept of *ostranenie* into poetics.

The representation of the usual as strange, as seen anew, as if at a remove—this was something I regarded as a phenomenon shared by romantic, realist, and so-called modernist art.

Now I know that the concept of *ostranenie* is, firstly, wrong and, secondly, unoriginal.

Let's start with the second point.

Novalis says in "Fragments": "The art to make things pleasantly strange, to make them alien and at the same time familiar and attractive—this is what makes up Romantic poetics."[9]

---

[9] A back-translation from the Russian version cited by Shklovsky is used here to show in which form he encountered Novalis' thinking. See Robinson (80) on Novalis in Russian

Ergo, the observations, if not the term itself, were not new.

As for the wrongness of the term, it consists in this: I presented a stylistic device as the final goal of art, thus robbing art of its true function.

Moreover, the term *ostranenie* was self-contradictory at its very creation. The self-contradiction consisted in my simultaneous claim that art was "not an inscription but an ornament."

You can only subject to *ostranenie* and return to sensation things that exist in reality and that had already been experienced, as was made clear by all examples used. But art, according to my theory at the time, was not supposed to be connected to the phenomena of reality—it was supposed to be a phenomenon of language and style.

The false theory became self-contradictory even within a single article.

According to the theory which I have now restored in my mind, magnetic storms were taking place in an artistic ether of sorts, storms which wouldn't even create a radio interference nowadays, storms that wouldn't have prevented anyone from sending telegrams.

According to this theory, the world of art appears to have been created only once. After that, works of art did nothing but change their clothes and confront each other.

Now I know that art is based on the desire to enter life. Seeing and touching life, let us not claim that it doesn't exist, let us not give up the attempts to comprehend the world for the sake of delayed sensation, which is actually the final stop preceding comprehension. Let us not restrict the human mind, let us not limit our own cognition.

Let us look at mankind making its way toward comprehension, let us understand wherefore we change the world, how we comprehend

---

translation, and specifically on the translators' decision, probably political, to avoid *ostranyat'* as a translation of *befremden*.

and transform it, let us place art at the head of the human cognitive attack.

The mind can grow blunt like the tooth of a beaver gnawing wood—but it can also grow sharper with work, with comprehension.

But let us leave beavers in their nature reserves; let them live in peace and nurse their children, holding them in their wet paws. Let us return to literature.

Chekhov writes in a letter: "I'm tired; I cannot, like Levitan, turn my paintings upside down in order to get my critical eye unused to them."

New comprehension of things does indeed sometimes require the destruction of old links. When a writer wishes to destroy the coherence of a world view that had become alien to him, he creates a new way of seeing by using a character who tells about usual things in an astonished manner, as if they were absurd.

Here is how a Persian named Usbek describes Christian rites in Montesquieu's *Persian Letters* (letter 35): "Their baptism is an emblem of our ablutions; and their only error consists in ascribing to that first ablution an efficacy which enables them to omit all others."[10]

The concept of baptism is reduced to a contact with water. Baptisms, like ablutions, are regarded as a kind of bathing; from this view, it is indeed strange that a baptism is only conducted once.

This is a usual device not only for satirical authors but for all writers striving to see things outside of false traditions.

You can take a usual form of address and renew it, reinstating and intensifying the seemingly lost meaning of the attribute. Thus, let us return *ostranenie* to its functional role.[11]

---

[10] Translation by John Davidson.

[11] The word *sluzhebnoy*, rendered here as "functional," can be used in linguistic contexts (*sluzhebnye slova* means "function words"), but also to mean "work-related." Thus, the final sentence suggests that *ostranenie* has a job to do.

Letters to Nikita Shklovsky (1965–1969/2002)[1]

05.10.1965

[…]

My dear boy, do learn some languages.[2] Your granddad feels like an idiot. It might be okay to make mistakes in writing (even after school) but it's not okay to be ignorant of foreign languages. Particularly for me.

I'll tell you all when I come back.

I kiss your mommy Varya, and dear Kolya. I kiss your grandmother's hands. Best regards to [her sister] Talya.

Today, they made me tea with cold water because I didn't speak the language. They asked me three times, and then they did it.

Your granddad, Viktor Shklovsky

---

[1] Source: "Pis'ma vnuku" in *Voprosy Literatury* 4 (2002).

[2] The plea is repeated again and again; Shklovsky often said how much he regretted his lack of foreign language skills. As regards orthographical mistakes, *ostranenie* is Shklovsky's most famous one.

05.10.1966

Yalta.

Dearest Nikitochka and Kolya.[3]

I'm writing the book, and it's beginning to take shape.[4] Just write your book, Kolya, you can always strike out things later. Don't try to write The Book. It can never be written. The Book of Kings in the Bible is full of unfairness, of cruelty, but it's still a good book.

One should write a lot: 0,999 out of any 1 will disappear.

One should live as if there were no death. It will find us, but we will find the grids of crystals on which to build future moments.

Dear Nikita, my very good boy, there are good people around you. This is happiness.

It is happiness when bird cherry trees are abloom, half submerged in water, on river banks.

I have never sailed, I shall never see islands with coconut palms.

I beg you, please do the looking at life for me.

Take care, my dear, my dearest boy.

I kiss you all.

I'm writing well.

Vitya.
Viktor Shklovsky.

---

[3]Even in the context of such a diminutive-happy language as Russian, the variety of pet names Shklovsky uses for his grandson Nikita is striking, which is why they are preserved in translation.

[4]Shklovsky was working on *Tetiva* (*Bowstring*).

19.04.1968

Nikitochka, my dear friend!

You wrote me a good letter.

I keep working, rewriting, rethinking, making mistakes and learning. "A little dog remains a pup right until it dies."[5] The big dog doesn't lose his sense of smell until he dies; he keeps learning.

I think at night. By the morning, everything's forgotten. But then I begin to write and remember things again.

I thought the apple trees had finished blossoming. They thought differently. The peach trees have shed their lilac blossoms, the almond and plum trees have long lost theirs, but the apple trees by the Dorsan Mountain are still in bloom.

They must be using the old calendar.

The sea is filled not with white horses but with white elephants, small and furry, herds of them run on and on in thin lines right up to the horizon.

[…]

02.04.1969

Yalta.

Dear Nikitenok.

I've been in Yalta for two days now.

On our way to the Crimea, there was more and more snow. It was now high and solid, now stripy. Then it stuck to the windows and crawled down, crying.

---

[5] A more frequent version of the Russian saying Shklovsky is citing says "… until it grows old."

The train was filled with writers, writesses, writerlings, and whistlers.[6]

[…]

They feed us according to the "eat up what's on the table" doctrine, but they put laurel leaves in the soup, and I think of the Olympic Games and Dante.

There've been storms here; the embankment is all crumpled up. But I haven't seen it yet. I keep sleeping. I keep sleeping. The doctor had a look at my heart. It sounds better and clearer than before. That's because I nibble my medicine. So things aren't so bad. The book is still crawling through the publishing house. I remember what I wrote but I don't know what it means.

Perhaps the book is bitter and intelligent. In any case, nobody ever cooked such a soup before.

I love you very much. More than anyone. More than anyone.

Don't be afraid of exams and people. They pass like a common cold, not like a case of sinusitis. Though sinusitis passes, too.

The ravens have grown bigger during my one-year absence. They have a life of their own. They live for a hundred years because they don't read newspapers and don't watch the news. They grow. I've known them for 15 years, they keep growing. I'd love to write, to finish a book, to grow. To understand what it is that I've been doing all my life.

[…]

---

[6] Apart from neologisms to denote bad writers (and perhaps also typists), Shklovsky uses what appears to be a variation on the common slang word for "informant."

20.07.1969

[…]

I was creating a science. Between 1914 and 1926, it was success all the way. Nothing but victories. I grew spoilt; I forgot all about ordinary work, immediately became the chairman of the OPOYAZ, a leader. The fact that I didn't speak any foreign language cut me off from the world. Then I went off into literature and cinema; again, I was lucky, and again, I misused my easy success. I misused my luck. I held my opponents in contempt and usually didn't even read them. Censorship and the need to make money played a role here, too, albeit a secondary one. At the end, I have lived a squandered, very difficult and contradictory life. I burned a great talent in a stove. Sometimes, you have to stoke a stove with furniture, after all. Eisenstein claims that the cement for buildings in Middle Asia was sometimes mixed with blood. I missed the time to study philosophy. I made my way without a map. Then, disappointment came. Silence. And that which I've called "potboiler work" in one of my later books. International recognition came 25 or even 35 years late. Today, I'm recognized. Today, my former friend Roman Jakobson claims that he—and not I—created what was called "the formal method" and what gave birth to structuralism. This is a late and unnecessary argument; people write about it a lot. My friend, young Nikita Shklovsky-Kordi. My dearest person on Earth. You need to study widely. You've scooped up some poetry. You've learned to love music. I, an old man, can tell you that you have enough time to learn philosophy. I think it a great pity that I failed to read Hegel and Marx when I was young, that I only read Lenin 20 years ago. And this despite being very widely educated. The sea is wide. Let us swim together. And here comes more advice from an old man. Keep in mind, I'm about 76,7 years old. Don't miss your first love. Don't be greedy about it. Don't be afraid of life.

The air will hold you if your wings put it in motion.

[…]

Bowstring. On the Dissimilarity of the Similar (1970)[1]

[...]

Mayakovsky's and Khlebnikov's poetry—and the visual arts of the time—wanted to see the world in a new way, and changed the very sound of poetry to do so.

But in our arguments we saw that we were not alone, that the poets and prose writers of the past also wanted to speak in new ways because they had their own ways of seeing.

In 1916, the theory of *ostranenie* appeared. In it, I was trying to generalize the way of experiencing and showing phenomena. Everything in it was connected to time, to pain and inspiration, to astonishment about the world. But at the same time I wrote: "A literary work is pure form; it is not a thing, not a material, but the relation of materials. Like any other relation, this one is zero-dimensional. The scale of the work, the arithmetic value of the

---

[1] The book's title and concept is based on Heraclitus, Fragment 51: "Men do not know how what is at variance agrees with itself. It is an attunement of opposite tension, like that of the bow and the lyre. People do not understand how that which is at variance with itself agrees with itself" (translation by John Burnet). Source: *Tetiva. O neskhodstve skhodnogo.* Moscow: Sovetskiy Pisatel', 1970.

numerator and denominator, does not matter; what matters is their relation. Jocular, tragic, world-wide and room-wide works; a world juxtaposed to a world, a cat juxtaposed to a stone—they are equal."[2]

There is a tiny fruit fly called drosophila.

The wonderful thing about it is that it's very short-lived.

When crossbreeding these tiny beings, the results can be studied very exactly and quickly.

There has been a time in our country when people were told: "You spend time breeding drosophilae, but they produce neither meat nor milk."

But breeding drosophilae is a way to find out the laws of genetics. As Vladimir Mayakovsky put it, "life appears in a new dissection, and tiny things make you understand great ones."

If, in art, we juxtapose a cat to a cat or a flower to flower, the artistic form is created not only by the very moment of this intersection;[3] these are the detonators of great explosions, entries into cognition, intelligencers of the new.

Rejecting emotion or ideology in art, we also reject the study of form, the very goal of this study and the way toward experiencing, sensing the world. We separate form and content. This provocative formula is, in fact, a formula of capitulation; it cuts up the sphere of art, destroying the unity of experience.

Drosophilae are sent to space so that we can understand how space influences a living organism, and not in order to provide them with a fun trip.

---

[2] Shklovsky suggests that the passage is immediately connected to "Art as Device", but he is actually quoting a later article, "Literature Beyound "Plot".

[3] The Russian *skreshchivanie* means both "interbreeding" and "intersecting"; thus, the passage is referring back to the "useless" drosophilae.

You can send a cat to the moon, or some drosophilae, but all their journeys have a goal.

Art learns by creating new models and by using old ones in new ways. Art progresses by changing. It changes its method, but the past does not disappear. Art is moving, reusing its old dictionary, rethinking its old structures—and it also, in a way, stays immobile. It stays immobile and at the same time it changes rapidly, not for the sake of change, but in order to make things experienced in their difference via their movement, their transposition.

[...]

Juxtaposition creates energy which remains in every artistic work and in every splinter of an artistic work; if it remains a work of art, it creates a new unity.

A cane, a stick is a unity. It is "one stick." A sinew, a string is a unity. A stick bent by a string is a bow.

It is a new unity.

This unity is the original model of an artistic work.

This thought can be elucidated by an excerpt from [Plato's] dialogue "Phaedo": "first the lyre, and the strings, and the sounds exist in a state of discord, and then harmony is made last of all, and perishes first."[4]

The harmony of a bow is a bent stick, a stick bent by the bowstring; the harmony of a bow is unity and opposition.

This is kinetic energy ready to become dynamic.

[...]

Ostranenie is often constructed like a riddle: it transposes the characteristics of an object. But the main function of *ostranenie* in Tolstoy is [the awaking of] conscience.[5]

---

[4]Translation by Benjamin Jowett. The Russian version Shklovsky uses is very close.

[5]"Consciousness" might seem like a better choice of word here; it is worth pointing out

More on that further on.

Tolstoy often illuminates things as if they were seen for the first time by listing their qualities instead of calling things by their names. In one description, for instance, he does not say "birch" but "a big curly-headed tree with a luminously white trunk and branches."

This is a birch, it can only be a birch, but it is described by a person who is wondering at this unusual tree and does not seem to know its name.

In February 1857, Tolstoy writes in his diary: "Anderson's fairy tale about the clothes. The goal of literature is to make people understand things so that they believe the child."

He is talking about "The Emperor's New Clothes." The world must be shown outside of the usual associations: the grandeur of the ceremony should not conceal the fact that it is headed by a naked man.

Tolstoy goes on in early March; the diary entries immediately follow each other:

"The pride and the disdain for others of a man who holds an ignoble monarchic position is akin to the pride and independence of a whore."

This entry is a key to understanding Tolstoy's *Resurrection*. The point is not that Nekhlyudov seduced a girl and thus made her a prostitute.

The point is that so-called respectable people surrounding Katyusha are for Tolstoy akin to a proud prostitute; they are compared to her and thus changed in our perception.

[...]

---

that this is not a translation mistake. Shklovsky uses the word *sovest'* (conscience), yet what immediately follows deals not with morals (the point stressed in his later writing) but about refreshing experience (the point of his early essays).

In my youth, I denied the notion of content in art, believing that art was pure form.

My comrades at the Moscow linguistic circle headed by Roman Jakobson said that literature was a linguistic phenomenon; they repeated the same thing in Prague and are still repeating it in detail in an article on Pushkin's poetry.

I can cite Einstein's *Autobiographical Notes* once again here: "Our thinking mostly proceeds leaving out symbols (words) and, moreover, unconsciously."

We asserted that language was one of many structures, and that art used other structures, too, different signal systems with different interrelations.

At the time when I claimed that art was free of content and beyond emotion, I myself was writing books that were bleeding—*A Sentimental Journey* and *Zoo*. *Zoo* has the subtitle "Letters not about Love" because it was a book about love.

In it, love is expressed in many different indirect ways, illuminating everything. The dialogue between a man and a woman illuminates time.

This dialogue is rather rich in content, and the people mentioned are not only real but alive today.

The tile which I knocked out of a stove in a quarrel is real, though it is not mentioned in the book.

Art reflects people, but the way of perception is changed like the way a beam of light is refracted in a prism; people are refracted by the optics of art, refracted in order to become newly visible—to become experienceable.

Creating a work of art means, first of all, creating a model of the world; then this model is studied, using artistic methods, within the work of art. To do this, writers not only use their own experience; they connect to the totality of human experience. This human experience helps us to perceive phenomena clearer and in more detail.

The strange ability of art not to grow old, the fact that we can today read Homer, the Bible, and the Gilgamesh epic, which was written many thousands of years ago, is based on the fact that artistic comparisons reveal the essence of things. An author enters the world as a young person, or as a baby, but he begins to study the world using the experience of mankind, he compares and grows wiser; he becomes astonished.

His astonishment changes human experience. Chinese poets, too, use the wonder of comparison to think.[6]

Epochs collide in art. They both foresee themselves and experience/outlast themselves in art.[7] What we call genre is really the unity of collision.

I believe that every work of art stands in opposition to something else because every work of art is a link in a process of self-contradiction.

Don Quixote stands in opposition to the chivalric romance. Sterne's novel stands in opposition to the adventure novel. Diderot's *Jacques the Fatalist and his Master* opposes, step by step, the prerevolutionary novel.

Here, the structure of the old novel is destroyed from the very start. There isn't even a hint of an introduction; the protagonists have no names. The text begins as follows: "How did they meet?—By chance, like all people.—What were their names?—That's none of your business.—Where did they come from?—From a neighboring village."

This text is grounded in the repudiation of old structures.

---

[6] In *Bowstring*, Shklovsky pays some attention to Japanese and Chinese poetry.

[7] The original *perezhivayut* can mean both "experience" and "outlast"; both meanings are relevant in context.

All coincidences and conditions which formed the foundation of the old novel are rejected; the text says that the people you meet in it are not the people you expect, not the people you know from previous adventures.

Diderot's novel is an antinovel. Chernyshevsky's novel [*What Is to Be Done?*], constantly arguing with the reader, carries in it Diderot's experience and stands in opposition to the usual novel. It has the reality of the future. Today, it is antireal; this is why it contains dreams.

Eisenstein's, Pudovkin's, Dovzhenko's films with their slow action and changed laws of editing were experienced as the defiance of old structure.

Each man, when he grows old, experiences a moment when he rejects fashion, when he sees new fashions as a mistake and won't give up his old narrow trousers and his old-fashioned hat.

I have dealt with art history enough to understand this.

New skirts are too short for me.

Art is a way to experience and understand the world. To this end, it constructs its contradictions. This is what I failed to understand; this was my mistake. This contradiction lay in the very concept but I couldn't see it back then.

On the one hand, I claimed that art was outside emotion, that it was merely the collision of elements, that it was geometrical.

At the same time, I talked of *ostranenie*, i.e. the renewal of experience. I would have to ask myself, then: what is it that you're going to enstrange if art does not express reality? The experience of what did Sterne and Tolstoy want to return?

The theory of *ostranenie*, which was taken up by many, including Brecht, speaks of art as a form of cognition, a method of exploration.

Art changes, genres collide in order to preserve the experience of the world, in order for information—instead of the sensation of traditional form—to keep coming from the world.

[...]

Energy of Delusion. A Book on Plot (1981)[1]

[…]

The book I am writing as an old man is called *The Energy of Delusion*.

These are not my words but Tolstoy's.

He hoped fervently that delusions would never disappear. They are the tracks left by the search for truth. They are mankind looking for the meaning of life.

We work on drafts written by other people. Unfortunately, I'm unfamiliar with the elements[2] of this art, and I am too old to learn. Time puts on its iron shackles.

But I want to understand the history of Russian literature as a history of movement, as the movement of consciousness—as defiance. Let us keep one other thing in mind.

There were many circles, steps, levels in Dante's *Inferno.* People lived here, imprisoned for life, punished differently for different sins.

But "circles of hell" are not only an ingenious plan of a literary work; they are also traces of different perceptions of time in the great city of Florence.

---

[1] Source: "Energiya zabluzhdeniya. Kniga o syuzhete." *Izbrannoye v dvukh tomakh*. Moscow: Khudozhestvennaya Literatura, 1983.

[2] Shklovsky uses the word *nachala*, which usually means "beginnings," but it is also used in textbooks titles; Euclid's *Elements* is *Nachala* in Russian.

There, people who had inherited different past experiences go on arguing beyond their deaths.

[...]

My book is called *Energy of Delusion.*

These are Tolstoy's words from a letter written to N. Strakhov on April 8, 1878.

Here are these words: "Everything seems ready for me to begin writing, to fulfil my earthly duty, but I'm missing the push of belief in myself, in the importance of the work; I'm missing the energy of delusion ..."

[...]

The energy of delusion—the energy of free search—never left Tolstoy.

He begins writing about Kutuzov with *War and Peace* in mind.

The character scheme he creates is wrong, though he includes real facts, real character traits.

But the energy of delusion, the energy of trying, the energy of exploration makes him describe Kutuzov anew and this time truly. This takes years.

He wants to find out the essence of Alexander I, but the energy of delusion, the energy of search deletes the solemn image of Alexander as the great historical force of good—and the hero disappears, the figure retreats into the remotest corners of the novel.

Tolstoy wanted to make Andrey Bolkonsky the center of the novel, an aristocrat understanding everything, making sense of everything that happens. This didn't work out.

What worked instead was another person—Tushin.

Andrey Bolkonsky wants to see Tushin ironically, he talks to him "as if he was Chinese," as if he belonged to another tribe, alien and worthy of no interest.

But he does become interested.

And prejudice collides with truth in this novel, seemingly by chance.

At first, when planning the novel, Tolstoy was interested in Anatoly Kuragin, wanting to show him as a heroic folk figure. But at the end he emerges as someone who enjoys life—who enjoys life at other people's costs, a calm liar.

The energy of delusion is the search for truth in the novel.

In the first drafts, Anna Karenina is a homely, fat woman, not at all graceful, though charming.

She is outside of intellect.

She has a plump, reasonable, good-natured husband; he is much older than she. She falls in love with a young man, younger than her. She is a woman guilty before her husband. She is the kind of woman whom Dumas fils would have called a female of Cain's seed. This is a French solution. Dumas' solution, in any case.

The novel's epigraph—"Vengeance is mine, I will repay"—sounds like an amnesty.

You don't need to kill her; her conscience will.

But truth is stronger than prejudice.

By and by, Anna Karenina becomes fascinating. And Lev Tolstoy writes to his friend Alexandrina Tolstaya—a strange woman with whom he exchanges Rousseau-style letters—that he had adopted Anna as a daughter, that she had become his own.

Following several attempts and drafts, Karenin is rehabilitated: the old husband turns out to be human, not a machine. But he also turns out to be a weak delusion, a man whose kindness and whose suffering were not needed.

Literary history is the history of character search. We could even say that it is a collected history of delusions.

There is no contradiction in the fact that a genius is not afraid to get lost—talent will find a way out; more than that, we can say that talent demands delusions, for it demands food, tension, material, it demands a labyrinth of connections in which to find its way.

[…]

All characters in *Anna Karenina* have inner worlds of their own, internal monologues of their own.

The most tragic monologue is Anna Karenina's.

For she blames everyone, even herself.

Alexey Karenin's internal monologues are different.

He is trying to acquit himself as if he was an institution.

He is trying to excuse himself with formal response letters.

Only Anna's lethal illness takes off his mask: he speaks differently, he is imagined differently.

He is a man who could have been good, but he is imprisoned in his own bureaucratic office.

Tolstoy's greatness, which denies easy description, is that he warms this man in his own hands, with his own breath—there, beyond the walls of his shell.

In the whole of *Anna Karenina*, the author himself does not speak.

This is true if we discount Levin's reflections, if we believe that Levin is not identical to Lev Tolstoy, if we understand how he is characterized by Tolstoy—he has his farm, his cares, his troubles.[3]

Anna Karenina is another person.

She thinks in an "internal monologue."

This becomes particularly apparent in the final scenes, when this woman quarrels with her beloved, with the man for whom she had remade her life.

---

[3] The idea that Levin is a transparent stand-in for the auctorial voice is commonplace in Russian literary criticism; his name is only one among many reasons for it.

She sees the world, but she sees it at a remove, as if separated from yesterday and from today.

She sees herself from without.

The way passing housemaids appraise her lace. The way people show themselves to her, trying to appear aristocratic, to speak good French. All things, even the billboards, which are no help in thinking, strike her with their sudden senselessness.[4] The drunks, the ice cream vendor, the man bringing a note from Vronsky—they are all reconsidered in her internal monologue.

Tolstoy turns his thinking over to other people. It is as if it was him dying with fever. It is him who pities and almost loves the old Karenin, but Karenin thinks for himself, and so does Vronsky.

I am trying to make a point.

The novel *Anna Karenina* is built around internal monologues, around people failing to understand each other.

This might sound strange, but rereading Tolstoy surprises me more often than reading Dostoyevsky [for the first time]. In Dostoyevsky's books, all characters think alike, as if they had only ever read a single author—Dostoyevsky.

[4] In the original (and also in other editions), "*veshchi, dazhe vyveski kotorykh ne pomogayut myslit*": "things whose very billboards are no help." This might be a metaphor but is more probably a typo; with one letter changed, the passage would mean what it does in the present translation. Shklovsky is referring to the following passage in *Anna Karenina*: "Without replying how she would live without him, she began reading the billboard. 'Office and depot. Dentist. Yes, I'll tell Dolly everything.'" Without this context, the phrase must be puzzling, which is perhaps why in Avagyan's translation of *The Bowstring*, the relevant phrase is rendered as "even the signboards are repulsive."

Part Five

On the Theory of Prose (1983)

Part Five: Introduction

Like *Hamburg Score*, Shklovsky's *On the Theory of Prose* (*O teorii prozy*) is actually two different books. One was published in 1925 (followed by a reprint in 1929), the other one appeared in 1983. This choice of title is typical of the older Shklovsky's relationship to his early writing. On the one hand, the mature publication appears to negate the very existence of the formalist volume by taking its place; on the other, the new book calls attention to the old one. Some early texts are included in the 1983 collection; others are discussed, debated, and promoted. Both the references to the 1925 volume and the usurpation/repetition of its title may reflect either genuine reconsideration on Shklovsky's part, or an attempt to reembrace formalism while pretending to conform to Soviet norms (cf. Sheldon, "Ostensible Surrender")—or, quite probably, a mixture of both.

The 1925 book was published in Benjamin Sher's translation in 1990 (Shklovsky, *Theory of Prose*); the 1983 one never appeared in English. It is a 384-page collection that includes chapters on topics as diverse as Shakespeare, cinema, and the Chinese novella. The present selection can accommodate but a very small part of this panoply, concentrating on Shklovsky's reconsideration of formalism and on the concept which has made his name, *ostranenie*.

These are essays rather than articles, perhaps even something of a more experimental and mixed genre. Sweeping statements such as "everyone knows how an uranium bomb works" and aphorisms along the lines of "all art is delayed enjoyment"—vintage Shklovsky—are interspersed here with passages that are immensely personal and poignant: "I've been crying in the bathroom today. It hurts to be old."

The first essay to be excerpted here is called "The First Unsuccessful Blueprint of a Whale." The title condenses three lines from "Mayakovsky in Heaven," a poem by Mayakovsky that describes "an ancient blueprint/—no one knows whose—/the first unsuccessful project of a whale" lying around among other discarded attempts at Creation. Apart from many repetitions and long quotations, *On the Theory of Prose* includes very detailed summaries of fairy tales and other examples. Shklovsky seems to be enjoying the retelling of his favorite texts. The present selection shuns such passages, though they have their charm: the space of the book is finite, and Shklovsky's reflections are of greater interest than his summaries. Still, one out of many dozens of such summaries is included here, both because it is very typical of the book and because it deals with Chekhov's "The Darling," a short story which mattered greatly to Shklovsky. He identified himself with its protagonist, a woman who can only exist in relation to another person. Later in *On the Theory of Prose*, Shklovsky writes: "When I talk about the Darling, I know that I'm talking about myself." And, elsewhere in the same book, when talking of *Don Quixote*: "Of course, I'm a Sancho Panza. I've been following this knight for sixty years."

Shklovsky is Sancho to several writers: Cervantes, Tolstoy, Sterne. His summaries, growing longer and longer, look as if Shklovsky was trying to rewrite the books he is talking about, like Borges' Pierre Menard. He keeps returning to these authors, just as he keeps returning to his formalist work, explaining the genesis of the term *ostranenie* and talking about the relationship of the formal method and structuralism.

This last topic is at the heart of the next essay, "The Rhyme of Poetry. The Rhyme of Prose. Structuralism through the Looking Glass." It is a personal one: Roman Jakobson was one of his closest friends, and falling out with him was a heavy blow to Shklovsky. Discussing the differences between formalism and structuralism, Shklovsky refers to Dante and the Bible, and deliberates on the tense unity of a bow or a lyre (without explicitly mentioning his book on this topic, *Bowstring*). "Yet Another Foreword" (yes, this is indeed the title of an essay appearing in the middle of a book) opens thus: "There was a time when I followed Potebnya so fixedly that I even began to argue with him." This is a rather surprising admission almost seventy years after the publication of "Art as Device," in which the greatest compliment to Potebnya was that his theory was "least self-contradictory when discussing the fable."

"Sterne" features some wonderful examples of Shklovsky's imagery, reminiscent of his early novel *Zoo*, such as "stressing every 'o,' as if his words had wheels." As the title makes clear, it deals with one of the most important writers in Shklovsky's life and work; the other two, Tolstoy and Cervantes, make their appearance in the essay entitled "*Ostranenie.*" To a large part, "*Ostranenie*" is a polemic against Bakhtin, or rather, an attempt to stake territory: Bakhtin's carnivalization, claims Shklovsky, is actually his *ostranenie*. He goes on to pronounce that "the world of *ostranenie* is the world of the revolution"—incongruous or ingenious, this is certainly a striking statement. And perhaps not as flattering to the Soviet authorities as might be assumed: several lines earlier, Shklovsky states that "the world of poetry includes the world of *ostranenie.*" If so, revolution is only a poetic device.

Preface[1]

[…]

We don't know the fate of words among which we live.

In the same way, we don't know nature, which changes the world around us, counts out the seasons, tries us with the cold and the boredom of winter, and returns as words, words about which or in which I want to think. Not too long ago, I was astonished by a Chinese story. A man saw a butterfly in his dream; he woke up wondering whether it was him dreaming of a butterfly or perhaps a butterfly dreaming of him.

He was only a part of this unknown land's life; the winged one flew away.

What, then, are words?

Words are different; they depend on who is saying them.

They are brought in, as if uprooted, carrying a piece of the forest of thought in which they live and collide.

[…]

The most important thing about the fate of the word is that it lives in sentences. And in repetitions.

And brand-new rhymes rush lightly out to meet
the daring thoughts that surge, collide, collect;

---

[1] Source (for each chapter in this section): *O teorii prozy*. Moscow: Sovetskiy Pisatel', 1983.

your hand demands a quill, the quill a sheet,
a minute—and the verse will flow unchecked.

This is a building plan for the ship of poetry.[2]

The word liberates the soul from narrowness.

The poem speaks of physical movement that has been begun and not suppressed. Why are rhymes placed this way here, stressed; why are they placed like flags, like landmarks?

This is not because rhyming words sound similar but because a rhyme is a repetition, a return to a word already said; the rhyme expresses something like surprise at the fact that a word can sound so similar and yet have an entirely different meaning.

This search for meanings (through combinations of sounds), for the collision of meanings, is held up in poetry through rhymes, through the construction of strophes.

What about prose, then?

What is decelerated in prose?

What do Dostoyevsky and Tolstoy repeat in their unrhymed prose lines, made from simple words that appear to exist in simple relations?

They repeat circumstances. Prose returns to the origins of events. It reconstructs history.

What follows is a story which looks at these circumstances in detail, looks at them in their development. These repetitions (just like in poetry) create the fruitful slowness, the deep plowing of prose.

This is the kind of repetition used by prosaic episodes. It's like a man tracing back the steps of his life. Repetition is what the so-called plot shares with the so-called rhymes.

---

[2] The next lines in Pushkin's poem refer to a motionless ship waiting to sail away. Shklovsky cites this quatrain three times in the 1983 *On the Theory of Prose*. The translation here is by Alexandra Berlina; the excellent translations by Antony Wood and Peter France don't use rhyme the way Pushkin does—and for Shklovsky, the rhymes are the point here.

[…]

The thoughts, the hopes of mankind don't follow beaten tracks; they move along the bridges connecting islands of poetry.

At night, the iron arcs of bridges are raised or turned to let the ships into the sea.

Hamlet's father is killed. Hamlet must take revenge. But his father's ghost says that he must not take revenge the way Orestes did—he must spare his mother.

Hamlet tests his suspicion that his uncle was guilty of killing his father and usurping the crown. He uses drama to try his uncle. He thinks of Hecuba.

The actor, incidentally invited into the castle, speaks of Hecuba from his accidental stage. And these words resound with new pain in the suffocating dust of petty thoughts and petty detail.[3]

Art uses its living archive, which is many thousand years old and all-understanding.

Art renews the memory of mankind.

[…]

[3] In Russian, "pain" is followed by *o* (about), not *v* (in); this is probably a typo, but perhaps not—Shklovsky might be, unidiomatically, speaking of the pain *of* petty thoughts.

Words Free the Soul from Narrowness: About the OPOYAZ

[…]

Doctor Kulbin, my first friend and a student of Pavlov's, told me: "Everyone can walk a tightrope, thanks to the arrangement of the ear labyrinths, but most people don't know they can."

Kulbin helped me, he gave me money, he fed me. He told me: don't eat at cafeterias; onions are good for you; fifty kopeks a day are enough to live on.

A revolution is a time when everyone can walk a tightrope. When we forget that we can't.

Our school came into existence before the revolution, but the thunderstorm was already in the air.

It was a time when a big, stooping man with white hair and a soft voice, Velimir Khlebnikov, an ornithologist by education—a specialist in birds—called himself "The Chairman of the Globe." He asked nothing in return.

Another famous man, an acquaintance of mine, Tsiolkovsky, said that there would be only two kinds of government in future: a male and a female one. Geniuses, though, should live on their own, asking the government (either one, presumably) for nothing.

Tsiolkovsky was not unknown—he was known and disdained. People failed to notice and mention him on purpose. They laughed at him.[1]

Tsiolkovsky lived from a cabbage field that he worked himself. In all of Kaluga, a quiet city, he had only one friend—the apothecary, also a quiet man.

They told me to go and see Tsiolkovsky.

I didn't want to see him without bringing him money.

He was owed money; there was some contract.

This was, I believe, in 1928. I resolutely said that I wouldn't go to Kaluga without money.

After long negotiations, they gave me some documents, a contract and five thousand rubles. At that time, for Tsiolkovsky, it was a fantastic sum.

I arrived.

The wallpaper—cheap light-blue wallpaper—was glued directly onto the beams of his hut-like house, his izba.

In the house and in all of Kaluga, everyone was chopping cabbage.

The cabbage patches were so thick that one could hardly walk through them.

Tsiolkovsky said quietly:

—You have a high brow. You probably talk to angels.

—No, I don't.

Tsiolkovsky answered:

—I do, every day.

Perhaps I seemed like a savior angel to him. His son had shot himself from hunger.

---

[1] Tsiolkovsky worked as a high school math teacher; only in the 1920s, when he was in his sixties, were his contributions to rocket science and astronautic theory acknowledged. Part of the reason he was shunned were his exotic beliefs such as panpsychism and the conviction that humans would colonize the Milky Way.

[…]

We, the people of that time—you too, perhaps—were more amazing than happy.

As a young man, Evgeny Dmitriyevich Polivanov read *The Brothers Karamazov* and bet his school friends that he would lay his hand under a passing train and not jerk it away. The train cut off his left hand.

This brought him to reason, and he began studying. First, he studied Korean, then Chinese, then the Filipino languages; he knew all Turkic languages and used his remaining hand to state in questionnaires that he was "entirely ignorant of the Botocudo language." Now, the Botocudos are a South American people who pierce their lower lips with wooden sticks. "Should knowledge of the Botocudo language be required, I request three months advance notice," he went on in the questionnaire. Students still use this formula of his today, varying the name of the language.

This man, who went on to have a very difficult biography, and also another friend of mine, Lev Petrovich Yakubinsky, a student of the linguist Jan Baudouin de Courtenay—both of them noticed the same thing.

They noticed that prosaic speech exhibited the phenomenon of dissimilation: when identical consonants come together, then one of them changes to simplify speech.

Poetic language, on the other hand, condenses sounds, like a tongue twister: "Peter Piper picked a peck of pickled peppers" and so on.

This it to say, poetic language is impeded.

At the same time, Polivanov noticed that Japanese poetic language preserves sounds long lost in everyday Japanese.

Everyone knows how a uranium bomb works. There is a certain

quantity of uranium which can remain unchanged, but if two quantities come together, there is an explosion.

At the time, I was writing about *zaum'*—transrational language, about the languages of religious cults; I was a friend of Khlebnikov, Mayakovsky, Kruchenykh, Malevich, Tatlin, other people. They are no more.

Then we chanced upon the idea that poetic language in general differs from prosaic language, that it is a special sphere in which even the lip movements matter, like the world of dance, in which muscle movements give joy, or like visual art, in which seeing gives joy—and that all art is delayed gratification. As Ovid puts it in *Art of Love*: when you love, do not hasten your pleasure.

It was a very hungry time, the time of the revolution. We stoked our makeshift iron stoves with books. We read books for the final time, tearing them up page by page. We stoked the stoves with the torn-away pages.

We wrote books, too. Our own books.

They say about the people of my generation (who are often unhappy people) that we are the victims of the revolution. This is untrue.

We are the makers of the revolution, the children of the revolution.

Khlebnikov, and Mayakovsky, and Tatlin, and Malevich.

Malevich was a Bolshevik from the very first years of the revolution; he took part in the Moscow revolt; only three OPOYAZ members or so weren't Bolsheviks.[2]

What mistakes did we make? (Let's leave others alone.)

I said that art was beyond emotion, that it did not contain love, that it was pure form. This was untrue. There is a phrase, I don't remember who said it: "Revolutionaries refute, Christians renounce."

---

[2] One of these three was Shklovsky. He does not mention his role in anti-Bolshevik uprising here, about which he is so frank in *A Sentimental Journey*.

One's past is not to be renounced but to be refuted and transformed.

So then, we, and I in particular, noticed that these phenomena which happen in language—these complications and impediments, these sound patterns, concentrations, these rhymes, whose function is not only to repeat the sounds of a preceding line but also to recall the preceding idea, these artistic shifts—were not only a phonetic phenomenon but the essence of poetry and the essence of art.

It was then that I created the term *ostranenie*, and—I can admit today that I made grammatical mistakes back then—I wrote it with one "n." I should have used two, as in *strannyi* (strange).

And off it went with one "n," roaming the world like a dog with an ear cut off.[3]

Tolstoy did not believe in common sense, in the life that was around him; he described life not the way it was but the way it should be.

Ostrovsky said that one should write poetry using not only the language in which people speak, but also the language in which people dream.

Chekhov mentioned this shift, I can't remember where, but I have the quotation written down.

Chekhov said: "I'm tired, I've written a lot, and I'm beginning to forget to turn my stories upside down the way Levitan does with his pictures in order to liberate them from meaning and to see only how the spots of color relate to each other."[4]

---

[3]The image of the dog might be part of a pun connecting it to Bezukhov, who appears a few paragraphs later and whose last name translates as "Earless" (argues Naiman 346); Shklovsky's mistake in describing his mistake (it is actually orthographic, not grammatical) might be intentional.

[4]Shklovsky may have had the quotation written down, but this is a summary of his own. The exact quotation appears, for instance, in *Tales about Prose* ("Concept Renewal", cited in the present reader).

All my life I have been studying Tolstoy, and Tolstoy keeps changing for me; it's as if he was growing younger. He is always ahead of me.

Tolstoy was so young that he envied Chekhov, believing that Chekhov anticipated the new realism. When Chekhov died, Tolstoy said that he saw him in a dream, and in that dream Chekhov called Tolstoy's preoccupation—his preaching—the occupation of a fly. And I woke up to argue with him, said Tolstoy.

You need to doubt yourself till the very end, and you need to be inspired.

Mayakovsky said: "If you're feeling inspiration and, at that very moment, get run over by a tram, consider yourself lucky."

You need to try and surpass yourself, to step over your yesterday.

Tolstoy describes the battle of Borodino not from the perspective of an army commander but from that of Pierre Bezukhov, who seems to understand nothing of military affairs; he describes a war council from the perspective of a little girl lying on the stove ledge, looking down on the generals as if they were arguing peasants and sympathizing with Kutuzov.

Tolstoy doesn't seem to trust specialists.

Not so long ago, on the Black Drin river, I was listening to a Rumanian poetess who was reading—almost dancing—mournful poems, often using the word "hallelujah."

And I was wondering: had this not been done fifty years ago? This doesn't mean that this shouldn't be done anymore. It means that doing this is not enough.

Non-inclusion of meaning into art is cowardice.

The spots of color must be decomposed and then recomposed—not as a mirror image.

Once upon a time I wrote that art was beyond pity.

I was passionate, but wrong.

Art is the herald of pity and cruelty, the judge who reconsiders the laws according to which mankind lives.

I was restricting the sphere of art, repeating the mistakes of old aestheticists.

They believed that rhymes, meters, and stylistic devices were the matter of art, while the rest—Job's rage, the love between a woman and a man in "The Song of Songs," Childe Harold's pilgrimage, Pushkin's jealousy, Dostoyevsky's arguments—all this was but the mantle worn by art.[5]

This is wrong.

Art renews religions, testing feelings in its own court of law, art passes judgement.

We worked tremendously quickly, tremendously easily, and we had agreed that everything said within our team was unsigned—our common work. As Mayakovsky put it, let's add the laurel leaves of our wreaths to our shared soup.

Thus, a theory of prose was created by and by, in a hurry; but we did notice the deceleration in art, we did notice the artificial character of time, the way time in a literary text or drama differed from the time in the street, on the city clocks.

We noticed the meanings of the knots tied and untied by plots—entanglements, denouements—and in 1916, we began publishing the *Poetika* book series.

One article of mine written back then—"Art as Device"—is still in print, unchanged.

Not because it is impeccable and correct but because time writes with us the way we write with a pencil.

Many of the things we said back then are common knowledge today.

---

[5] This mixture of writers and characters chimes in with the fact that the crucial character of Shklovsky's own fiction was Viktor Shklovsky.

Often, when you say something new, first they tell you that you're lying—and then they tell you they've known what you said forever. The people you are talking to will claim to have always known all about it.[6]

The number of articles I have written is comparable only to the number of articles railing at me.

Roman Jakobson and I were in love with the same woman, but, as fate would have it, it was I who wrote a book about her.

This book tells about a woman who doesn't hear me, but I'm all around her name like the surf, like an unfading garland.[7]

[...]

What am I guilty of? First of all, I know a considerable deal, but at the same time I know little. I wasn't familiar with philosophy. And so I believed that I was discovering everything for the first time.

For this, I was beaten terribly, because those who beat me didn't even know as much as I did.

But they had negative intuition. I've been given this expression as a gift.

They had instinct. People who live outside of truth like to throw stones at it.

The stones were rather weighty.

We were going through whistling and guffaws.

When people pass an exam, they usually say something like "I passed structural resistance" in the same tone of voice in which they say "I passed the salt."[8]

---

[6] "To truth only a brief celebration of victory is allowed between the two long periods during which it is condemned as paradoxical, or disparaged as trivial", writes Schopenhauer (cited here in John Payne's translation), and proceeds: "The former fate is also wont to befall its author". Shklovsky's long life enabled him to experience both fates.

[7] Elsa Triolet, the addressee of *Zoo*.

[8] The original pun is on *sdal*, which can mean "passed" (an exam) and "checked in" (a coat).

My advice is: don't pass over what you have learned.

When you defend your thesis, don't defend it—attack. Else, you'll lose the meaning.

This is because we are stronger, because a man who is free from fear, who can see himself, who can feel himself, who knows that he must be understood—he is almighty.

I was crying terribly when writing the final pages of Tolstoy's flight [in his biography]: he was so famous that he had nowhere to go.

He could not change the world, and neither could he find a quiet place in the world to be good on his own, to be good alone.

[…]

At night, while we were walking the embankments of Petersburg, which wasn't yet called Leningrad, Blok told me that this was the first time that he heard somebody saying the truth about poetry; he also added, though, that he wasn't sure if poets should know the truth about themselves.

Poetry is complex, mobile, its different layers are so contradictory; these contradictions are poetry itself.

We do need to analyze poetry. But we need to analyze it like poets, without losing the breath of poetry.

What is the relationship between formalism and structuralism?

We argue; these are two conflicting schools. Tynyanov is dead, so is Eikhenbaum, Kazansky is dead, Polivanov is dead, Yakubinsky is dead.

To my joy, I see new poets, new arguments. If you ask me about my attitude toward art, I'll say this: I feel greedy about it, the way one feels about youth.

I need to tell a sad story now. I had a friend, Roman Jakobson. Then we quarreled. We had been friends for forty years.

I believe that quarrels are unavoidable.

We are formalists—this name is incidental. I, Viktor, could have been called Vladimir, or Nikolai.

We did deal with form, though. And we happened to say many unnecessary things about form. Once, I said that art was a sum of its devices, but if this was so—why, of all things, addition? Why not multiplication, or division, or simply interrelation? It was just something said in a hurry, for an article.

The structuralists tease a text apart, into layers, then they find solutions for the layers one by one. Art is more complex than that. Still, the structuralists, and our Tartu school in particular, have done a great deal.

[…]

We might count words and letters as much as we wish, but if we don't see the thinking in this argument, the wrestling right at the edge of the mat, we'll never understand art.

We do need to count. The structuralists do it. Before that, we need to read.

You cannot understand Dostoyevsky without knowing his epoch, without knowing that Russia was pregnant with a great revolution; you cannot read Tolstoy without knowing what he means when he says that social revolution is not "something that might happen" but "something that cannot *not* happen."

You can analyze neither Tolstoy nor Dostoyevsky without knowing this. Why did Raskolnikov kill an old woman of such a weight and height that her throat looked like a rooster's? Why did he kill her with an ax? Carrying an ax in the street is inconvenient, and he didn't even have one handy. Raskolnikov borrowed the ax from the yardman. Though he could have killed the old woman with a stone, a weight.

What is behind this? What is behind the need for this crime? Why didn't Dostoyevsky use a detective novel, why didn't he ask who had killed, who had committed the crime, but asked instead what crime was?

When Raskolnikov arrives at the penal colony, the convicts tell him: "That's not what the gentry is supposed to do, walking around with an ax."

The ax was the peasants' only weapon.

Chernyshevsky was calling to take up the ax; axes are mentioned in *The Possessed.*

The devil appears before Ivan and tells him that he's freezing. He had been flying through the air wearing a suit and a bowtie (he also had a tail like a big dog). He says that it's as cold out there as in Siberia, where girls, in jest, like to make a guy kiss an ax so that his lips freeze to it.

Ivan Karamazov is so mad that he's talking to himself; he asks: what kind of ax?

And the devil answers: an ax, if it has sufficient initial speed, will become a satellite of the Earth, and the calendars will say at what time the ax ascends, and at what time the ax descends.

Around Dostoyevsky's world and around Tolstoy's world, an ax is flying.

[…]

Dostoyevsky and Tolstoy never talked to each other, and this wasn't a matter of chance.

Dostoyevsky wrote about Tolstoy, and what he said was good. Tolstoy never wrote about Dostoyevsky, but what he said about him was right. He said that Dostoyevsky's characters did everything suddenly, "all at once."

These words, "all at once," are really permanently present in Dostoyevsky. Tolstoy says that every character in Dostoyevsky who is supposed to do one thing is bound to do something completely different "all at once."

But "all at once" does not only refer to unexpectedness. This phrase also means a joint action, an abrupt joint action.

"Turn about all at once!" means that everyone is supposed to turn about.

Tolstoy's and Dostoyevsky's worlds were twofold.

Tolstoy knew that the social revolution was not merely likely but bound to happen.

But he existed in the old world, he wanted to go on existing in it, and at the same time he argued against it; he argued against the laws of the old world while trying to defend them.

There was another world, though, the world of Dostoyevsky.

The second universe of its time. Dostoyevsky's "all at once" is an intrusion of that world into this one.

Let's not picture art as a one-story house.

Contradiction appears in order to reveal, "all at once," another reality.

Dostoyevsky wrote not only for his own time, but for an astonished Earth, and his "all at once" became real.

This is why Dostoyevsky became a maker of great art. What interests me is a world that is being concealed, predicted, foreseen, analyzed, that exists in the past, but that is not yet revealed.

What interests me is the world, and how a model of the world is created.

Einstein said that the strongest impression of his life was Raskolnikov, followed by the discovery of the law of relativity.

[...]

The Rhyme of Poetry. The Rhyme of Prose. Structuralism through the Looking Glass: A Farewell

[…]

For years now, I've been spending every day writing *On the Theory of Prose*; this is an argument of the heart and a remedy against my pain in the heart.

What I wrote in 1925 has changed—the way life itself has changed.

I write every day.

I'm not in a hurry. I'm almost ninety: who'd rewrite this book?

Structuralism is still a strong, persistent movement in Europe; it has been arguing with me for over forty years.

The structuralists, headed by Roman Jakobson, say that literature is a linguistic phenomenon.

Roman is no more—the argument remains.

[…]

You can't analyze a single position as if all movement had stopped at your command; you need to analyze movement by comparing contradictory phenomena.

You can't analyze the whole, the ever-changing whole, by placing a part of it into a jar filled with formalin while saying, like a spell, that you're only doing this "for a minute," that you realize you're only dealing with a part, that you can't work otherwise.[1]

If you can't, then you can't.

You shouldn't kill movement, i.e. life.

Why? Because otherwise the word carries no identification; it has no passport stating its age and sex.

Every word is loaded by the circumstances of the text.

[...]

Shklovsky wrote the book "How *Don Quixote* is Made."

Eikhenbaum wrote "How 'The Overcoat' is Made."

But let us ask: what are 'The Overcoat' and *Don Quixote* made *for*? To what aim—or, rather, why—is the protagonist wearing such contradictory armor? Where is he going?[2]

Why does Dostoyevsky say that, when the skies roll up like a roll of parchment, mankind will put Cervantes' book on the table?

Whom will it try to justify by doing so, and before whom?

Note that Pushkin had no abandoned manuscripts—unfinished ones, yes, but not abandoned.

---

[1] Using "formalin" as the preserving agent might be a pun suggesting that formalism was as "guilty" as structuralism.

[2] The interest in this question is sincere. Talking to Vitale (90), Shklovsky says: "[Eikhenbaum] wrote an extremely interesting essay, 'How Gogol's "Overcoat" is Made.' Interesting and important, focused on *skaz*, oral speech in Gogol. Gogol began with the word, of course, there's no arguing that. But beyond that, in Gogol, there is the revolt of the little guy."

Because what Pushkin gets into is not a mirror image of life but the argument of life and an argument with life.

Structuralist theory is interesting in its exactness. It resembles the work of wood carvers. They ornament the wood, and, in its own way, this is great work.

But we, the ones who have lived for decades on our own territory, know the rumbling of history; we hear the roll call of epochs at our door.

[…]

Let us take *Eugene Onegin*. This text's composition owes much to Sterne, it uses plot permutations typical of his work.

Pushkin was familiar with Sterne. It is important to keep that in mind: the device is reconsidered, but the connection is preserved. The construction of the novel's story makes sense both on its own, within the novel, and in relation to Sterne, i.e. beyond the novel but within its literary sphere.

The text is not isolated; it doesn't exist apart from its series, from its system and the system's system.

Another problem. What is a text with a "torn off" ending, an unfinished text?

"At this point, imagination left me," says Dante at the end of *The Divine Comedy*. *Onegin* is cut short, *The Hero of Our Time* has no ending, *Dead Souls* seems incomplete, "The Resurrection" as well as *Crime and Punishment* are not finished.

These works of art give us endings which are cut short as if with the same promise: the characters' lives will go on; the telling of the story has suddenly stopped, but it is not exhausted, it has not exhausted the material and the biographies.

Well then, what is this incompleteness—is it a phenomenon of content or of structure?

[…]

Jesus' disciples ask him: "Teacher, why do you speak in parables?"

It follows that the parable was perceived as an alien form, an unusual form.

This is the motivation for the inclusion of alien material. Jesus begins a parable, a comparison, with a particular case and makes his way to the general situation, widening the scope. The transition is stressed by the disciples' initial lack of understanding. The genre shift is accentuated.

When we say this we realize that we are talking about the true structure of the text.

Thus, we need to point out the device's purpose in terms of meaning.

Let's say, we have the aesthetics of a bridge over a river. This is a structure. The dome of a building is a different structure; they have elements in common, but they have different intentions. Aesthetically, they are perceived differently. Similar elements are transformed in them.

When Dante describes heaven, he slides into describing pictures within a moving drum. What he is describing are paintings in the tholobate of a church. It is as if Dante was working together with Giotto.

The motivation of arrangement in visual, plastic art is transferred onto verbal art. Without this transfer, the structure of the text is unclear.

This is why you can't reduce analysis to the naming and listing of separate parts without bringing them together in their unique semantic relations.

Doing so is like constructing a grammar of analysis, which is in itself neither bad nor unimportant. But the complex unity of texts, which exists beyond doubt, is lost.

The unity pointed out by structuralists is merely the surface of a phenomenon they failed to comprehend.

An example of unity is a bow or a lyre. The bow is the interrelation of a flexible branch and a bowstring. The new is created as an independent form. It means that the bow is there to shoot. Like every structure, it has a direct intention.

The lyre is a bow made to produce sounds; its strings are differently tuned. It has a different task, a different goal, which is why the same element can give rise to different forms, different structures.[3]

[...]

---

[3] Here, Shklovsky is summing up the key idea of his earlier *Bowstring. On the Dissimilarity of the Similar* (1970).

The First Unsuccessful Blueprint of a Whale: Chekhov's "Darling"

[...]

Tolstoy said that, purely in terms of art, Chekhov was more gifted than he was. But Chekhov didn't write religiously, he didn't show people the right path.

As a young writer, Anton Chekhov published a short story entitled "The Darling." This was the nickname of the title character, a retired collegiate assessor's daughter. Her father had left her a small inheritance. Her house was on the outskirts, where the gypsies wandered, but it was a solid house.

Her last name was Plemyannikova.

She was a quiet, good-natured, compassionate young girl with a naïve smile. Her neighbors called her "Darling."

Plemyannikova rented out a room in her house.

She fell in love with a tenant, Kukin, the director of a provincial theater. Plemyannikova took pity on Kukin. The town garden with its open stage was right beside her house, and Kukin kept complaining about the weather getting in the way of his performances. The theater had no roof; Kukin cried, shook his fist at the skies and said that he's hampered in his attempt to create real art, to outdo Shakespeare.

The woman began talking in his language and about his affairs, she pitied him, she railed at the public.

Plemyannikova took pity on her tenant, and her pity was such that they married. Kukin loved his wife; when he got a proper look at her neck and her full shoulders, he threw up his hands in delight and said "Darling!"

Thus, this woman's nickname was confirmed by her husband.

But he went to Moscow to look for artists and died; the widow received a telegram with an ingeniously added misprint: "Ivan Petrovich died suddenly today … Fuferal Tuesday."[1]

The woman had already learned to love the theater. She was used to the theater the way one gets used to an umbrella or a dog. She also loved the man, purely, in her own way. She loved him together with his profession, she always said: "Ivan and me …"

Some time passed after Ivan's death.

On her way from church, Plemyannikova met the woodyard manager Pustovalov.

She fell in love with him—so badly that she now only ever talked of promissory notes and of the rising prices for wood planks.

She never went to the theater anymore.

She loved her husband. With him, she prayed to God for a child.

They lived in absolute harmony for six years.

He died.

She cried.

The house was empty.

She rented out a room to a veterinary. When she learned that he was divorced, she said: "Vladimir Platonych, you should make up

[1] *Khokhorony* instead of *pokhorony* (funeral); published English translations include such versions as "funreal," "wuneral," "tuneral," "huneral" and "fufuneral."

with your wife. Forgive her for your son's sake! The little boy surely understands everything ..."

They began living together, and she talked of nothing but animals diseases.

The veterinary was angry about it.

He left with his regiment. A few years later he returned and brought his boy—and the woman learned to love him very much.

She read his schoolbooks with him, and the words "an island is defined as a piece of land surrounded by water" became a holy truth to her.

The woman learned to love the boy and everything he did, be it right or wrong. Chekhov himself learned to love a child like this, a boy whom he took in. He didn't have a child of his own.

The Darling entered other people's lives the way a seed enters the soil.

With enough rain, grass will start growing and filling the earth.

This text was a favorite of Tolstoy. He reread it four times, out loud. He said that the Darling was the ideal woman. That this was how life should be lived.

What happened to Tolstoy's wife?

She became friends with Dostoyevsky's widow who published her husband's books, which turned out to be very lucrative. Sofia Tolstaya, too, began to publish, and also to sell apples. There were wonderful apples growing on their estate. She also sold books by weight because counting them would have cost a lot of time.

She had seemingly found herself: she published books.

Besides, she had cows, and she let students live in the yard. She sold them butter.

She had entered another person's life. This is a very usual story.

Most often, women enter a life and remake it the way they'd remake an old dress.

Dostoyevsky's widow wasn't a bad person, either. She was a businesswoman. She bought up summer cottages. She was trying to get hold of a whole uninterrupted street of houses.

The war began.

Dostoyevsky's widow found herself in the Crimea. There, she wasn't buying anything, but she was still very busy. She wanted her son, her beloved boy, to have his own stable full of racing horses. She had entered another person's life, her boy's.

This is not a happy story. What is surprising is not that a woman is colored by the light refracted from her husband.

Why does Tolstoy condemn Anna Karenina but lauds the Darling, Kukin's widow, almost falling in love with her?

Actually, it is not women but us men who fall in love with another person's life. We change it, we sacrifice things to it. After all, we need something to grow on.

Something to join. The astonishing thing is that we color the things we do.

[…]

Pushkin told his wife: "[When I'm dead], you'll go live in the village for four years, and then you'll marry a nice man."

Not even Odysseus talked like this when leaving for the Trojan War.

This is a new fidelity.

A new belief in the future.

A new belief that already exists.

Tolstoy approves of the Darling.

He says that the Darling is a heroine just like Sancho Panza—a friend following a knight.

[…]

The Links of Art Do Not Repeat Each Other. Once Again, on the Dissimilarity of the Similar

Sterne

The young Lev Tolstoy translated Sterne. He was learning English, and he was also learning from Sterne.

In the diary which he kept as a volunteer in the Caucasus, he quotes Sterne: "If Nature has so wove her web of kindness that some threads of love and desire are entangled with the piece—must the whole web be rent in drawing them out?"

Preceding the quotation, there is a note in Russian: "Reading Sterne. Delightful."

Side by side with Tolstoy's translations from Sterne are his first attempts at writing. These are journeys far into the future. Here is Tolstoy's unfinished piece "Yesterday's Story."

In it, Tolstoy wants to express thoughts as they are before they reach the soul. The manuscript consists of thirteen separate pages torn out from a large notebook. They express the entanglement of thoughts, the contradiction between words—words as formulae, as words of etiquette—and the acts of the body.

A man declines to stay in the house of the woman he loves. He politely declines the invitation, but his body sits down and puts his hat on the floor, just as politely, and thought appears only after the movement, belatedly: what is to be done now, following this strange contradiction?

Sterne is not just someone who was born 270 years ago, who wrote centuries before us. He is a man whose attempt to understand literature and himself we still haven't comprehended. Since that time, no one's feet have trod the path of Sterne.

[…]

What is wrong and what is right in my old book about Sterne (which you will probably never read—but then again, you might)?[1]

I was right in describing the construction of Sterne's novel, and I was more or less right in describing the construction of Don Quixote's path. However, I did not explain where these constructions come from, what ravines art passes on its way, what wounds it heals.

There was an old man by the name of Jambul whom I met by the snow-crowned mountains of Kazakhstan. He counted his years according to the lunar calendar, not the solar one. The lunar year is shorter, I believe. Jambul wanted to reach life's roundest figure—a hundred years.[2]

He understood Russian, and perhaps he spoke it, as well.

---

[1] You might: versions of Shklovsky's booklet on *Tristram Shandy* (published by the OPOYAZ in 1921) are included in *Theory of Prose* in Benjamin Sher's translation (chapter "The Novel as Parody"), and in a translation by Lemon and Reis in *Russian Formalist Criticism: Four Essays* ("Sterne's Tristram Shandy").

[2] Twelve lunar months make up 354 days; Jambul would need to live to almost ninety-seven.

In the East, people sometimes hide their knowledge in order to be able to listen to the same speech twice—first, in an alien language, then in one's own.

The old man told me: art is a way to console without deceiving.

The *akyns* [Central Asian singer-poets] turn around splinters of old epic tales and renew them, like blinded Samsons.

Art is not a way to console; the old man mentioned consolation to console me.

Art is a way to reveal and renew reality. It constructs its own reality side by side with the reality of the world; it's closer to its source than a shadow is to the object which conceals part of the ground from the sun.

Art constructs ways of cognition, removes the white noise, turns it into speech fit to carry a message.

Art changes its forms the way a forest, with passing years, changes not only its trees but its whole vegetation system.

[...]

When I was writing my book on Sterne in 1921, I had borrowed the novel from Maxim Gorky and, to his horror, returned it swollen with hundreds of bookmarks. He said, stressing every "o," as if his words had wheels:

—Possibly it is not that bad that you, Viktor, have spoiled this volume so quickly.

But I hadn't spoiled it. I just hadn't finished revealing Sterne's essence.

I remember myself laughing at old professors who write footnotes to novels, saying that they jump over the horse while trying to mount it and end up as pedestrians on the other side.[3]

---

[3] For instance, in "Literature Beyond 'Plot,'" excerpted in the present collection.

In order to mount a horse or that "hobbyhorse" Sterne keeps talking about, in order to understand the essence of a work, you need not only to put your foot into the stirrup but also to grab the steed by the mane.

[...]

Wonder, or, as I put it a long time ago, *ostranenie* (this term, in changed form, reached Brecht, probably via Sergey Tretyakov, an LEF comrade of mine)[4]—the ability to wonder and the changing ways of creating wonder—connects many artistic phenomena.

A long time ago I said that art was unbound, that it had no content. These words could be celebrating their golden wedding anniversary now, their 50-year jubilee. These words are wrong.

When talking about *ostranenie*, you have to understand what it works for.

Scientists discover new things in the world, and are themselves surprised at it.

[...]

In the Footsteps of Old Discoveries and Inventions

[...]

Socrates says that the peculiarity of the written word was born from visual art, that it only seems to be alive but cannot reply. Once written down, it remains unchanged. Speech, on the other hand, is not the memory of wisdom but direct contact with it, it is wisdom itself: "nobler far is the serious pursuit of the dialectician, who, finding a

---

[4]This suggestion, made so many decades after the fact, could be based on second-hand sources such as Bernhard Reich's account (371).

congenial soul, by the help of science sows and plants therein words which are able to help themselves and him who planted them, and are not unfruitful, but have in them a seed which others brought up in different soils render immortal, making the possessors of it happy to the utmost extent of human happiness" (Plato).[5]

Today, new methods of information still hold on to the old forms of light reading and theater dramaturgy.

In this way, in Socrates' times, recreational prose held on to the depiction of court speeches. Real people, such as Lysias, wrote literary speeches for real court processes.

Perhaps I'm writing somewhat incoherently because I'm talking about an art form just about to be born. Its birth was preceded by a growing interest in living speech.

The Institute of the Oral Speech was founded in Petrograd, today's Leningrad: men such as [the lawyer] Koni and [the linguist] Shcherba taught there. At the same time, oral stories appeared. You know, that is what Irakly Andronikov does. It was hard for him to enter literature, and the Writers' Union in particular: both he and his genre were unprovided for.

Today, though, the image which can ask questions and reply to them all by itself has great opportunities.

But people don't know that they can find their living past in television, that television is the place to continue what had been called, somewhat patronizingly though not without respect, folklore.

New art, art which uses new tools, is unstoppable. Book copyists burned down the first printing establishment in Moscow on the Varvarka street: this was a useless and contemptible act.

Today, a TV set is to be found in every room, standing in the corner like a punished child—but it is quite blameless.

---

[5]Translation by Benjamin Jowett.

The Problem of Time in Art

[...]

Pushkin spent seven years writing *Eugene Onegin*. It took Tolstoy ten years to write *The Cossacks*.

We, the readers of *Eugene Onegin*, perceive it as a whole thing, as if it was written all at once. But there is also the author, who is a human being, surrounded by all kinds of change; he writes bits and pieces of text which have different directions, both intentionally and not. Time, the time it takes to write a text, influences—and often defines—its development, its results. In literature, time leads the way, defines the perspective. In literature, time is often the main reason for textual change.

[...]

The novel is intended to be read in a particular period. At the same time, the novel shows how humans and the world change under the influence of time.

Birth, education, enrichment, ruin, travel, inheritance—all these are phenomena of time in a novel.

In Dickens' *Dombey and Son*, the very title features time.

A man and his son. A generation.

But the novel, and in particular the English novel, goes even further. A man grows old, loses all his money, and gains it again. *Dombey and Son*: the mention of the son suggests that the bankrupt company will regain its money.

Don Quixote is not only a novel about a particular man; it's also a survey of that man's country.[6]

---

[6] Shklovsky occasionally treats time and space as interchangeable.

Pushkin said that *Eugene Onegin* was built around the calendar. We can specify that it's built around the seasons.

Autumn, winter, spring—these are changes of the viewpoint from which life is presented, these are changes of perspective.

Why am I saying this?

We live in the moment.

Yury Olesha creates a good graphic image of this when he says how stealthily the moment creeps upon a boy when he finds himself being called an old man; he, a boy, is suddenly addressed this way in the street.

The boy is already on the threshold of time.

Now I need to create a passageway, long and seemingly invisible for the reader—I will move my thought over onto a perpendicular path.

The characters in the texts are people from different times.

From different moral epochs.

This is probably why they find it so hard to live together.

[…]

The Lungs Are for Breathing. Thoughts Out Loud

Yet Another Foreword

[...]

There was a time when I followed Potebnya so fixedly that I even began to argue with him.

When looking for the ancestors of modern machines you can end up, via the wooden pumps of salt wells, with the reed pipes through which water was pumped out of rivers dangerously filled with evil spirits and simply with crocodiles.

The old does not disappear. It is resurrected, often even in seemingly unnecessary detail. History preserves traces of every house so reluctantly destroyed by time.

What we could discover is that myths were attempts to understand something—or else, not to understand, but to cover the old, the way people in the mountains cover dangerous areas with rugs and cloths.

When a Crimean from the House of Giray was leaving the city of Bakhchysarai (the one celebrated by Pushkin), leaving his palace whose fountain was crying instead of playing, the people remembered that he was kin of the Khan and threw their last cloths under the hoofs of his horses and donkeys.

Or else, we could think of Pushkin's repeated dreams.

Dreams are drafts which were never destroyed, only elevated.

Dreams don't survive the day, or they rarely do, but they are remembered.

Dreams can be read as presentiments, predictions—the drafts of history.

The Romans held up the movements of their legions because of inauspicious dreams, because of birds flying strangely, in unusual ways and directions.

We could comprehend history, literature as the history of paths not yet comprehended.

Some dreams have come true.

I'm writing a new book on the theory of prose.

This book is all about old, forgotten pathways, about woods in which some tribes were hidden once upon a time, about holes in rocks in which people lived and learned, in the dark, to paint the white rocks black, to draw, doubling their memories by virtue of an image. They learned to make drafts, they were almost realists.

We speak of "wandering plots." Yes, plots do wander. Children, too, wander the streets. I myself wandered once, and knocked on drainpipes, which answered in differently pitched voices.[1]

Unspoken, deceptive decisions.

Deceptive monkey bridges made by interweaving opposing branches. Stones leaning against each other as shelter against predators and the wind.

These stones are forerunners, contemporaries, and polemists of architectural arcs.

[1] "Wandering plots" (sometimes rendered as "migrant plots"), standard plot variations traveling through different languages and literary epochs, were a key concept in formalism, for instance in *Morphology of the Folktale* (Propp), available in English. The mention of drainpipes might be an allusion to Mayakovsky's poem "And could you?" which ends with "And you, / could you play / a nocturne on the flute of a drainpipe?"

I'd like to open old graves. Old human graves.

As early as the Paleolithic times, skeletons of dead people were colored in red ochre.

People eat, and a part of their food ends up on the earth, ingloriously.

Grass grows thicker in such places.

But pathways need to be cleaned.

There was a time when angels looked more like animals than like people, though even back then they had wings. Their portraits are a matter of art because they are the forerunners of the game killed by a hunter.

Humans broke their knowledge into shards in order to learn to talk, to talk out loud.

Or else, to construct a whole, a unity from the shards.

There are places in the mountains where the rocks respond to a shout by a landslide.

There, the stones teach you poetry, teach you how to rhyme.

The pathways near habitations must be clean.

The nightingale does not sing to seduce its lover.

No, the nest is already built; the eggs, laid with care and pain, are already in it. The nightingale sings songs of the future, but there are neighbors and enemies around, and it doesn't always sing for pleasure.

[…]

You need to learn to return to things you've done, to return if only in order to grow disappointed in them, in youth, which is very often wrong but has good eyes.[2]

---

[2] The Russian *khotya by* usually means "if only"; however, it could also mean the opposite in this context: that disappointment is the main goal of return.

Passing through the lungs, blood is enriched . No author can avoid repetitions.

I'm saying this fully aware of the distance between myself and the authors I quote. Repetitions of landscapes, descriptions of delight, descriptions of events are unavoidable, and each writer has their own.

Blok has a Petersburg of his own, a city which he's been seeing through the same window for years.

Mayakovsky was the protagonist of his own lyrical drama, a drama he told to himself, changing the hopes and disappointments; one of his poems ends with:

Take my gift, darling,
I might not be able to come up with anything else.

This is an endorsement not of obsessive thoughts but of necessary steps taken by humans on their way up, for their own sake, for the sake of attentive thought and inspiration, which, as Pushkin said, is needed for both geometry and poetry, for a walk in the city and a conversation with your children who've heard you so often but still don't understand you.[3]

[…]

The eternity of art is the eternity of change. It is an eternity trying on new possibilities.

The history of human change—not the history of aging, but that of change—is the unity of art.

Having gone through all the circles of hell, being in the wrong, demanding love, Anna Karenina ends up in a painted world.

---

[3]The verse quotation is actually from the penultimate stanza of Mayakovsky's "Backbone Flute"; as regards Pushkin, Shklovsky doesn't make clear the quotation ends with poetry and geometry; the rest is his own.

In it, everything is unnatural, everything is wrong, and two women at the Obiralovka station say, respectfully, that her lace is real.

Andrey Bolkonsky hurls himself, carrying the banner, toward his Toulon, and then, dying, he hears his idol, Napoleon, and sees him against the backdrop of the sky, and understands what life is, and what is unreal.[4]

Art tries on the possibilities of the world by using the coincidences of the world, by using madness, the descriptions of insanity—in other words, *ostranenie*, i.e. the world placed on a different foundation.

[…]

Prose appeared after poetry

Poetry had its rhythm, its own way of impeding, constraining meaning. What did art find to make up for the mass disappearance of rhythm and meter, of the constraints conveniently placed in speech itself?

Art gave birth to the plot. A plot is an impediment, a riddle. It is a form of deceleration, just like the superimposition of certain sounds.

Plot, then, is an event, an event made complicated. Plot is younger than rhythm. It is a way to put things into their place. To complicate them.

Stories are told about funny things, coincidences, wonder, surprise. This is when prose is created.

Another source is the court appeal. In order to talk in court, you needed to talk well; those who weren't good orators engaged people to write appeals, which were very much like books.

---

[4]In *War and Peace*, and particularly for Bolkonsky, "Toulon" is a metaphor for military success. The name of the station "Obiralovka," is derived from *obirat'*, to fleece someone.

Court speeches were written by specialists; people repeated what they had written. A man complaining about his wife's infidelity says that his house has creaky stairs—he says he heard them creaking and found the lovers in flagrante.

Socrates condemned these first hired prose writings.

This is one of the first realistic details of a psychological novel ever written down.

[...]

Ostranenie

Ostranenie is seeing the world with different eyes.[5]

Jean-Jacques Rousseau, in his own way, estranged himself from the world; he lived apart from the state.

The world of poetry includes the world of *ostranenie.*

Gogol's troika, which is rushing over Russia, is Russian because it is sudden. But it's also international; it's flying over Russia, and Italy, and Spain.

It is the movement of new literature proclaiming its very self.

A new view of the world.

Ostranenie is a matter of time.

Ostranenie is not only a new way of seeing; it is also the dream of a new world, sunny only because it is new. Mayakovsky's many-colored, belt-free shirt is the festive garment of a person firmly believing in tomorrow.

---

[5] Here, as well as in the title and elsewhere in the 1983 collection, Shklovsky's original mistake is corrected by the editor; *ostrannenie* is written the way correct Russian demands. The present anthology uses *ostranenie* throughout, unless Shklovsky discusses this very word and its orthography. So many alternative translations exist already, that producing even more confusion while arguing for the use of the original term in English seemed counterproductive.

The world of *ostranenie* is the world of the revolution.

Dostoyevsky says of Cervantes that *Don Quixote* is one of those books written many centuries in advance. Don Quixote could intercede for a boy who hadn't been paid but he couldn't save the boy from a beating because he believed, or rather assumed, that the world wasn't malicious.

The Pickwick Papers became a sought-after book when another Samuel appeared along with Pickwick, a poor young man who talks in a folksy way, in his own way—and who sees the necessity for fairness in his own way.[6]

But what could Charles Dickens do?

The great consoler, he could only save one boy per book.

I keep thinking about the time of writing. What creates good literary language?

The correction of the first impression. A person sees something and then he corrects what he sees. He washes the past clean from the usual, he shuns the eternal room, the eternal apartment, even the eternal family—and finally he reaches what is most important.[7]

Lev Tolstoy's work is an ingenious attempt to see the world as if it had never been described before. His work required much rewriting, and the result teaches people to see.

The thing that we call an image, sorting it into different categories and classes, was originally not an image but a sideways step made in order not to step on what had been done before. It is an attempt to leave behind the repetitiveness of existence.

---

[6] *The Pickwick Papers* did indeed become a publishing hit with the introduction of Sam Weller in chapter 10.

[7] When Shklovsky says *chelovek* (human, person), he often means a particular person, sometimes himself. The fear of a lack of change and of family in particular was certainly his own: in a letter to Jakobson, he writes "in a family, husband and wife have to make up for deficits every day" (included in *The Third Factory*).

It is from literature that writers learn to write. For they learn to push themselves off literature. The history of literature is partly the history of fighting against yesterday. One of Tolstoy's earliest attempts is entitled "Yesterday's Story".[8]

This title plays down its own meaning.

One contests the very fact of seeing. One begins with a description. One begins with the description of a birth, committing what can be called a terrible breach against his separation from the world. One airs out his feelings.

Andersen's fairy tale, one you must all be familiar with, the fairy tale about the princess and the pea, is a tale of how to remain sensitive in life.

People like their own traces.

A Caucasian tradition said that you shouldn't be able to feel the wooden floor of a room. People walked on carpets; when the room was being tidied up, the carpets were rolled up into special holes, very wide holes in the walls. People walked in their rooms wearing very soft boots custom-made by shoemakers who measured the naked foot. People wore narrow boots made from thin leather. The houses built on the shores of the Black Sea stood on strong low piles. These piles were not rammed in; they were like hands holding up the floor.

Today, people travel pushing themselves off the earth with wheels.

There is also another point. Aleko, the character of Pushkin's poem [*The Gypsies*], carried the author's name. Aleko is short for Alexander.

Gypsies lived in carts, they walked on torn rugs; they considered it disgraceful to let anyone walk on the floor over you, this was like letting people walk on your head.

---

[8] *Istoriya vcherashnego dnya*" can mean both "The History of Yesterday"/"Yesterday's Story" and, dismissively, "A Thing of the Past."

This is why I repeat that people like their own traces.

You cannot tread literary language with another person's feet.

Every person has a gait of his own, which he knows.

If he doesn't know it, doesn't feel it—it is as if he didn't exist.[9]

[…]

Language is so carefully protected by different academies because it's impossible to stop grass from growing and wilting.

Khlebnikov believed that reconsidering the phenomena of the world was the meaning and the task of art.

Literature is an argument, an argument between interpretations, theories, world views.

When history opens up frozen rivers, the floes argue with each other, they break and rustle, and hit the foundations of the Neva bridges, and smash into pieces; sometimes, the frost takes holds of them, and everything freezes over again.

[…]

[When I was a child] we were visiting someone who had a magic lantern, and I took a piece of that transparent film with pictures on it, a piece about two—no, three—fingernails long.

My crime was revealed.

My mother did everything short of pulling out her hair.

She screamed that her son was a thief, that he was stealing already, that she was about to go drown herself and god knows what else.

She was an ordinary woman, after all.

I think she never forgave me.

---

[9] This harks back to the entry from Tolstoy's diary which formed the basis to the theory of *ostranenie*: "the whole life of many people is lived unconsciously, it is as if this life had never been."

A confession is a clever thing.

Like a vessel to be held under something which gets squeezed out all by itself.

You talk—and you feel better.

You feel reborn, liberated.

Look at all Anabaptism sects, all these rebaptism stories—they were invented because a child is not the same person as the grown-up he will become.

The Brahmins have the golden ring of the holy cow through which they drag a person, as if newly bringing him into life.[10]

This is the true role of art, its true image.

A chain of such golden rings is the history of art.

[…]

Prose needs details, it needs the unexpected, because these things increase attention. Prose was born by the campfire, when people made a stop in the desert. They talked about the extraordinary, in prose. These were tired people talking, and keeping the listeners' attention was difficult. This is why prose was often intimate and often talked about unaccustomed things.

The prosaic phrase is founded on communication. It needs to contain information. Traditionally, it began with describing who is talking, and to whom.

Travels, stops on the way, talks on the deck, conversations while waiting for a ship to arrive. Conversations on piers, conversations about the dead, praising the dead and parting from them, changing

---

[10] Sic. One of the closest rituals to what Shklovsky describes is the coronation ceremony for Hindu maharajas that involved a ritual bath in a golden effigy of a cow, which meant a rebirth. There are also rituals connected to golden rings, such as writing a mantra on a child's tongue with a golden ring to initiate him or her into learning.

relations, conversations about the most wonderful and the most terrible things in human life—all these are the themes of prose.

The theme of prose is an argument about guilt and about finding a doctor who will heal the diseases.

Prose likes the unexpected. It says things which make people stay at the campfire, listen on, add their own input.

The reader holds on to the pages of books and manuscripts the way a child holds on to the dress of his mother while she consoles him.

[…]

The world itself is founded on contradiction.

Rivers flow down, rays of energy pierce immense spaces, rocks and races change.

What Bakhtin calls the culture of laughter, claiming this term for himself like a newly discovered continent, was created neither sooner nor later than other cultures. It is hardly right to define the epoch of masks as a carnival phenomenon, for we are familiar with very old masks—cultural (geographically speaking), comic, and otherwise. African masks are not a parody of anything, they are art, and this art is not comic.

This art is what I had called *ostranenie* back in 1914.

When Bakhtin talks about Rabelais—in great, perhaps exhaustive detail—he hardly seems to notice how old medieval clerical notions are dislodged.

Bakhtin remarks that Rabelais creates carnivalization in a world in which people exert themselves and wish to change the level of tension, as if entering a different world. A society in which youths are thrown into a fiery oven is replaced, in Europe at least, by a less religious world.

It seems to me, though, that the two worlds coexist in art.

Bakhtin mentions the fact that Shakespeare's tragedies always feature jesters or characters which play a similar role. They are necessary. A special dramatic type was needed to play these roles, and actors who played jesters received more money and had the right to improvise on stage, to change the text, to introduce new jokes.

If we take such a seemingly familiar spectacle as a circus show, we shall see that in it, the comical, the parodic coexists with the frightening, forming a stripe pattern: clowns and wild animals side by side.

[…]

What do an author's old books look like for him, I'm asking myself.

They don't disappear.

But their fates change.

The book on the theory of prose published in 1925 (and written in 1920) should be included as a footnote to this one, the larger one.[11]

After all, everything is born small and then develops.

"Art as Device" is like a Rubik's cube: you can turn it this way and that.

Reality, meanwhile, is life talking about life.

I've been crying in the bathroom today. It hurts to be old. "Don't; in just two years you achieved a great deed."[12]

Those two years don't count.

Those two years are standing in line.

---

[11] A part of it was actually included in *O teorii prozy* published in 1983.

[12] It is not clear which years exactly Shklovsky has in mind, but he appears to be referring to his most productive years, shortly before and after the revolution. Among the many members of the Russian intelligentsia who believed that the elder Shklovsky had sold out or lost his talent, the kinder ones liked to remind him and each other of his past deeds. However, this could hardly console Shklovsky, who agreed with Mayakovsky: "you can tell me the cruelest things, but never say that my latest book is worse than the previous one" (Viktor Shklovsky, *O Teorii Prozy* [1983] 79).

Only that which you feel right now counts.

[…]

The human brain is a very strange construction. It knows more than it knows. The human brain can think seemingly at random. It can create convoluted solutions.

Einstein said: we don't think in words; otherwise, a person making a discovery wouldn't be so astonished.

But let us return to our topic. To the theory of prose.

Novels and stories are created as if beyond their creator's knowledge.

The writer Tolstoy is many times more intelligent than the count Tolstoy, the owner of a small estate, the man who preaches non-resistance but is weak in his beliefs. When he heard false news of another attempt to shoot [the reactionary prime minister] Stolypin, he said with displeasure: "So they've missed again …"

[…]

A long time ago, I wrote a book called *On the Theory of Prose*, compiling it from many articles.

Tatyana Larina could say to Onegin: "Onegin, back then, I was younger,/I was a better person then."[13]

I, too, haven't grown any younger since I wrote on this old topic, and neither has the topic itself.

The laws of art are the laws of internal human need, the need for a change in tension.

With the help of art, humans have built a world in order to comprehend it. They were magnanimous. They were almost equal

[13] Translation by Alexandra Berlina; despite several English versions which have Tatyana saying that she had been better-looking back then, she actually is talking about her moral character. Is Shklovsky implying the same about his own?

but they already had wars and prevented the warriors from sleep by beating the newly invented drums. At their own loss, they were conquering sleep but they couldn't conquer death. However, they did create magnanimity.

Art makes life denser.[14] Having found no continuity in life, mankind is looking for the word that could push away the inevitable.

Art needs compaction. Meaning. It needs incidents. Coincidences. Events that stand out among the usual. This is how people hope to achieve immortality.

So far, the game seems lost, but it isn't over.

[…]

In Reply to a Questionnaire

[…]

I was told how many lines I was supposed to write: apparently, a succinct answer was expected.

But if I could answer, and succinctly at that, I'd never need to write anything else again.

The question is this.

What is the difference between a fact of prose and a fact of poetry?

The first difference is age. The primary fact is older.[15]

Secondly, they are related: the poetic fact is the awareness of the primary fact.

---

[14] Shklovsky spoke no German but he might have known that the word "Dichtung" (poetry, literature) is connected to "dicht" (dense).

[15] *Pervichnyi* means "primary" and not "the former," but it seems to refer to prose here. However, in many other articles—including some published in *O Teorii Prozy* (1983)—Shklovsky says the opposite. Possibly, he is talking about literature as opposed to life rather than prose and poetry in the present passage.

[…]

Thirdly, the poetic fact is, to put it very modestly, an edited fact.

It's color, paint.

It's subordinated to the newly found image. It's painted in new colors. It's part of a great reality. It's a fact.

But at the same time it's a stroke of the paint brush.

[More Thoughts Out Loud][16]

[…]

Thoughts are not solitary in art.

Solitude in art is as sad as throwing a ball against a haystack: the hay is elastic, and the ball doesn't rebound.

In art, thoughts marry.

Alexei Maximovich [Maxim Gorky], of whom I can say now, fifty years after our separation, that he was right when he fell out with me (he suffered much from me: everyday thoughtlessness and the ability to wonder through another's window are difficult), talked often and with pleasure about the future successes of other people.

After all, I myself am only a letter in the book of time.

And I want—I'm trying—to restore my line.

I don't want you to succumb to a fit of madness and become reasonable.

Prose fills us with parallelisms which seem to be parallel but are not supposed to feel parallel, or rather, they're supposed to feel complexly parallel.[17]

---

[16] Some subchapters of *On the Theory of Prose* (1983) have no title; this one has been added in translation in accordance with the main chapter heading, hence the square brackets.

[17] *Slozhno-parallelnyi* (lit. complexly parallel) is a rare technical term usually translated into English as "multiple" (e.g. "multiple converter"). The root *slozhno-* also appears at the

When creating a book, you need to create confusion:

—there's nothing;

—there's light.

This is how the Bible is constructed.

---

beginning of Russian linguistic terms denoting complexity and multiplicity, such as the terms for complex and compound sentences.

Part Six

In 60 Years: Works on Cinema (1985)

Part Six: Introduction

Viktor Shklovsky: A Reader encompasses seventy years of scholarship. So far, this was presented chronologically. This last chapter, however, is a history of Shklovsky's writing in miniature, from 1919 to 1984. Apart from biography and history, the present anthology so far was dedicated to literary studies, with occasional forays into visual art and theater. But film criticism and scholarship took up most of Shklovsky's time, particularly in later years. This wasn't an entirely deliberate decision; Shklovsky began to work in cinema mostly because he needed the money. *Zoo* includes this work in a rather unflattering list: "The deaths of friends bent my soul. The war. Arguments./Mistakes. Injuries. Cinema."

Still, he did grow fascinated with film. He was, for instance, "one of the first to get excited about animated films, convinced 'that they have possibilities that are, as yet, untapped … Maybe cartoons can be combined with regular films?' Indeed, when Shklovsky died in 1984, aged 91, having avoided every purge endured by the ranks of Soviet artists, *Who Framed Roger Rabbit?* was already in development at Disney" (Norton). The best of Shklovsky's writing on cinema is guided by genuine interest and closely interconnects with the rest of his work.

The present selection follows the collection *In 60 Years: Works on Cinema* (*Za 60 let: Raboty o kino*), which was published posthumously but selected under Shklovsky's guidance. The collection takes up 516 pages, including eight pages of very small print listing more of Shklovsky's publications on cinema. Only a small part can be reproduced here, with a few texts that have already appeared in English included due to their importance. A recent translation of Shklovsky's early book on film (*Literature and Cinematography*) features "On Cinema" and "The Plot in Cinema"; there is a considerable amount of Shklovsky's writing in *The Film Factory* (Christy and Taylor), including "Poetry and Prose in Cinema." Still, the majority of the texts presented here have never been translated into English before.

Throughout the collection, there is Shklovsky's trademark aphoristic style: "art—as I haven't proved in the previous lines—is advanced by irony." There are his favorite examples, for instance, sexualized folktales, such as the one about "the hare that abused a fox in a most strange way." There is the strong interest in empirical research on the human body and mind, with Shklovsky explaining how our visual perception ensures that "onscreen, blowing your nose works much better than dancing." The collection's foreword is a manifesto on the value of both repeating and contradicting oneself—an idea that, self-serving or not, became crucial to the late Shklovsky. "On Cinema" explains the concept of indirect inheritance in art both earlier and clearer than the better-known "Literature beyond 'Plot.'"

"Talking to Friends" illustrates that, in 1939, Shklovsky could only talk to friends obliquely, if he wanted to do so in print. He seemingly sarcastically compares formalist conversations with those led by the inhabitants of Swift's flying island—but also speaks of "returning the sensation of reality to the artist," without directly mentioning *ostranenie*. He appears to denounce stream of consciousness writing, claiming that "a writer of genius [Tolstoy] had considered and discarded what another writer [Joyce] did later." However, those familiar with Shklovsky's earlier work know that he loved Tolstoy's story referenced here. In 1970, he would again compare it to *Ulysses*—this time without criticizing either (Shklovsky, *Tetiva* 60).

"Chaplin as Policeman" begins with a comparison which is at the heart of automatization and hence *ostranenie*: "As unfamiliar to me as the back of my hand. That's what we should be saying about what is alien." "On Cinema Language" puts forth the theory that film can be poetic or prosaic. "On Film Reassembling" describes the fascinating practice of editing foreign films to change their plots. "Happy Fable-land" ridicules Hollywood happy endings, but also appeals to the Russian love for American literature as an argument against the Cold War. Apropos of wars, Shklovsky writes: "I fought in World War I and the civil war, I saw World War II. But I never guessed that cities and countries—the whole world—could be conquered so quickly." He is talking about television.

In one of the last texts Shklovsky ever wrote, a letter which serves as an afterword to *In 60 Years: Works on Cinema*, he says: "The life I lived was, of course, wrong. But in another life I wouldn't have done what I have done."

Introduction (1985)[1]

[...]

There are many repetitions in my articles.

The way of thought is a winding way. Repetitions are stops alongside it. They are moments when you check your course against the stars, which are not always visible to those walking beside you.

Repetitions mean that the conversation topic isn't a matter of incident.

They are the traces of attempts to get closer to the object.

The traces are loopy, but the object becomes clearer and clearer, seen many times and from different points.

Eyesight can deceive.

But it gets better along the way. It grows wise with work.

My dear compiler, please don't throw out the repetitions—without them, the topographical map doesn't shows the terrain relief.

My dear editor, without the repetitions the readers will only receive a contour map.

Contour maps are good for geography lessons, to test the pupils' memory.

What I want to give to the readers is a relief map of my journeys. A map showing the development of Soviet cinematography.

---

[1]Source (for each chapter in this section): *Za 60 let. Raboty o kino.* Moscow: Iskusstvo, 1985.

This is not about geography. This is about history.

The pencil that tries to correct it slips and breaks, leaving not a scratch.

Let us leave everything as it was, so as not to repeat old mistakes.

Those who venture farther than us see things anew.

They make new mistakes.

Without mistakes, there would be no discoveries.

One shouldn't be afraid of one's previous self. Or ashamed of one's past.

No apologies are accepted anyway.

Others will explain you.

Others will want to understand your journey, will follow into your footsteps. Still, they'll find their own way.

[…]

On Cinema (1919)

Art history has a very important feature: in it, it's not the eldest son who inherits seniority from his father, but the nephew who receives it from his uncle.

I'll open the brackets of my prosaic metaphor.

Medieval lyric poetry descends not directly from the classical tradition but from a younger line—the folk song, which existed during the heyday of classicism as a parallel, "junior" art form. This is proven by the canonization of a new form unknown to old art in its upper layers, namely the rhyme. The development of the novel is the canonization of the novella and the anecdote, which lived below "literature."

This happens as follows.

Outliving the old forms, "high" art reaches an impasse. The tension of the artistic atmosphere weakens and begins to let in elements of non-canonical art, which usually has worked out new artistic devices by this stage.

As an analogy—not a parallel—we can point to the similarity between this phenomenon and the change of the culturally hegemonic tribe or class. Today's cultured mankind is not a direct descendant of the Sumer-Akkadians.

This is why it is so dangerous when the older layer of art begins to mentor the younger one. Great opportunities can be lost this way. A turbine prototype represented a higher technology than any state-of-the-art steam engine, and it would have been a deeply harmful, regressive business to try and furnish it out with a crank.

This is why it pains me so to see what people are doing to cinema, attempting to make it rhyme with theater and literature.

Old theater, which has gone dry, and old literature, which is drying out, are taking it upon themselves to "improve" cinema. With due respect to the comrades in cinema studies I must point out that this closely resembles the epoch of Nicolas I when all soldiers were made to wear boots of the same size.

Apparently, our cinema scholars proceed from the assumption that an artwork consists of form and content, and that any content can be given any form. Thus, any literary plot can be made into a film. In yesterday's great art, narrative literature was represented mainly by the psychological novel and the novel of manners: therefore, these are supposed to become the prototypical genres of literary cinema. Scripts based on old novels are written, followed by new novels in the same vein.

Meanwhile, if cinema was left alone or handed over to people eager to comprehend the forms offered by its own technical (and therefore also artistic) opportunities, then it could not only develop on its own terms but also replace the kind of theater that is now drying out and refresh art with newly created forms.

[…]

The Plot in Cinema (1923)

To do real work in cinema theory, one should begin by collecting all the existing films, or at least a couple of thousands.

Classified, these films would produce the kind of mass material that would make it possible to establish several absolutely exact laws.

It's a great pity that institutes for art history and academies are more interested in the Atlantis and the Pamir excavations.

Cinema was created before our very eyes, its life is the life of our own generation, we can follow it step by step.

Soon, the material will become immeasurable. It's sad and boring to think that we all know how important it is to study contemporary phenomena of art history, and yet that we never do so.

This kind of work cannot be done by one person; it needs qualified assistance, financing, perhaps experiments.

The groundwork for solving some questions of aesthetics could be laid in experimenting upon the audience with films made for this purpose.

What makes people cry?

What makes people laugh?

Under which circumstances does the comic become tragic?

[...]

The detective novel triumphed as "the novel about a detective" and not "the novel about a criminal" because the novel concentrating on the criminal, a descendant of the adventure novel, decelerates action merely by accumulating challenges in the protagonist's path. "The novel about a detective," on the other hand, enables entirely new constructions. We first see the crime as a mystery, then we are given several possible solutions, and finally the true picture is established. Thus, the detective novel is a mystery novel with a professional mystery solver.

Cinema is a triumph of the plot shift. What we usually see first is a sequence of incomprehensible scenes, which are subsequently explained by a protagonist; this motivation is not an account of past events, as in novels, but a pure plot shift: it is as if a part of the film was cut off from the beginning and placed at the end.

In this, cinema is certainly stronger than literature. It is much weaker in the domain of hints, which literature traditionally uses to support the interest toward the mystery's solution. Cinema does not allow for ambiguity.

The novel also often uses parallelisms to decelerate action. In such cases, the hero or heroine of one plot line is left alone at the most critical junction, and we turn to the other, parallel line. Thus, the books six and seven in *The Brothers Karamazov* are rammed shut at the moment of greatest suspense (the preparation of Fyodor Pavlovich's murder). In *Crime and Punishment*, too, two themes—Raskolnikov's and Svidrigailov's fate—keep interrupting each other.

Arguably, *King Lear* uses the same technique of two parallel intrigues.

In cinema, the interruption of one action by another is canonical. But it differs in its structure from the interruption in the novel. In the novel, one narrative situation interrupts another. Plot lines take turns. In cinema, the interrupting segments are much shorter, they are exactly this—segments of film reel; we usually return to the same episode. A very typical kind of interruption in cinema is the motif of "help being late." The hero or the heroine is about to be killed, "meanwhile …"—and we learn that the victim's friends don't know about the terrible situation, or are unable to help. Now, we see the murder scene again, etc.

[…]

Chaplin as Policeman (1923)

As unfamiliar to me as the back of my hand.

That's what we should be saying about what is alien.

If women know themselves, this is only because they often change their dresses.

We've marked time with the notches of days in order to feel its movement.

Love exists as long as there is a difference, as long as there is wonder or separation.

Art is, at its root, ironic and destructive.

If it does build its little houses, this is because houses that haven't been built cannot fall.

Sophocles' tragedy *Oedipus* is ironic because Oedipus creates his own ruin while trying to solve the mystery of the curse upon the city. [Gogol's] *The Government Inspector* is ironic; the only reason the play exists is that Khlestakov is not really an inspector.

A human being in the wrong place—this is the oldest theme in art.

Slandered virtue, kings robbed of their kingdoms, weak-willed avengers, soft-hearted murderers, frail old men imagining themselves to be knights of la Mancha—these are the usual characters.

Another frequent feature in art is the description of events from the perspective of a person to whom they are alien, who doesn't understand them.

This is how Voltaire describes the life in contemporary France in *L'Ingénu*, this is how Chateaubriand describes French life in *Les Natchez*, this is how Tolstoy always wrote.

Being in the wrong place, not recognizing things—this is the eternal topic of art.

In Mark Twain's story *The Prince and the Pauper*, a boy finds himself in the king's palace by chance and cracks nuts with the Great Seal.

Robinson [Crusoe] isn't an exception. Admittedly, he behaves very reasonably on the desert island; he creates a life for himself—but he does so on a desert island and not in London, where he could be living if there wasn't his passion for travelling.

Thus, art—as I haven't proved in the previous lines—is advanced by irony.

One of the ways to create an ironic construction is to create a type.

Very often, an artist who has created a certain type finds it hard to lose, so that the type is transferred from scene to scene, from novel to novel.

This is done partly to save artistic material and to avoid beginning every text with the exposition of the type, but also for another reason.

It is important for the artist to carry one unchangeable yardstick through the changeable worlds of his works.

[…]

Not only Chaplin but also his main partners—the blonde (the love object) and the giant (the adversary)—wander from film to film without changing their make-up. What changes are the motivation of their relationships and the methods of collision. Apparently, the prettiness of the blonde, which makes her a love interest, and the immense height of the adversary are the optimal combination for creating a conflict around Chaplin's distinctive figure.

The giant defeated by cleverness is another literary topos, as old as the animal epos. What comes to mind are the frogs that lure an elephant into their swamp, the fox that abused a wolf and the hare that abused a fox in a most strange way (in *Russian Censored Tales*). In the domain of human relationships, the weak who defeats the strong is a beloved figure. David and Goliath are, of course, a classic variation of this theme.

However, we find much closer parallels to Chaplin's feat in German fairy tales about the brave tailor. Here, we see a weak man defeating a giant with cleverness, and not with the national weapon.

[...]

The Semantics of Cinema (1925)

[...]

According to recent research, we experience moving objects rather than single stationary objects replacing each other not because of eyesight physiology but because of our psychology. We tend to see change rather than exchange; thus, if the same letter appears on the screen in different fonts, we will see it as modulation, a gradual change. If, on the other hand, we project onto the screen letters that are very similar in their form but correspond to different sounds, then the moments of transformation will be much more apparent to us.

Expanding the distance between frames, moving them further apart, we don't destroy the experience of continuity but merely make this perception difficult. One can go as far as making the audience faint by forcing it to spend too much mental energy on connecting the fragments flashing before it. Movement in cinema is very interesting in regard to the perception of movement in general. It relates to reality the way a broken line relates to a curve. Our knowledge about what the character is doing onscreen helps our perception. Meaningful movements, particular actions appear to fill up the space between frames, simplifying perception, which is why pure movement, such as ballet, suffers most in cinema. Onscreen, blowing your nose works much better than dancing.

Cine-eye and the whole "kinoki" movement do not want to understand the essence of cinema.[1] Their eyes are placed unnaturally far from their brains. They don't understand that cinema is the most abstract of all arts, close in its essence to certain mathematical devices. Cinema needs action and meaningful movement the way literature needs words, the way a painting needs semantic meaning. Without it, the spectator becomes disoriented; his view loses direction.

In painting, shadows are a convention, but they can only be replaced by another convention. Cinema needs to accumulate conventions, they'll work the way case endings work in language.

The primary material of cinema is not the object, but a particular way of filming it. Only the cameraman's individual approach can make a film scene tangible.

This said, it is quite possible for a writer to work not with single words but with more complex pieces of literary material. Introducing an epigraph, the writer contrasts his whole work with another. Inserting documents, letter fragments, newspaper excerpts into his text, the writer doesn't stop being an artist but merely applies the artistic principle to another sphere. Lev Tolstoy's "What For?" consists of quotations by Maximov, but they are selected and juxtaposed by Tolstoy. He considers this text his own.

[…]

---

[1] Dziga Vertov's *Kino-Glaz* (Cine-Eye) ideas included an attempt to abstain from creating meaning, e.g. by working with ready film fragments; they gave rise to cinéma vérité and the Dziga Vertov Group, formed in 1968 by French filmmakers such as Godard and Gorin. Vertov claimed to be "a mechanical eye" decades before Isherwood (followed by Van Druten) called himself a camera.

Poetry and Prose in Cinema (1927)

[...]

In film making, we are still children. We're only just beginning to consider the object of our work, but we can already say that there are two cinematographic poles, each with its own laws.

Charlie Chaplin's *A Woman of Paris* is certainly prose; it's based on semantic meanings, on things made clear.

[Dziga Vertov's] *A Sixth Part of the World*, even though it was made by order of the [state export agency] Gostorg, is a poem, an ode.

[Vsevolod Pudovkin's] *Mother* is a centaur of sorts, and centaurs are weird animals. The film begins as prose with convincing captions (which fit the frame rather badly), and ends as purely formal poetry. Repeated frames and images that become symbolic support my conviction that the essence of this film is poetic.

Let me repeat: there is prosaic cinema and poetic cinema, and this is the main distinction. Prose and poetry differ from each other not in rhythm, or not only in rhythm, but in the prevalence of formal technical aspects (in poetic cinema) over semantic ones, with formal elements replacing semantics and providing compositional solutions. Plotless cinema is "poetic" cinema.

On Re-editing Films (1927)

[…]

One very bad Italian film, I recut seven times. In it, a countess was defamed before her lover, a fisher. The defamation was a cinematographic kind of tale. I made the slander true, and turned the truth into the woman's attempt at self-justification. In the Italian film, the woman became a writer and kept dangling her manuscripts in front of everyone she talked to. I had to transform the manuscripts into mortgage notes. The woman's character was entirely inhuman and impossible to motivate. I had to make her hysteric.

In another film, I turned two twins—a good and an evil one—into a single person with a double life, an insidious villain. At the end of my film, he died for his brother, and all his relatives turned away from him.

[…]

There is an invention by Vasiliev that I consider a masterpiece of film work. He wanted a man to die, and the man wasn't dying. He chose a moment when his intended victim was yawning, took that frame and multiplied it, so that the action stopped. The man was frozen with his mouth open, all that remained was to add a caption: death by heart failure.

This device was so unexpected that nobody protested.

Almost all filmmakers worked in re-editing before they went on to direct; it is a great filmmaking school. I had to re-edit and remake the plots of Russian films, adding continuity shots, and I know now how weakly particular actions are connected to particular meanings in cinema.

Lev Kuleshov once said that a man before a plate of soup and a man in sorrow have almost the same facial expression. In order to give the external expression of an emotion a certain meaning, one needs to know the person's experiences and feelings.

In *The Song of Roland*, Roland blows his horn so strongly that blood begins to seep from his ears; Charlemagne hears him from afar, but people reassure him that Roland is merely hunting.

There is also a novella, a much more cinematographic one.

At a ball, a duke brings into the hall a bottle in which some kind of jester is wriggling wildly. He's being very funny, making all kinds of unusual movements. Only later does everyone find out that the bottle had been corked up tightly, that the man in the bottle had been suffocating and pleading for help.

[...]

Five Feuilletons on Eisenstein (1926)

What is Eisenstein good and bad at?

Eisenstein is good at working with things.

Things work wonderfully in his films: the battleship really becomes the work's protagonist. The cannons, their movement, the masts, the stairs—they all perform, but the doctor's pince-nez works better than the doctor himself.

The actors, the "models"—or whatever you call them—don't work in Eisenstein's films.[1] He doesn't want to work with them, and this weakens the film's first part. Sometimes, Eisenstein is good at showing human beings: it is when he interprets them as quotes, when he shows them in standard ways. Barsky (*Potemkin*'s captain) is good, as good as a cannon. The people on the stairs are good, but the stairs themselves are best of all.

The stairs are the plot. Its landings play the role of decelerating points, and the stairs—the stairs, down which the carriage with the baby is rolling, gaining and losing speed by turns—are organized according to laws cognate to Aristotelian poetics: a new form gave birth to dramatic peripeteia.

[1] Eisenstein advertised for "naturally expressive actors," whose main work was supposed to consist in being themselves.

[...]

Was the color red—the color on the flag, rising over *Potemkin*'s mast—necessary? I believe it was. You can't reproach the artist if the people watching his film applaud the revolution rather than his work.[2]

A well-illuminated red flag is always flying over the Kremlin. But the people walking down the street don't stop to applaud it.

Eisenstein colored in the flag audaciously, but he had the right to this color.

To be afraid of audacity, to be afraid of simple effective devices in art—this is vulgar. To color in a flag on the film reel, once—this was brave.

[2] Many critics accused Eisenstein of vulgarity for coloring in—by hand—the red flag at the end of a black-and-white film.

Talking to Friends (1939)

[…]

I believed that there were no more plots, that plots were merely motivations for tricks.

We [the formalists] were claiming that there was nothing behind the text, nothing beyond it.

But we didn't see the text, we didn't see color. We saw only the junctions of paint, and in literature, we loved rough drafts best of all.

This is how the Proletkult performed Ostrovsky's *Enough Stupidity in Every Wise Man.* Every aspect of the play was developed and parodied, but the play didn't exist.

Neither did the world.

The world didn't exist as a whole; it was experienced as a collection of objects for parody. Young "eccentrics" performed the civil war in their conceptual costumes.[1] They couldn't get hold of the epoch without a conceptual subtext.

This resembles the Chinese who have to find a phonetically similar hieroglyph for each syllable if they want to reproduce a European word.

---

[1] The "Eccentric Actor Factory" (FEKS) existed in Petrograd from 1921 to 1926; Eisenstein's "models" vs. "eccentrics" were two conflicting acting schools of the 1920s.

[…]

Art finds itself thematically locked in.

Art has lost its humanity. Cinema actors are being filmed from different angles like samovars. The actor has become an isolated human being among things.

On Swift's flying island, people decided to replace words with showing things. They carried things around with them and led long formalist conversations in the street, arranging their props.

Not all things, not all people were cinema-compatible.

Look how in Abram Room's rather banal *Death Bay*, the director's handwriting grows livelier when he peoples the ship with freaks.

This new sharp tone returns the sensation of reality to the artist, who had lost it in its usual form.

Riffraff bursts into Eisenstein's *Split.*

The riffraff live in barrels. The barrels are dug into the ground, though even a kitten knows that you can only hide from rain in a barrel or box if it lies on its side.

But the effect of the freaks' sudden appearance (a hundred people instantaneously appear right out of the earth) is so great that verisimilitude goes flying into the editorial waste-basket.

[…]

Not everything that is easily possible is worth doing.

Our country has fallen in love with Joyce. Now, Tolstoy, before *Childhood*, wrote a text entitled "Yesterday's Story." It hadn't been published before; now, it appears in the first volume's addendum.

Tolstoy based this text on internal dialogue.

He described only a few hours, but they took up a lot of space.

He based his text on the intersection of different planes, such as the contradictions between the semantics of different languages. Let me quote an excerpt:

> How I love to have her speak of me in the third person. In German this is rude, but I would love it even in German. Why can't she find a decent way to call me? I see how awkward it must be for her to call me by my name and title. Is this really because I … "Stay for dinner," said her husband. Busy with my reflections on third person formulas, I didn't notice that my body, having already politely made its excuses, put down its hat again and made itself comfortable in an easy chair. It was clear that my consciousness was taking no part in this foolishness.[2]

A writer of genius had considered and discarded what another writer did later.

Joyce's text moves, the way a blind man moves along a wall, along an altered plot of Ulysses' travels.

The things of the external world are destroyed.

The fragmented consciousness does not serve to test the world; it becomes the content of the artwork.

But it can only live and move if it leans on existing art, on its destruction.

[…]

[2] Translation by Alexandra Berlina; a version of the full text by George Kline is available at en.wikisource.org/wiki/A_History_of_Yesterday.

Happy Fable-land (1948)[1]

As children, we were reading Mark Twain and rafting with Huckleberry Finn on an American river, the Mississippi.

We were rafting with Jim, a Negro who had placed his faith in a white boy.

Huckleberry Finn believed what he was told, but he found the strength and courage not to write a letter about a runaway Negro on his way to the free states. He had found in himself enough faith, and power, and simple human ethics to fight against the ethics of slaveholders.

I'll be talking to Huckleberry Finn's compatriots, to Americans who, as children, read the same books as I did, and who probably comprehended them the way I did.

Miss Watson freed her Negro before dying, but before that, she was going to sell him; Tom Sawyer helped the flight of a slave who was already free. He took on risks, but he did not take on new ethics. This is why Huckleberry Finn is braver than Tom Sawyer. He is closer to the future.

How well does Mark Twain describe the Mississippi! The river is

---

[1] This article's title, "*V nekotorom gosudarstve*," is a fairy-tale formula that could also be rendered as "in a kingdom far away." However, Shklovsky is referring to Thackeray's "happy, harmless Fable-land" here.

wide. Someone says something about the night, laughing, far away. On the raft, you can hear every word.

This is how we hear the words of art that are oceans and centuries away: they are spoken quietly, but still they reach us.

Crossing centuries, the words of Sancho Panza, who judged according to the laws of common sense, reached Mark Twain, and he, an American, described the Englishman Tom Canty, who finds himself on the throne and makes laws of sense and justice.

Twenty years ago, my friend Mayakovsky was crossing the ocean toward America. Over the ocean, it was raining. The thread of rain had sewed the sky to the water, and then the sun rose, and a rainbow emerged, shining, over the ocean, mirrored in water—the steamer was entering a festive many-colored circle.

Once upon a time, people believed that a rainbow meant hope.

There was a war. The rainbow of peace didn't remain for long over the burnt-out earth, over the ocean that saw battles.

The sky is stormy, and familiar clouds are forming.

But the ocean is not too wide for words.

Mayakovsky loved the Brooklyn Bridge the way a painter loves Madonna; he loved New York, he admired the masts of ships passing by, he listened to the houses in the city responding to faraway trains, the way crockery in its cupboard responds to your footsteps by tinkling.

The best poet of our time loved New York the way one loves a forest, he loved this city in its busy autumn weekdays, he loved thunderstorms in New York.

We understand America.

[…]

Dickens and Thackeray both complained about the necessity to create happy endings.

Thackeray called the land of false happy denouements in feel-good bourgeois novels a "happy, harmless Fable-land."

American films, as we all know, always end well, with very few exceptions. These few are very good.

Chaplin's screenplays do not end in fun. The happy ending in *The Gold Rush* is a straight-out parody. It's constructed as a pauper's dream. Only we don't see the pauper wake up.

But I'll be talking about American popular cinema here. This kind of cinema deals with the happy Fable-land, now geographically pin-pointed.

It's in America.

Even if the film doesn't play in America, the protagonist is at least on his way there; in *Casablanca*, whose screenplay is very cleverly written, the whole pathos, the whole goal consists in an American visa.

American popular films resemble each other the way detective novels do.

A successful film immediately spawns sequels and turns into a series.

A film that has attracted an audience immediately gives birth to a parody.

A popular parody, in its turn, gives rise to endless sequels.

This is half-folklore, but it has its authors. It's fixed, organized, directed. The author is the owner of the film company.

Dickens knew America. He wrote: "The most terrible blow ever struck at liberty would be struck by this country. This blow will result from its inability to be worthy of its role as 'the world teacher of life.'"[2]

---

[2] This quotation, for which Shklovsky gives no source, sounds very much like Chesterton's summary of *American Notes* in his book *Charles Dickens* (which Shklovsky read; he cites in *Tales about Prose*): "In one of his gloomier moments he wrote down his fear that the

Quoting these words by Dickens, I'm ready to restrict their application. We all understand the importance of progressive American literature and technology; we are aware of the diversity of American characters. But the lessons the world learns from American cinema have been for the worse, for a long time now.

Of American cinema technique and, in particular, screenwriting technique, I can say this: it very skillfully brings the most diverse phenomena of world literature to the level of harmful vulgarity.

[…]

---

greatest blow ever struck at liberty would be struck by America in the failure of her mission upon the earth" (Chesterton). The text of *American Notes* doesn't contain the exact phrase Shklovsky claims to be citing, though it does feature many passages such as "with sharp points and edges such as these, Liberty in America hews and hacks her slaves; or, failing that pursuit, her sons devote them to a better use, and turn them on each other" (Dickens).

What the Character Knows and What the Audience Knows (1959)

Even in our best films, the characters often seem to know everything about themselves.

A negative character might not know himself fully, but the positive one certainly does know the final truth about himself and about everyone around him. This truth is offered to the audience as the film's conclusion.

Meanwhile, this perspective is unscientific. It equates objective existence in the world with a person's, albeit a very intelligent person's, self-understanding. But what we call human psychology must be differentiated from deep relations with reality, which are often beyond control.

The audience sees the character in a series of connections and circumstances; it knows him better than he knows himself.

We empathize with the character—we often feel pity for him—because he doesn't know what we know.

Chapaev doesn't know how much work, how much self-restriction and strain he is to go through as a Red Army commander. The audience knows. The audience knows the future. In *Chapaev*, the audience sees and comprehends its past. This is why Chapaev's utterances reveal his character but do not constitute the film's moral. They are more than a moral: they lead us into the process of a new moral's creation.

In Ekaterina Vinogradskaya's film *Member of the Government*, the heroine's story consists in her constant elevation. Her horizon grows, but it grows without her full awareness. This is why the audience finds itself seemingly ahead of the heroine but also capable of following her—precisely because it knows her future.

The transition from a witty situation or a conflict to the intelligently developed plot must be imperceptible though predetermined.

Too often, we rob the audience of the joy of discovery.

[…]

The Emergence of the Word (1963)[1]

We, the cinematographers of the older generation, have lived through a rare phenomenon: we have seen an art form being born and dying. In our lifetime, imaginative cinema emerged as new art that claimed a place beside old art, sometimes even contesting this place. And in our lifetime, it was all over. I'm talking about silent cinema.

By and by, silent cinema developed its own language. First, the missing words were replaced by exaggerated gestures. By and by—this happened very characteristically in Russian cinema—acts, not gestures, began to replace words. Situations were created in which the spectators seemed to construct the text. The captions didn't replace speech; they were short, aphoristic, and constituted what could be described as lines shared by the filmmaker and the characters.

Rendering actors speechless, silent cinema raised the importance of subtle facial and body expressions—not gestures, but the figure as a whole, the actor's behavior as a unity expressing the meaning of the action.

The word doesn't replace action; it has its own, more complex task: it deepens and changes the action's meaning. The speeches of

---

[1]In the original, the reference to Shklovsky's first published article is even clearer: "*Poyavleniye slova*" (The Emergence of the Word) sounds similar to "*Voskresheniye slova*" (Resurrecting/resurrection of the Word).

messengers in antique tragedies conveyed actions which remained unseen; they commented without showing.

By 1925–1930, silent cinema had reached international success and united the world in what might be called graphic language. The whole world was learning how people lived, behaved, loved, cheated, suffered from jealousy in different countries.

Silent cinema had to express complex ideas without a voice, without words. Film editing emerged as a technical tool: initially it had to do with combining close-ups with long shots, it was a concession to the specifics of the camera lens. But later, editing was reinterpreted as a means of expression. Showing a part instead of the whole, emphasizing crucial details, cinema developed a language of its own, which included editing. In language, we point to one feature of an object in order to define the object as a whole. In filming, the director produced an impression of the whole by showing a hand, a pair of eyes, or a thing used by a character. Thus, the filmmaker taught the spectator to see, compare, and comprehend.

Technology knows no mercy; it is as if accomplishments were irreversible. I'll explain my use of "as if" later.[2]

The silence of the film reel was masked by sound illustrations. They hovered near the screen, half-improvising, half-repeating. The sounds of the piano didn't quite reach the spectators' consciousness, but they were necessary.

The great composer Shostakovich worked as a pianist in the cinema "The Light Reel" on the Nevsky in Leningrad when he was a boy. This brought in good money. Besides, the work allowed the

---

[2] The article never directly refers to this "*kak by*" (as if) again; the explanation is apparently to be found at the very end of the article: "New inventions never destroy old achievements, they merely narrow down their use."

boy genius to improvise freely. Later, he greatly enjoyed writing film music.

Nobody else remembers this, probably, but I know for sure that a fire once started in that cinema while Shostakovich was working. A flame appeared under the screen, and the musician saw it. If he had stopped playing, the spectators would have panicked. Back then, fires were frequent in cinemas. Shostakovich went on playing, and the fire was extinguished quietly. The smoke rising from the pit joined the fluttering shadows that always live in the blue cone extending from the projector to the screen. But this is not what I meant to talk about—I merely wanted to mention the quiet heroism of the cinema mechanic and the cinema musician. That tribe was dedicated to its work.

And then, sound came. This happened sometime about 1927. It came from America. It turned out that sound could be recorded on the film reel. The new electronic world, the world approaching cybernetics and mastering the atom, mastered speech and sound on the way; it mastered the art of creating likenesses.

The emergence of the word in cinema looked rather pathetic. First, it seemed that sound must have a special motivation to appear onscreen. What followed were films about singers. I remember one about a Jewish boy who first sang in the synagogue and then became an opera singer; his father was devastated, he died, and the young man came to sing the kaddish in his father's house. The film was very sentimental, very uncinematographic, and enjoyed much success.[3]

[…]

Don't be surprised at the deafness of my questions, my blindness, my

---

[3] Shklovsky appears to be referring to Alan Crosland's *The Jazz Singer* (1927).

inability to see: I was finding it hard to leave behind me the skills of a silent cinema screenwriter.

Everything turned out differently at the end. Many achievements of silent cinema returned to the talking pictures. New inventions never destroy old achievements, they merely narrow down their use.

We are all living through yet another turning point now. Television, despite its restricted camera field, is already forcing out the cinema, the newspaper, and the book. Theater fought against cinema, and theater survived. Cinema is now fighting against television: it probably will survive, as well. These means of human self-expression will coexist, just like painting, graphic art, and sculpture do.

Return the Ball into the Game (1970)

I saw two films by the brilliant director Antonioni. One of them is called *Eclipse*. A man and a woman can't sort out their relationship. We see their things, their successful and unsuccessful financial operations. We see their decisions, made but unrealized. At the end we're shown water flowing out of a big barrel.

But this is not the saddest film. Antonioni has made another very famous one, *Blowup*. Here it is, as a simple content summary, (but keep in mind that the path of events along which I'm leading you ends in a cul-de-sac):

A young, very talented photographer is looking for sensations. He makes many pictures; his clients demand the story of a murder: a corpse whose picture can be printed in the paper.

The photographer takes a snapshot. He blows it up. Suddenly, it emerges that there is a corpse in the garden, under the trees. Another blowup. The corpse is found. Then, a woman appears, wishing to buy this picture. We see how the theft of the picture is organized. All this is rather disconnected and very difficult. The picture is stolen. The reporter goes to see the place where the corpse had been: there is no corpse. He goes to see his friends who like him well. They are busy with what, in cinema today, carries the short name "sex."

They aren't interested in him or the blowup: the sensation didn't come off.

On his way, the reporter sees a group of young people. They travel in fancy dress, in parody costumes, singing something.

Then, this crowd is playing tennis: we clearly hear the rackets sharply, skillfully hitting the balls.

Then we comprehend that they are playing without a ball.

There is no goal, no ball, only the ghost of a sound.

Nobody is interested in the end of the detective story, the solution of the crime. There might be a newspaper, there might be a picture, but that's it. The denouement disappears. There is no ending …

A film by Pasolini ends differently. Its title could be translated as *Birds and Birdies*.[1] The story is about Francis of Assisi sending monks to preach Christianity to birds. The monks arrive in the modern world.

They find some hawks and turn them Christian; then they find sparrows, and the sparrows, too, receive the revelation.

But the Christian hawks eat the Christian sparrows: this is their nature.

The monks pray. Around them, a monastery emerges and does a brisk business in faith. The monks leave.

They see terrible things, needless births, needless deaths. They see a Chinese man for whom a beggar woman is getting a swallow nest from the top of an old house. The monks' guide through the world of lawless sadness and strange entangled paths is a raven who is given them by fate. The raven keeps sidling, looking for something. In the end, the hungry travelers eat the bird.

This is, schematically, the film's ending.

We have lived for millennia, and we haven't been living in vain. We

---

[1] *Uccellacci e uccellini* could also be rendered as *Big/Bad Birds and Little/Good Birds*; in English, the film is known as *The Hawks and the Sparrows*.

don't believe that raven soup is a tasty dish; we don't believe in the sublimity of ironic denouements.

But private denouements, the denouements of particular cases seem to be replaced by comparative denouements.

Our scope of thinking is growing ever larger.

Conflicts take place not only between individuals but between generations, between social systems.

Irony won't help. It will save neither Antonioni, nor Pasolini, nor Fellini—an immensely gifted man who made a whole film about being unable to make a film about a man making a model of a rocket which is supposed to carry him off into another world.

The way of Gilgamesh, who crossed an ocean with a pole, seems difficult to his descendants.

Poems are written about poems being written.

Novels about novels, screenplays about screenplays.

Tennis is being played without a ball. But the journeys of Gilgamesh, Odysseus, Pantagruel, even of Chichikov [from *Dead Souls*]—they all need a goal.

Return the ball into the game.

Return the deed into life.

Return meaning not to the reaching for records but to movement itself.

Unread Dream (1984)

[...]

In Plato's dialogue "Phaedrus," there is that conversation. Socrates tells a legend about the invention of numbers, games, and writing.

Writing is defined as a means of conserving knowledge, a means of remembering and reminding.

Socrates comments that writing cannot be really considered an invention because it does not create anything new. We write down what we said or thought. Letters, these signs that assume formation on paper in dense rows, cannot talk and cannot contradict you.

I will add that they kill the living, sounding word; they flatten it, making it fit under the cover.

But Socrates failed to notice a crucial feature of writing. It does not only preserve our knowledge (losing some aspects). It also gives a greater number of people the opportunity to share in this knowledge. Socrates views knowledge as a privilege of the aristocracy.

Writing, on the other hand, knows no class distinctions.

The system of depiction created by silent cinema (which, I'll add, has been so thoroughly forgotten by television) was panhuman and universally comprehensible.

But I seem to be getting ahead of myself.

Printing prompted the democratization of knowledge. Printing assured the victory of revolution.

Television went even further.

The following story once happened to Dickens. The great writer often performed readings of his work. Once, the Queen of England, desiring to witness one, invited him to the palace. Dickens' reply was simple: he sent her a ticket to his reading.

Admittedly, this story has nothing to do with television.

[...]

If we compare the art of cinema to the invention of writing, the frame to the letter, the sign, the hieroglyph (this comparison was widespread in the 1920s), then television is comparable to the invention of book printing.

Writing put the living sound of the word into a little box. Printing left the word even further behind. It also separated itself from the figurative quality of letters, which once had been drawings depicting particular things. The letter, the piece of type, is far removed from a drawing on stone.

Television has disseminated the achievements of cinema, churning out copies. It uses what has already been done, often without noticing, without thinking. The culture of framing and cutting is lost.

Gogol's Petrushka reads syllable by syllable and is astonished to see words emerge from single letters.

We aren't astonished at this anymore. We read automatically, without noticing the words, without finishing them, the way we say "h'lo" instead of "hello."

This is how we watch television.

This probably also happens because television is a specific art form, one we don't yet understand. What we must use in TV work is not what unites it with other art forms but what sets it apart.

[...]

Today, television is more widespread and influential than books, cinema, and theater. Young and audacious, it's forcing out related and unrelated art forms.

I'm afraid that soon it might force out itself.

Its invasion, the invasion of TV, was uncoordinated and highly active. This is how the Huns conquered Rome, avalanche-like, leaving the Romans no time to come to their senses.

Cinema was at the avant-garde of this invasion. It galloped by like the herald of a fire brigade. In old Russia, fire brigades had heralds. Their job was to ride in front, blowing their horns, warning everyone to step aside.

Television has crept into our homes without asking our consent, without as much as talking to us beforehand. Even a thief doesn't come quite without notice—we can hear him force the door.

We let television sit at our table. We wear it on our head. We've been converted to a new faith, replacing the toppled crosses with TV antennas on the roofs of our houses.

I've seen a lot in my lifetime. I fought in World War I and the civil war, I saw World War II. But I never guessed that cities and countries—the whole world—could be conquered so quickly.

We were not prepared for this. We were dumbfounded; for a long time, we were disputing if television would destroy everything we had created.

A genie who took no orders from us had broken free from his bottle.

Today, we're all used to the TV screen. Television is part of our life. It all seems very simple to us now: you come in, you turn it on, you turn it off. Or (worse): you arrive, you place your camera in the street and just start filming.

It's not as simple as that. We haven't yet conquered television. Its fate reminds us of Plato's warnings.

[…]

A Letter to Evgeny Gabrilovich (1984)[1]

[...]

Einstein wrote: "Forgive me, Newton."

Einstein looks into Newton's mirror and knows: there is another one beyond it.

Only the greatest trees can nod at each other with such joy.

The world isn't flat.

Space is curved, but this is beyond my understanding.

The life I lived was, of course, wrong. But in another life I wouldn't have done what I have done.

I had that term, *ostrannenie*.

They printed it with one "n." This is how it started. Actually, there should have been two terms.

I only corrected this recently, in my book *Energy of Delusion*. These two words coexist now—*ostranenie* and *ostrannenie*, with one "n" and with two, with different meanings but with the same plot, a plot about the strangeness of life.

You think you're finishing a thing.

But you're just beginning.

[...]

---

[1] Gabrilovich (1899–1993) was a Soviet screenwriter, one of the very few acquaintances of Shklovsky whose life experience was comparable to his own in regard to both length and variety: Gabrilovich went from being a member of "The First Soviet Eccentric Jazz Band" to a socialist realist specializing in films on Lenin. In the 1970s, Gabrilovich intended to make a film about Shklovsky, but this never happened.

Works Cited

Adamovich, Georgiy. *Literaturnye zametki*. St. Petersburg: Aleteya, 2007. Print.

Alloy, L. B. "Induced Mood and the Illusion of Control." *Journal of Personality and Social Psychology* 41 (1981): 1129–40.

Alloy, L. B., and L. Y. Abramson. "Depressive Realism: Four Theoretical Perspectives." *Cognitive Processes in Depression*. Ed. L. B. Alloy. New York: Guilford Press, 1988. 223–65.

Aristotle. "Poetics." Project Gutenberg, 2008. Web. www.gutenberg.org/files/1974

Avenarius, Richard. *Filosofiia kak myshlenie o mire*. St. Petersburg: Tipografiya Son'kina, 1899.

Belinkov, Arkady. "Sobiraite Metallolom!" *Vremya i my* 7 (1976): 149–64.

Belinkov, Arkadiy, and Natal'ia Belinkova. *Rasprya s vekom*. Moscow: Novoye literaturnoye obozrenie, 2008.

Belozerskaya-Bulgakova, Lyubov'. *O, myod vospominaniy!* New York: Ardis, 1969.

Berberova, Nina. *Kursiv moy*. New York: Russica Publishers, 1983.

Berezin, Vladimir. *Viktor Shklovsky*. Moscow: Molodaya Gvardia, 2014.

Berlina, Alexandra. "Faith and War Made Strange: *Ostranenie in Slaughterhouse-Five*." *Amerikastudien / American Studies* 62.1 (2017): forthcoming.

Berlina, Alexandra. "Make it strange, make it stony: Viktor Shklovsky and the horror behind *ostranenie*." *Times Literary Supplement* (2016): 13–15

Berlina, Alexandra. "To Give Back the Sensation of Life: Shklovsky's *Ostranenie*, Cognitive Studies and Psychology". *Journal of Literary Studies* 11/2 (2017): forthcoming.

Boym, Svetlana. "Estrangement As a Lifestyle: Shklovsky and Brodsky." *Exile and Creativity: Signposts, Travelers, Outsiders, Backward Glances*. Ed. Susan Rubin Suleiman. Durham, NC: Duke University Press, 1998. 241–62.

Boym, Svetlana. "Poetics and Politics of Estrangement." *Poetics Today* 24.4 (2005): 581–611.

Brooker, Peter. "Key Words in Brecht's Theory and Practice of Theatre." *The Cambridge Companion to Brecht*. Ed. Peter Thomson and Glendyr Sacks. Cambridge: Cambridge University Press, 1994. 185–200.

Bulgakov, Mikhail. *Belaya gvardiya. Master i Margarita*. Moscow: Olma Press, 2003.

Bykov, Dmitry. *Orfografiya*. Moscow: Vagrius, 2003.

Cassedy, Steven. *Flight from Eden: The Origins of Modern Literary Criticism and Theory*. University of California Press, 1990.

Chesterton, G. K. *Charles Dickens*. Whitefish: Kessinger Publishing, 2005.

Christy, Ian, and Richard Taylor, eds. *The Film Factory: Russian and Soviet Cinema in Documents 1896-1939*. London: Routledge, 1994.

Chudakov, Alexander. "Dva pervykh desyatiletiya." *Gamburgskiy schet*. Moscow: Sovetskiyi Pisatel', 1990. 3–32.

Chudakov, Alexander. "Sprashivaya Shklovskogo." *Literaturnoye obozreniye* 6 (1990): 101.

Chukovsky, Korney. *Polnoye sobraniye sochineniy*. Vol. 11. Moscow: Agenstvo FTM, 2013.

Coleridge, Samuel Taylor. *The Works of Samuel Taylor Coleridge, Prose and Verse: Complete in One Volume*. Thomas, Cowperthwait, 1840.

Dickens, Charles. *American Notes for General Circulation*. Project Gutenberg, 1996. Web. http://www.gutenberg.org/files/675

Diez, Friedrich. *Leben und Werke der Troubadours*. Leipzig, 1829.

Eco, Umberto. *The Name of the Rose*. Boston: Houghton Mifflin Harcourt, 2014.

Eikhenbaum, Boris. "Kak sdelana 'Shinel' Gogolya." *Poetika*. Petrograd: 18-aya gosudarstvennaya tipografiya, 1919. 151–66.

Eikhenbaum, Boris. *O literature*. Moscow: Sovetskiy Pisatel, 1987.

Emerson, Caryl. "Shklovsky's *ostranenie*, Bakhtin's *vnenakhodimost*" ("How Distance Serves an Aesthetics of Arousal Differently from an Aesthetics Based on Pain"). *Poetics Today* 26.4 (2005): 637–64.

Erlich, Victor. "On Being Fair to Viktor Shklovsky or the Act of Hedged Surrender." *Slavic Review* (1976): 111–18.

Erlich, Victor. *Russian Formalism: History and Doctrine*. Berlin: De Gruyter Mouton, 1955.

Fauconnier, Gilles, and Mark Turner. *The Way We Think: Conceptual Blending and the Mind's Hidden Complexities*. Basic Books, 2008.

Fielding, Henry. *Tom Jones*. Gutenberg Project. Web. www.gutenberg.org/files/6593

Frezenskiy, Boris. *Sud'by serapionov. Portrety i syuzhety*. Moscow: Akademicheskiy Proyekt, 2003.

Galushkin, Alexandr. "Footnotes." *Gamburgskiy schet*. Moscow: Sovetskiy Pisatel', 1990.

Galushkin, Alexandr. "Razgovory s Viktorom Shklovskim." *Novoye Literaturnoye Obozreniye* 131.1 (2015): Web. http://magazines.russ.ru/nlo/2015/1/19g-pr.html

Ginzburg, Lidiya. *Zapisnyye knizhki. Vospominaniya. Esse*. St. Petersburg: Iskusstvo SPB, 2001.

Gorman, David. "Shklovsky at 115." *The Minnesota Review* 70 (2008): 133–40.

Grosse, Erns. *Proiskhozhdenie iskusstva*. Moscow: M. & S. Sabashnikovy, 1899.

Gul, Roman. *Zhizn' na fuksa*. Moscow: Gosudarstvennoye Izdatelstvo, 1927.

Haber, Erika. *The Myth of the Non-Russian: Iskander and Aitmatov's Magical Universe*. Lanham: Lexington Books, 2003.

Hansen-Löve, Aage Ansgar. *Der russische Formalismus*. Wien: Verlag der Verlag der Österreichischen Akademie der Wissenschaften, 1978.

Jakobson, Roman. "O pokolenii, rastrativshem svoikh poetov." *Smert' Vladimira Mayakovskogo*. Berlin: Petropolis, 1931.

Jangfeldt, Bengt. *Mayakovsky: A Biography*. University of Chicago Press, 2014.

Kalinin, Il'ya. "Viktor Shklovskiy, ili Prevrashcheniye poeticheskogo priema v literaturnyi fakt." *Zvezda* 7 (2014): Web. http://magazines.russ.ru/zvezda/2014/7/11k.html

Kaverin, Veniamin. *Epilog*. Moscow: Moskovskiy Rabochiy, 1989.

Kaverin, Veniamin. *Skandalist, ili vechera na Vasil'yevskom ostrove*. Leningrad: Izdatel'stvo Pisatelei, 1931.

Khmel'nitskaya, Tamara. "Neopublikovannaya stat'ya o V. Shklovskom." *Voprosy literatury* 5 (2005): Web. http://magazines.russ.ru/voplit/2005/5/hm2.html

Khodasevich, Valentina. *Portrety slovami*. Moscow: Galart, 1995.

Koestler, Arthur. *The Act of Creation*. London: Penguin, 1995.

Konetsky, Viktor. *Ekho*. Moscow: Tekst, 2005.

Kozakov, Mikhail. *Tretiy zvonok*. Moscow: Vagrius, 2004.

Lachmann, Renate. "Die Verfremdung und das Neue Sehen bei Viktor Šklovskij." *Poetica* 3 (1970): 226–49.

Lazarev, Lazar'. "Zapiski pozhilogo cheloveka." *Znamya* (2001): Web. http://magazines.russ.ru/znamia/2001/6/lazar.html

Lemon, Lee, and Marion Reis. *Russian Formalist Criticism: Four Essays*. Lincoln: University of Nebraska Press, 1965.

Lomonosov, Mikhail. *Kratkoe rukovodstvo k kransorechiyu*. St. Petersburg: Akademiya Nauk, 1748.

Loseff, Lev. *On the Beneficence of Censorship: Aesopian Language in Modern Russian Literature*. Munich: Otto Sagner, 1985.

Mandelstam, Nadezhda. *Vospominaniya*. Moscow: Soglasie, 1999.

Mandelstam, Osip. *Sobraniye sochineniy*. II. Moscow: Art Business Center, 1993.

Mayakovsky, Vladimir. *Polnoye sobraniye sochineniy*. Vol. 12. Moscow: Khudozhestvennaya Literatura, 1949.

Morson, Gary Saul. "The Russian Debate on Narrative." *Literary Theory and Criticism: An Oxford Guide*. Ed. Patricia Waugh. Oxford: Oxford University Press, 2006. 212–22.

Nabokov, Vladimir. *Nikolai Gogol*. New York: Penguin, 2013.

Naiman, Eric. "Shklovsky's Dog and Mulvey's Pleasure: The Secret Life of Defamiliarization." *Comparative Literature* 50 (1998): 333–52.

Nepevnyy, Vladimir. *Viktor Shklovsky i Roman Jakobson. Zhizn' kak roman*. Russia: n.p., 2009. Film.

Norton, James. "Against the Poverty of the World: Viktor Shklovsky and the Critical Mass." *Vertigo* 4.2 (2009): Web. https://www.closeupfilmcentre.com/vertigo_magazine/volume-4-issue-2-winter-spring-20091

Ognev, Vladimir. *Figury ukhodyshchey epokhi*. Moscow: Gelios, 2008.

Otter, Samuel. "An Aesthetics in All Things." *Representations* 104.1 (2008): 116–25.

Ovsyaniko-Kulikovsky, Dmitrii. *Yazyk i iskusstvo*. St. Petersburg: Akademiya Nauk, 1895.

Paulmann, Inge. "Anmerkung." *Texte der russischen Formalisten II*. Ed. Wolf-Dieter Stempel. München: Wilhelm-Finck-Verlag, 1972.

Plato. *Phaedrus*. Trans. Benjamin Jowett. The Internet Classics Archive, 2009. Web. classics.mit.edu/Plato/phaedrus.html

Pogodin, Alexandr. *Yazyk kak tvorchestvo*. Kharkov: Tipografiya Men'shova, 1913.

Polivanov, Evgenii. "O zvukovoy storone poeticheskoy rechi." *Poetika: Sbornik po teorii poeticheskogo iazyka (I)*. Petrograd: n.p., 1916.

Potebnya, Alexandr. *Iz lektsiy po teorii slovesnosti*. Kharkov: Tipografiya Schastni, 1894.

Potebnya, Alexandr. *Iz zapisok po teorii slovesnosti*. Kharkov: Tipografiya Sil'berberg, 1905.

Propp, Vladimir. *Morphology of the Folktale*. Trans. Laurence Scott. Austin: University of Texas Press, 1968.

Reavey, George, and Marc Slonim, eds. *Soviet Literature: an Anthology*. London: Wishart, 1933.

Reich, Bernhard. *Im Wettlauf mit der Zeit*. Leipzig: Henschel, 1970.

Robinson, Douglas. *Estrangement and the Somatics of Literature: Tolstoy, Shklovsky, Brecht*. Baltimore: Johns Hopkins University Press, 2008.

Romanov, Evdokim. *Belorusskiy sbornik 1–2*. Kiev: Tipografiya Kul'zhenko, 1886.

Rose, Margaret A. *Parody: Ancient, Modern and Post-modern*. Cambridge: Cambridge University Press, 1993.

Rozanov, Vasily. *Opavshie Listya*. Petrograd: Tipografiya tovarishchestva Suvorina, 1915.

Rozanov, Vasily. *Uyedinennoye*. St. Petersburg: Tipografiya tovarishchestva Suvorina, 1912.

Runes, Dagobert D. *Dictionary of Philosophy*. Whitefish: Kessinger Publishing, 2010.

Rybnikov, Pavel. *Pesni, sobrannye P.N. Rybnikovym*. Ed. Alexey Gruzinskiy. Moscow: Tipografiya A. Semyona, 1916.

Sadovnikov, Dmitriy. *Zagadki russkogo naroda*. St. Petersburg: Tipografiya Lebedeva, 1895.

Sarnov, Benedikt. "Rossiya – rodina mamontov." *Lechaim* 9.137 (2003): Web. http://www.lechaim.ru/ARHIV/137/sarnov.htm

Scholes, Robert. *Structuralism in Literature: An Introduction*. New Haven: Yale University Press, 1974.

Schwartz, Evgeny. *Zhivu bespokoino ... Iz dnevnikov*. Moscow: Litres, 2000.

Sheldon, Richard. "The Formalist Poetics of Victor Shklovsky." *Russian Literature Triquarterlyterature triquarterly* 2 (1972): 351–71.

Sheldon, Richard. "Viktor Shklovsky and the Device of Ostensible Surrender." *Slavic Review* 34.1 (1975): 86–108.

Sheldon, Richard. *Viktor Shklovsky: An International Bibliography of Works by and about Him*. New York: Ardis, 1977.

Shelley, Percy Bysshe. *The Selected Poetry and Prose of Shelley*. Wordsworth Editions, 1994.

Sher, Benjamin. "Translator's Introduction: Shklovsky and the Revolution." *Theory of Prose*. Champaign: Dalkey Archive Press, 1991. xv–xxi.

Shklovsky, Viktor. "Art as Device." *Theory of Prose*. Trans. Benjamin Sher. Champaign: Dalkey Archive Press, 1991. 1–14.

Shklovsky, Viktor. "Art as Technique." *Russian Formalist Criticism: Four Essays*. Trans. Lee T. Lemon and Marion J. Reis. Lincoln: University of Nebraska Press, 1965. 3–24.

Shklovsky, Viktor. *Bowstring: On the Dissimilarity of the Similar*. Trans. Shushan Avagyan. Champaign: Dalkey Archive Press, 2011.

Shklovsky, Viktor. "Energiya zabluzhdeniya. Kniga o syuzhete." *Izbrannoye v dvukh tomakh*. Moscow: Khudozhestvennaya Literatura, 1983.

Shklovsky, Viktor. *Energy of Delusion: A Book on Plot*. Trans. Shushan Avagyan. Champaign: Dalkey Archive Press, 2007.

Shklovsky, Viktor. *Gamburgskiy schet* [1928]. Leningrad: Izdatel'stvo pisateley, 1928.

Shklovsky, Viktor. *Gamburgskiy schet* [1990]. Moscow: Sovetskiy Pisatel', 1990.

Shklovsky, Viktor. "Iskusstvo, kak priem." *Poetika*. Petrograd: 18-aya gosudarstvennaya tipografiya, 1919. 101–14.

Shklovsky, Viktor. *Izbrannoe v dvuhk tomakh*. Moscow: Khudozhestvennaya Proza, 1983.
Shklovsky, Viktor. *Khod konya*. Moscow/Berlin: Gelikon, 1923.
Shklovsky, Viktor. *Literature and Cinematography*. Trans. Irina Masinovsky. Dublin: Dalkey Archive Press, 2008.
Shklovsky, Viktor. *O teorii prozy* [1925]. Moscow/Leningrad: Krug, 1925.
Shklovsky, Viktor. *O teorii prozy* [1983]. Moscow: Sovetskiy Pisatel', 1983.
Shklovsky, Viktor. "Pamyatnik nauchnoy oshibke." *Literaturnaya Gazeta 4* (January 27, 1930): 1.
Shklovsky, Viktor. "Pis'ma vnuku." *Voprosy Literatury* 4 (2002): Web. http://magazines.russ.ru/voplit/2002/4/sh22.html
Shklovsky, Viktor. "Pochta veka." *Grani* 207–8 (2002): 392–3.
Shklovsky, Viktor. *Povesti o proze*. Moscow: Khudozhestvennaya Literatura, 1983.
Shklovsky, Viktor. *Sentimental'noye puteshestviye*. Ber lin: Gelikon, 1923.
Shklovsky, Viktor. *Tekhnika pisatel'skogo remesla*. Moscow/Leningrad: Molodaya Gvardia, 1927.
Shklovsky, Viktor. *Tetiva. O neskhodstve skhodnogo*. Moscow: Sovetskiy Pisatel', 1970.
Shklovsky, Viktor. "The Resurrection of the Word." *Russian Formalism: A Collection of Articles and Texts in Translation*. Ed. Stephen Bann and John E. Bowlt. Trans. Richard Sherwood. New York: Barnes and Noble, 1974. 41–7.
Shklovsky, Viktor. *Theory of Prose*. Trans. Benjamin Sher. Champaign: Dalkey Archive Press, 1991.
Shklovsky, Viktor. *Tretya Fabrika*. Moscow: Krug, 1926.
Shklovsky, Viktor. "Verstovyye stolby rifmuyut dorogu." *Arion* 2 (1994): Web. http://www.arion.ru/mcontent.php?year=1994&number=126&idx=2433
Shklovsky, Viktor. *Voskresheniye slova*. Petrograd: 18-aya gosudarstvennaya tipografiya, 1914.
Shklovsky, Viktor. *Za 60 let. Raboty o kino*. Moscow: Iskusstvo, 1985.
Shklovsky, Viktor. *Zhili-byli*. Moscow: Sovetskiy Pisatel', 1966.
Shklovsky, Viktor. *Zoo. Pis'ma ne o lybvi, ili Tretya Eloiza*. Berlin: Gelikon, 1923.
Shklovsky, Viktor, and Alexander Maryamov. "Budu pisat' pismo. Filma podozhdet." *Novyy Mir* 11 (2012): Web. http://magazines.russ.ru/novyi_mi/2012/11/p10.html
Shulman, Eduard. "Shklovskiye korotyshki." *Voprosy iazykoznaniia* 2 (2008): n.p.
Spencer, Herbert. *The Philosophy of Style*. Auckland: The Floating Press, 2009.
Steiner, Peter. *Russian Formalism. A Metapoetics*. Ithaca, NY: Cornell University Press, 1984.
Storbeck, Justin, and Gerald L. Clore. "On the Interdependence of Cognition and Emotion." *Cognition & Emotion* 21.6 (2007): 1212–37.

Striedter, Jurij. *Literary Structure, Evolution, and Value: Russian Formalism and Czech Structuralism Reconsidered*. Vol. 5. Cambridge, MA: Harvard University Press, 1989.

Striedter, Jurij. *Texte der russischen Formalisten I*. München: Wilhelm-Finck-Verlag, 1969.

Todorov, Tzvetan. "Poetic Language: The Russian Formalists." *Literature and its Theoretists*. Ed. Tsvetan Todorov. London: Routledge, 1988. 10–28.

Todorov, Tzvetan. *Théorie de la littérature: textes des formalistes russes*. Paris: Seuil, 1965.

Tolstoy, Lev. "Dnevnik." *Letopis'* 12 (1916): 354.

Tompkins, Jane P. *Reader-Response Criticism: From Formalism to Post-Structuralism*. Charles Village: JHU Press, 1980.

Trotsky, Leon. "Formal'naya shkola poezii i marksizm." *Pravda* 166 (July 26 2015): 1.

Turgenev, Ivan. "Hamlet and Don Quixote." Trans. Moshe Spiegel. *Chicago Review* 17.4 (1965): 92–109.

Tynyanov, Yuri. *Poetika*. Moscow: Nauka.

Tynyanov, Yuri. *Problema stikhotvornogo yazyka*. Leningrad: Academia, 1924.

Vatulescu, Cristina. "The Politics of Estrangement: Tracking Shklovsky's Device through Literary and Policing Practices." *Poetics Today* 27 (Spring 2006): 35–66.

Veselovsky, Alexander. *Sobraniye sochineniy*. I. St. Petersburg: Imperatorskaya Akademiya Nauk, 1913.

Veselovshy, Alexander. *Tri glavy iz istoricheskoi poetiki*. St. Petersburg: Imperatorskaya Akademiya Nauk, 1913.

Vitale, Serena. *Shklovsky: Witness to an Era*. Trans. Jamie Richards. Champaign: Dalkey Archive Press, 2013.

Yakubinsky, Lev. "Skoplenie odinakovykh plavnykh v prakticheskom i poeticheskom yazykakh." *Poetika: Sbornik po teorii poeticheskogo yazyka (II)*. Petrograd, 1917. 15–23.

Zelenin, Dmitriy. *Velikorusskie skazki Vyatskoi gubernii*. Petrograd: Tipografiya Orlova, 1915.

Index